FREE Study Skills DVD Offer

Dear Customer,

Thank you for your purchase from Mometrix! We consider it an honor and privilege that you have purchased our product and want to ensure your satisfaction.

As a way of showing our appreciation and to help us better serve you, we have developed a Study Skills DVD that we would like to give you for <u>FREE</u>. **This DVD covers our "best practices" for studying for your exam, from using our study materials to preparing for the day of the test.**

All that we ask is that you email us your feedback that would describe your experience so far with our product. Good, bad or indifferent, we want to know what you think!

To get your **FREE Study Skills DVD**, email <u>freedvd@mometrix.com</u> with "FREE STUDY SKILLS DVD" in the subject line and the following information in the body of the email:

    a.   The name of the product you purchased.

    b.   Your product rating on a scale of 1-5, with 5 being the highest rating.

    c.   Your feedback. It can be long, short, or anything in-between, just your impressions and experience so far with our product. Good feedback might include how our study material met your needs and will highlight features of the product that you found helpful.

    d.   Your full name and shipping address where you would like us to send your free DVD.

If you have any questions or concerns, please don't hesitate to contact me directly.

Thanks again!

Sincerely,

Jay Willis
Vice President
<u>jay.willis@mometrix.com</u>
1-800-673-8175

PSAT Exam
SECRETS

Study Guide
Your Key to Exam Success

PSAT Test Review for the
National Merit Scholarship Qualifying Test (NMSQT)
Preliminary SAT Test

Published by
Mometrix Test Preparation
PSAT Exam Secrets Test Prep Team

Written and edited by the PSAT Exam Secrets Test Prep Staff

Printed in the United States of America

This paper meets the requirements of ANSI/NISO Z39.48-1992 (Permanence of Paper).

Mometrix offers volume discount pricing to institutions. For more information or a price quote, please contact our sales department at sales@mometrix.com or 888-248-1219.

*PSAT/NMSQT is a registered trademark of the College Entrance Examination Board, which was not involved in the production of, and does not endorse, this product.

ISBN 13: 978-1-61072-790-7
ISBN 10: 1-61072-790-8

Dear Future Exam Success Story:

Congratulations on your purchase of our study guide. Our goal in writing our study guide was to cover the content on the test, as well as provide insight into typical test taking mistakes and how to overcome them.

Standardized tests are a key component of being successful, which only increases the importance of doing well in the high-pressure high-stakes environment of test day. How well you do on this test will have a significant impact on your future- and we have the research and practical advice to help you execute on test day.

The product you're reading now is designed to exploit weaknesses in the test itself, and help you avoid the most common errors test takers frequently make.

How to use this study guide

We don't want to waste your time. Our study guide is fast-paced and fluff-free. We suggest going through it a number of times, as repetition is an important part of learning new information and concepts.

First, read through the study guide completely to get a feel for the content and organization. Read the general success strategies first, and then proceed to the content sections. Each tip has been carefully selected for its effectiveness.

Second, read through the study guide again, and take notes in the margins and highlight those sections where you may have a particular weakness.

Finally, bring the manual with you on test day and study it before the exam begins.

Your success is our success

We would be delighted to hear about your success. Send us an email and tell us your story. Thanks for your business and we wish you continued success-

Sincerely,

Mometrix Test Preparation Team

Need more help? Check out our flashcards at: http://MometrixFlashcards.com/PSAT

TABLE OF CONTENTS

Top 20 Test Taking Tips

1. Carefully follow all the test registration procedures
2. Know the test directions, duration, topics, question types, how many questions
3. Setup a flexible study schedule at least 3-4 weeks before test day
4. Study during the time of day you are most alert, relaxed, and stress free
5. Maximize your learning style; visual learners use visual study aids, auditory learners use auditory study aids
6. Focus on your weakest knowledge base
7. Find a study partner to review with and help clarify questions
8. Practice, practice, practice
9. Get a good night's sleep; don't try to cram the night before the test
10. Eat a well-balanced meal
11. Know the exact physical location of the testing site; drive the route to the site prior to test day
12. Bring a set of ear plugs; the testing center could be noisy
13. Wear comfortable, loose fitting, layered clothing to the testing center; prepare for it to be either cold or hot during the test
14. Bring at least 2 current forms of ID to the testing center
15. Arrive to the test early; be prepared to wait and be patient
16. Eliminate the obviously wrong answer choices, then guess the first remaining choice
17. Pace yourself; don't rush, but keep working and move on if you get stuck
18. Maintain a positive attitude even if the test is going poorly
19. Keep your first answer unless you are positive it is wrong
20. Check your work, don't make a careless mistake

Reading Test

The reading portion of the PSAT consists of one 60-minute section. It will contain 5 single passages or passage pairs. There will be a total of 47 questions relating to these passages. The breakdown of passages and questions is in the table below.

U.S and World Literature	1 passage; 9 questions	20%
History/Social Studies	2 passages, or 1 passage and 1 pair; 9-10 questions each	40%
Science	2 passages, or 1 passage and 1 pair; 9-10 questions each	40%

The PSAT Reading Test will contain a range of text complexities from grades 9-10 and post-secondary entry. The passages will cover U.S. and World Literature, History/Social Studies, and Science. The test will also contain 1-2 graphical representations. These may include tables, graphs, and charts. They will vary in level of difficulty as well as data density, and number of variables.

Information and Ideas

The questions tested in this section will focus on the informational content contained in the text.

Reading Closely

These questions will focus on the student's ability to read a passage and extrapolate beyond the information presented. They will look at both the explicit and implicit meanings of the text.

Explicitly stated information
Identifying information stated explicitly in text means locating facts or opinions stated outright in the text and not requiring reader inference or interpretation. For example, when including factual information, an author might give specific names of people, places, or events; specific numbers; specific days of the week, names of months, or dates including the month, date, and year. In informational text, the author might state numerical measurements, e.g., the size of a room or object; the distance between places; how many people live in a certain locality; how many people die annually from a certain cause; or the date, time, and/or place a certain event occurred. Abraham Lincoln began his Gettysburg Address, "Four score and seven years ago," which today is archaic language but does not require inference or interpretation; even a reader unfamiliar with the meaning of "score" can easily look up and find it. In a fictional novel, the author might state how many people are invited to, or were in attendance at, a party or other event.

Drawing inferences from text
Some meanings in text are implicit rather than explicit; in other words, they are not directly stated (explicit), but implied (implicit). This means the reader needs to make an assumption or draw an inference based on what is actually stated. Inferring meaning is often described by the saying "reading between the lines," i.e., determining what is unsaid through carefully observing what is

said. For example, if an author writes, "Considering recent economic changes, what were once necessities are now luxuries for many businesses," the reader can infer that the "recent economic changes" the author refers to involve recession, not recovery or prosperity. Describing things formerly viewed as necessary but now as unnecessary implies worse, not better changes. Or a novelist might write, "Trembling and flushing, she asked breathlessly, 'You saw him? How is he? Did he ask how I am? Did he mention me at all?'" From the author's description of the character, the reader can infer she feels love/attraction for "'him'."

Determining Explicit Meanings

These questions will require the student to identify information explicitly stated in the text.

Explicit descriptors

Writers explicitly state not only factual information in their texts; they also explicitly state other kinds of information. For example, authors use description to give readers a better idea of the characteristics of whatever they are describing. If an author writes, "This sarcophagus is decorated with a vivid color illustration," the word "vivid" is more descriptive than factual. It communicates to the reader that the color illustration described is especially bright, vibrant, or intense visually. This is very helpful when there are no visual images of the object being described to accompany the text. Explicit descriptive words also apply to abstract concepts. For example, the author might write that the vivid color illustration depicts a famous figure's "brave actions." The word "brave" describes the actions of the person using an abstract concept. It communicates to the reader that the person's actions are considered brave or courageous by the author, and usually by other people as well.

Explicitly stated opinions

An essayist might state an opinion; for example, "These people were not treated fairly." Since readers are expected to be able to distinguish opinion from fact, the essayist need not write, "In my opinion, these people were not treated fairly." It is a common practice of authors, especially those writing argumentative or persuasive types of text, to state opinions the same as facts. Even though not proven factual, opinions are stated just as explicitly as facts in these instances. Writers state ideas explicitly in text as well. For example, an author might write about how people historically believed that the Earth was flat, or that the Sun revolved around the Earth. These are not factual, but not simply opinions either; they were the prevailing beliefs at the time, i.e., commonly held ideas. When an author explicitly states his or her *main* idea, he or she typically makes it the topic sentence of the paragraph, chapter, or piece. Topic sentences are also examples of explicitly stating ideas, i.e., expressing them directly in text rather than implying them.

Determining Implicit Meanings

The questions in this section will require the student to read the text and then draw inferences from the text and form logical conclusions.

Inferences

Inferences are educated guesses that can be drawn from the facts and information available to a reader. Inferences are usually based upon a reader's own assumptions and beliefs. The ability to make inferences is often called reading between the lines. There are three basic types of inference: deductive reasoning, abductive reasoning, and inductive reasoning. Deductive reasoning is the ability to find an effect when given a cause and a rule. Abductive reasoning is the ability to find a cause when given a rule and an effect. Inductive reasoning is the ability to find a rule when given the cause and effect. Each type of reasoning can be used to make logical inferences from a piece of writing.

Drawing conclusions

An essayist might state an opinion; for example, "These people were not treated fairly." Since readers are expected to be able to distinguish opinion from fact, the essayist need not write, "In my opinion, these people were not treated fairly." It is a common practice of authors, especially those writing argumentative or persuasive types of text, to state opinions the same as facts. Even though not proven factual, opinions are stated just as explicitly as facts in these instances. Writers state ideas explicitly in text as well. For example, an author might write about how people historically believed that the Earth was flat, or that the Sun revolved around the Earth. These are not factual, but not simply opinions either; they were the prevailing beliefs at the time, i.e., commonly held ideas. When an author explicitly states his or her *main* idea, he or she typically makes it the topic sentence of the paragraph, chapter, or piece. Topic sentences are also examples of explicitly stating ideas, i.e., expressing them directly in text rather than implying them.

Ways that drawing inferences are tested

One way a test might ask you to draw inferences or conclusions is asking what a character in text would likely react to a given event/circumstance based on a text passage. You would need to read closely for clues on which to base your inference. You might see a description of an earlier incident wherein this character reacted a certain way. For example, the author wrote, "The last time somebody hit her, she ran away." Based on this, you could infer she would do the same thing. Or one character says, "If he finds out what you did, he'll kill you," and the passage includes explicit description of the referenced character having killed people. You could then conclude if the third character finds out what the second character did, he will kill him or her. Some works, rather than providing a neat conclusion, seem to end in mid-action; yet readers can predict much from it. An excellent example of such a midstream ending inviting readers to infer conclusions is in Joyce Maynard's novel *Baby Love* (1981).

Using Analogical Reasoning

The student will be required to extrapolate information and idea from the text in order to answer these questions. They will also need to be able to this information and ideas to new, analogous situations.

Using analogical reasoning

Using analogical reasoning as described above involves thinking about situations that are comparable to one in the text and applying information from the text to those other parallel situations. For example, suppose a student reads that colonial Americans, dissatisfied with British laws and influenced by Enlightenment philosophy, wanted freedom to govern themselves instead of being ruled by the British monarchy, so they started the American Revolution to fight for their freedom and won, forming a democratic government. Suppose the student then further reads that the French, strongly influenced both by the same Enlightenment philosophy and by the Americans' success, started the French Revolution, also fighting for their freedom from an unfair monarchy, winning, and forming a democratic government. Then suppose the same student reads about people in other countries being ruled unfairly by a tyrannical monarchy. The student could reasonably apply the information about America and France to these other countries and expect revolutionary wars to break out in some of these other countries.

Extrapolate from text

Even fictional text can be applied to analogous situations, particularly when the author's knowledge of human nature is sound and some of the text elements can be applied across settings. For example, reading William Shakespeare's tragedy *Romeo and Juliet,* one might first observe differences from today's real world: It is set centuries ago, in another country, and involves a family feud, which is rare today. However, one could then observe similarities: The main characters are teenagers; they fall madly in love; their families prohibit their seeing each other; and their families dislike each other, which is commoner today than actual feuds. Teen suicide and teen suicide pacts occur today. Thus the student could extrapolate from this play, albeit fictional, that two teens today as fervently in love as Romeo and Juliet whose parents kept them apart, feeling there were no better options, might take the same actions. Despite today's technology, the chance/accidental element (lack of timely information) causing the double tragedy could equally occur today.

Example

Consider that a student reads in a biology text that mitosis is an asexual type of reproduction in which cells divide to produce more identical cells. The student reads further that mitosis takes place in all living organisms. From this information, the student can extrapolate that since mitosis occurs in all living organisms, mitosis must therefore occur in human beings. Since mitosis is an asexual type of reproduction, the student can further infer that mitosis is not the way in which humans reproduce sexually. By process of elimination, the student can then deduce that mitosis in humans must involve only the reproduction of cells within each individual human body. The student can further deduce that sexual reproduction in human beings must not be mitosis. The student cannot know that human sexual reproduction involves meiosis, or how this differs from mitosis, without reading about meiosis; however, he or she can determine all the aforementioned things just from reading about mitosis alone.

Citing Textual Evidence

These questions will ask the student to support their answer with evidence from the text. The student should be able to specifically identify the information in the text and be able to properly cite it.

Citing supporting evidence

Citing evidence from text that supports a point or claim in that text involves identifying which information is most directly related to that point or claim. As an example, if a writer makes the claim that the world population is increasing, that author might provide evidence to support this claim, such as census statistics from the past several consecutive years, decades, or centuries that give world population numbers larger than they were previously. In the same text, the author may also provide figures measuring poverty, hunger, and other ills related to overpopulation in certain parts of the world to make a case for the argument that population growth is bad and should be controlled. However, the student would be mistaken to cite those figures as evidence supporting the claim that the population is increasing; they are, rather, evidence supporting the claim that population growth is bad and should be controlled.

Citing information that is not informational or argumentative

Whereas informational and argumentative text may often use facts and/or figures as evidence to support various points or claims, fictional narration or description may use more descriptive details as supporting evidence. Moreover, the points or claims in such works may not be stated explicitly in words, but instead may be demonstrated through the actions or responses of characters. For example, an author of a play or novel may establish that a character is highly emotional by portraying or describing behaviors demonstrating this—e.g., flying into a rage, crying easily, becoming overjoyed readily, etc. The playwright or novelist need not write in another character's dialogue that this character is passionate or has mood swings; it is demonstrated through actions/behaviors. Subsequently in the play or novel, the character may do something which is not surprising but expected based on this established character trait. The character's previous actions are evidence supporting the credibility of the later action—i.e., it was "in character."

Steps to cite textual evidence
To cite evidence explicitly stated in text to support what they think about the text, students can take several steps. First, students should state their idea regarding the text. When answering a test question, students should also ensure his or her idea is or includes a restatement of the question. Then, to cite textual evidence supporting that idea, students can either paraphrase the evidence, i.e., restate or describe it in their own words; or quote part of the text directly, enclosing it in quotation marks and introducing it by referencing the paragraph or portion where it appears. Then students need to explain how the evidence they cited supports their idea about the text. For example, students might write that the evidence illustrates a similarity or difference between things, gives a reason for something, demonstrates a cause-and-effect relationship, explains what something means or how something works, etc. Students should also identify how the evidence cited contributed to their formulation of the idea answering the question. Students should cite at least two pieces of textual evidence per idea/question.

Determining Central Ideas and Themes

For these questions the student should be able to identify central ideas and themes that are explicitly stated in the text. They will also need to be able to determine implicit central ideas and themes from the text.

Determining the central ideas of a passage
Central ideas are what a passage is mainly about. They are why the passage is written. The main idea is often found in a topic sentence or even a concluding sentence, and there are supporting details found in the passage that expand upon the main idea. There can, however, be more than one central idea, and these main ideas can be related and intertwined. For instance, the main or central idea of a passage may be that rainforests are drying out. A related main idea might be that the result of rainforest destruction is a loss of wildlife. These two central ideas are obviously related, and the passage may present both of them by focusing on one in one part of the passage and the other in another part of the passage. Another way they could be related is in a cause and effect relationship, with the loss of rainforests being the reason for losses of wildlife. It is important to always check to see if there is more than one central idea in a passage.

Read the excerpt below. Identify and discuss the main idea.

Students who have jobs while attending high school tend not to have as much time to complete their homework as other students. They also do not have time for other activities. We should try to persuade our young people to concentrate on doing well in school, not to concentrate on making money. Having a job while you are a student is harmful.

The main idea of the excerpt is actually the last sentence: "Having a job while you are a student is harmful." This is what the excerpt is mostly about. The other sentences contain supporting information: students who have jobs don't have as much time for homework; students with jobs

Copyright © Mometrix Media. You have been licensed one copy of this document for personal use only. Any other reproduction or redistribution is strictly prohibited. All rights reserved.

don't have time for as many activities. These are both supporting details that tell more about the main idea. The third sentence deals with a persuasive argument; it is another kind of detail. Only the last sentence tells what the excerpt is mostly about. Main ideas are sometimes found in a topic sentence at the start of a text or in the concluding sentence, which is the case in this excerpt.

Theme

As opposed to a main idea, themes are seldom expressed directly in a text, so they can be difficult to identify. A theme is an issue, an idea, or a question raised by the text. For instance, a theme of William Shakespeare's *Hamlet* is indecision, as the title character explores his own psyche and the results of his failure to make bold choices. A great work of literature may have many themes, and the reader is justified in identifying any for which he or she can find support. One common characteristic of themes is that they raise more questions than they answer. In a good piece of fiction, the author is not always trying to convince the reader, but is instead trying to elevate the reader's perspective and encourage him to consider the themes more deeply.

5 Steps to identify the main idea or theme

As with all learning and development, reading should begin with concrete and gradually progress to abstract. Students must identify and understand literal information before they can make inferences. The first step is to identify the most important nouns and verbs in a sentence and define what the sentence is about. The second step is to identify the most important nouns, verbs, and adjectives in a whole paragraph, and define what that paragraph is about. The third step is to read brief passages, all of which use topic sentences with literal meanings. Students should be able to identify topic sentences not only at the beginning, but also anywhere else in a paragraph. In the fourth step, students can begin to make inferences by reading a single paragraph and then determining and articulating what the main idea is that the paragraph implies. The fifth step involves reading passages with more than one paragraph, gradually and slowly increasing the length of passages and identifying the implicit main idea each time. Students should be able to infer the main idea in shorter texts before proceeding to longer ones.

Summarizing

These questions will test the student's ability to identify a summary of a text after reading the text. The student should be able to identify a reasonable summary of the text or of key information presented in the text.

Summarizing

It is also helpful to summarize the information you have read in a paragraph or passage format. This process is similar to creating an effective outline. To begin with, a summary should accurately define the main idea of the passage, though it does not need to explain this main idea in exhaustive detail. It should continue by laying out the most important supporting details or arguments from the passage. All of the significant supporting details should be included, and none of the details included should be irrelevant or insignificant. Also, the summary should accurately report all of these details. Too often, the desire for brevity in a summary leads to the sacrifice of clarity or veracity. Summaries are often difficult to read, because they omit all of graceful language, digressions, and asides that distinguish great writing. However, if the summary is effective, it should contain much the same message as the original text.

Activities to help students learn to summarize

For students to be able to identify good summaries of text or its key information, it will help if they learn how to summarize these themselves. Although they will find recognizing good summaries easier than making their own summaries, both processes require identifying subject matter through locating representative words and recalling significant information. One activity in which students can practice summarizing skills and teachers can provide scaffolding and guidance is using an ABC Chart. This is a simple square grid containing smaller squares, each labeled A, B, C, etc. through Z. Students read a passage; the teacher guides them to recall important phrases and words in the text, write each one on a Post-it Note, and attach it to the square labeled with the first letter of the phrase/word. Students should try to recall as many details, facts, etc. as possible. Then they remove the Post-it Notes from the chart and stick them randomly on the board. The teacher helps them arrange the notes in some pattern—e.g., into a web, by ideas; or chronologically along a timeline, etc. This helps students organize their thoughts.

Understanding Relationships

Texts will contain many different relationships between individuals, events, and ideas. These questions will test the student's ability to identify explicitly stated relationships as well as determine implicit ones.

Textual features that help identify relationships

Authors use various relationships as ways of organizing, presenting, and explaining information. For example, describing cause-and-effect relationships is a common technique in expository/informational text. The author describes some event(s), and then either explicitly states or implicitly establishes factors causing them. When authors use comparison-contrast, they typically compare similarities between/among ideas/things using similes (stated comparisons), metaphors (implied comparisons), and analogies (comparisons of similarities in two unrelated things). Authors identify contrasts by describing opposing qualities/characteristics in things/ideas. One example of using sequence or order is arranging events chronologically, beginning to end. Students can recognize sequential organization by observing specific dates, times, and signal words including "first," "before," "next," "then," "following," "after," "subsequently," "finally," etc. Sequence can also be spatial or by order of importance. Authors introduce some problem, describe its characteristics, and then offer solutions in problem-solution relationships. Descriptive writing provides sensory details to make information realer and easier for readers to imagine. How-to/instructional texts use serial directions to provide information.

Compare and Contrast

Authors will use different stylistic and writing devices to make their meaning more clearly understood. One of those devices is comparison and contrast. When an author describes the ways in which two things are alike, he or she is comparing them. When the author describes the ways in which two things are different, he or she is contrasting them. The "compare and contrast" essay is one of the most common forms in nonfiction. It is often signaled with certain words: a comparison may be indicated with such words as *both*, *same*, *like*, *too*, and *as well*; while a contrast may be indicated by words like *but*, *however*, *on the other hand*, *instead*, and *yet*. Of course, comparisons and contrasts may be implicit without using any such signaling language. A single sentence may both compare and contrast. Consider the sentence *Brian and Sheila love ice cream, but Brian prefers vanilla and Sheila prefers strawberry*. In one sentence, the author has described both a similarity (love of ice cream) and a difference (favorite flavor).

Cause and effect

One of the most common text structures is cause and effect. A cause is an act or event that makes something happen, and an effect is the thing that happens as a result of that cause. A cause-and-effect relationship is not always explicit, but there are some words in English that signal causality, such as *since*, *because*, and *as a result*. As an example, consider the sentence *Because the sky was clear, Ron did not bring an umbrella*. The cause is the clear sky, and the effect is that Ron did not bring an umbrella. However, sometimes the cause-and-effect relationship will not be clearly noted. For instance, the sentence *He was late and missed the meeting* does not contain any signaling words, but it still contains a cause (he was late) and an effect (he missed the meeting). It is possible for a single cause to have multiple effects, or for a single effect to have multiple causes. Also, an effect can in turn be the cause of another effect, in what is known as a cause-and-effect chain.

Text sequence

A reader must be able to identify a text's sequence, or the order in which things happen. Often, and especially when the sequence is very important to the author, it is indicated with signal words like first, then, next, and last. However, sometimes a sequence is merely implied and must be noted by the reader. Consider the sentence He walked in the front door and switched on the hall lamp. Clearly, the man did not turn the lamp on before he walked in the door, so the implied sequence is that he first walked in the door and then turned on the lamp. Texts do not always proceed in an orderly sequence from first to last: sometimes, they begin at the end and then start over at the beginning. As a reader, it can be useful to make brief notes to clarify the sequence.

Interpreting Words and Phrases in Context

These questions will ask the student to determine the meaning of words and phrases from the text. The student must use context clues to help determine the meaning of these words and phrases.

Contextual clues

Look for contextual clues. An answer can be right but not correct. The contextual clues will help you find the answer that is most right and is correct. Understand the context in which a phrase is stated.

When asked for the implied meaning of a statement made in the passage, immediately go find the statement and read the context. Also, look for an answer choice that has a similar phrase to the statement in question.

Example:

In the passage, what is implied by the phrase "Churches have become more or less part of the furniture"?

Find an answer choice that is similar or describes the phrase "part of the furniture" as that is the key phrase in the question. "Part of the furniture" is a saying that means something is fixed, immovable, or set in their ways. Those are all similar ways of saying "part of the furniture." As such, the correct answer choice will probably include a similar rewording of the expression.

Example:

Why was John described as "morally desperate"?

The answer will probably have some sort of definition of morals in it. "Morals" refers to a code of right and wrong behavior, so the correct answer choice will likely have words that mean something like that.

Using word meaning

Paying attention to the phrase, sentence, paragraph, or larger context surrounding a word gives students two distinct advantages: One, it can help figure out the meaning of a new or unfamiliar vocabulary word by the information its context provides; and two, it can help distinguish

- 9 -

between/among different meanings of the same word according to which meaning makes sense within context. For example, when reading words like "nickelback" and "bootleg," if the surrounding context is football, these refer to an additional, fifth defensive back position played by a safety or cornerback and a play run by the quarterback, respectively; but if the surrounding context is rock music, "Nickelback" refers to the name of a Canadian band, and "bootleg" to unofficial or unauthorized recordings of musical performances. Students can look for contextual synonyms for unknown words; for example, a reader unfamiliar with the meaning of "prudent" may observe the words "careful," "cautious," "judicious," etc. Antonyms also help; e.g., if text says, "Smug? On the contrary, he's the most self-critical person I know." This informs defining "smug" as self-congratulatory/overly self-satisfied.

Rhetoric

The questions in this section will focus on the rhetorical analysis of a text.

Analyzing Word Choice

Authors use specific words, phrases, and patterns of words in their writing. The student will be asked to determine how these help to shape the meaning and tone in the text.

Rhetorical Analysis

When analyzing the rhetoric a text uses, students should aim to reveal the purpose of the text or the author's purpose in writing it; who the author's intended audience was; the decisions that the author made, and how these decisions may have influenced the final result of the text. Identifying the intended purpose and audience of a text is identifying two main components of its rhetorical situation, i.e., the circumstances wherein communication occurs, which serves as a major basis for rhetorical analysis. The third main component is the context. Context can include many factors, e.g., the occasion of the work; the exigency, i.e., what motivated the author to write the text; the media and/or venue of its original appearance; the historical background and even the state of the world relative to the text's topic. As an example, texts written respectively before and after 9/11/2001 on the topic of air travel would have some marked differences.

Word choice or diction in rhetoric

Word choice or diction affects the tone of a text and how readers perceive its meaning. Writers inform their diction in part by considering their intended audience and selecting words that will be understood by and appeal to this audience. For instance, language with more denotative meanings (i.e., straightforward dictionary definitions) is more suitable for informational texts, whereas language with more connotative meanings (i.e., words that carry implied associated meanings) is more suitable for descriptive and narrative texts to evoke images and emotions. As examples, describing a sound or noise as "extremely loud" or "at a volume of 100 dB" is more factual and denotative; describing it as "thunderous," "deafening," or in specific reference to a speaker's voice, "stentorian," is more descriptive, connotative, and evocative. Audience also influences the relative formality of diction. For example, more formal text appropriate for an adult professional academic audience might describe size as "massive," whereas more informal language appropriate for high school and younger students might use the blending neologism "ginormous."

How word choice or diction influence meaning and understanding

When writers use good judgment in word choice, they communicate their messages more effectively for readers to understand. Poor word choice, as well as not considering the intended audience in one's diction, can distract readers to the point that they miss the message. Readers can consider the denotations (dictionary definition meanings) and connotations (implied associated meanings) of words used in text, as well as the rhythm and force of words and whether the author uses words concisely, includes verbiage, or appears to have logorrhea. When analyzing word choice in a text, students can consider whether the author has selected words that are comprehensible to the identified reading audience; whether words are chosen with precision and specificity; whether the author selected strong words to express meaning; whether the author placed more emphasis on positive than negative words in text; whether/how often the author included words that are overused, making the language cliché or trite; and whether the text incorporates words that are obsolete today, which readers may not recognize or understand.

Analyzing Text Structure

For these questions students will be asked to answer questions about why the author structured the text a certain way. They will also be asked about the relationship between a particular part of the text and the whole text.

Elements to consider in analyzing text structure

Text structure is how a text is organized. In analyzing the overall structure of a text, the reader can consider its order, e.g., what is written first, what follows, and how it ends; and how its sections and chapters are divided. The genre or type of text is another consideration. For example, consider whether the text is fictional or nonfictional; prose, poetry, drama, or oratory; in fictional prose, whether a novel is a romantic, adventure, action, graphic, historical, fantasy, science fiction novel, etc.; in nonfiction, whether it is an essay; research article, journalistic article, opinion-editorial article; how-to manual; travelogue, etc. The relationship or pattern organizing the text may be a timeline sequence, logical sequence, a priority sequence, or spatial sequence; an analysis of the balance of forces; an analysis of similarities and differences/comparison-contrast; a process of problem, solution, and resolution; simply a list of items; or a piece that seems to jump around without order. Consider also what tone the language establishes; vocabulary and imagery used; and the accuracy of text mechanics (grammar, punctuation, spelling, etc.).

Organizational methods to structure text

Authors organize their writing based on the purpose of their text. Common organizational methods that authors use include: cause and effect, compare and contrast, inductive presentation of ideas, deductive presentation of ideas, and chronological order. Cause and effect is used to present the reasons that something happened. Compare and contrast is used to discuss the similarities and differences between two things. Inductive presentation of ideas starts with specific examples and moves to a general conclusion. Deductive presentation of ideas starts with a conclusion and then explains the examples used to arrive at the conclusion. Chronological order presents information in the order that it occurred.

Cause and effect and chronological order

Authors have to organize information logically so the reader can follow what is being said and locate information in the text. Two common organizational structures are cause and effect and chronological order. In cause and effect, an author presents one thing that makes something else happen. For example, if you go to bed very late, you will be tired. The cause is going to bed late. The effect is being tired the next day. When using chronological order, the author presents information in the order that it happened. Biographies are written in chronological order. The subject's birth and childhood are presented first, followed by adult life, and then by events leading up to the person's death.

Compare and contrast example

Read the following thesis statement and discuss the organizational pattern that the author will most likely use:

> Among people who are current on the latest technologies, there is a debate over whether DVD or Blu-ray Disc is a better choice for watching and recording video.

From the thesis statement the reader can assume that the author is most likely going to use a compare and contrast organizational structure. The compare and contrast structure is best used to discuss the similarities and differences of two things. The author mentions two options for watching and recording video: DVD and Blu-ray Disc. During the rest of the essay, the author will most likely describe the two technologies, giving specific examples of how they are similar and different. The author may discuss the pros and cons of each technology.

Chronological example

Read the following thesis statement and discuss the organizational pattern that the author will most likely use:

> Throughout his life, Thomas Edison used his questioning and creative mind to become one of America's greatest inventors.

Based on the thesis statement, the reader can assume that the author is most likely going to use chronological order to organize the information in the rest of the essay. Chronological order presents information in the order that it occurred. It is often used as the organizational structure in biographies as a way to logically present the important events in a person's life. The words "throughout his life" clue in the reader to the chronological organizational structure. The author will probably discuss Edison's childhood and initial inventions first and then move on to his later queries and inventions.

Example

Todd is writing an editorial on the need for more bus stops in his town. Discuss the type of organization he should use for his editorial and what each might look like.

Todd could organize the information in his editorial in a few different ways. An editorial is a persuasive text so Todd will want to keep that in mind. First, he could organize the information by making his most important points first, following with his lesser points towards the end. Alternatively, Todd could use a cause and effect structure. He could discuss the reasons that his town needs more bus stops and the effects they would have for the people living there. Finally, Todd could discuss the pros and cons of adding the bus stops, using a compare and contrast structure. The organizational structure Todd chooses will depend on the information he wants to write and the method he thinks will be most persuasive.

Part-whole relationships

Students should be able to recognize and explain how a portion of a text is related to the overall text to demonstrate they understand part-to-whole relationships when analyzing text. Every part of a text must serve essential purposes, including setting up/establishing the text at the beginning; fitting together logically with all other parts of the text; remaining focused on the point; supporting the overall text through introducing its topic, establishing evidence, supporting or countering a claim, outlining subtopics, aspects, or components, describing a characteristic or feature, etc.; and informing the reader—about the setting of the text, a character in it, a relationship between/among characters, a research study, an opinion, or something else relevant to the text. Test questions may ask about how words function within sentences, as these examples address; or sentence-to-paragraph relationships, which also include setup or setting the tone, logic, focus or point, including shifts in focus, and evidence supporting claims as functions; or paragraph-to-whole-text relationships, wherein paragraphs should establish a claim/situation; support or refute a claim; maintain focus; and/or inform readers.

Analyzing Point of View

These questions will make the student to determine from which point of view a text was written. They will also need to determine the influence that that this point of view has on the content and style of the text.

Point of view

The point of view of a text is the perspective from which it is told. Every literary text has a narrator or person who tells the story. The two main points of view that authors use are first person and third person. If a narrator is also the main character, or protagonist, the text is written in first-person point of view. In first person, the author writes with the word *I*. Third-person point of view is probably the most common point of view that authors use. Using third person, authors refer to each character using the words *he* or *she*. In third-person omniscient, the narrator is not a character in the story and tells the story of all of the characters at the same time.

Example

Read the following excerpt from Jane Austen's *Emma* and discuss the point of view:
> "Doing just what she liked; highly esteeming Miss Taylor's judgments, but directed chiefly by her own. The real evils, indeed, of Emma's situation were the power of having rather too much her own way, and a disposition to think a little too well of herself...."

To determine the point of view, you should first look at the pronouns used in the passage. If the passage has the pronoun "I" it is probably written in first-person point of view. In first-person point of view, the protagonist is the narrator. In the case of this excerpt, a narrator who is not the protagonist is telling the story. The pronouns used are "she" and "her," which are clues that someone is talking about the character rather than the character speaking for herself. This excerpt is written in the third-person point of view. An outside narrator is telling the story *about* Emma. Emma is not telling the story about herself.

How to determine point of view

In expository text, authors apply various strategies for communicating their points of view about specific topics. As readers, students can identify author point of view readily in some texts; however, they will have to analyze other texts closely to determine point of view. To discern author viewpoint, students can ask themselves four questions: (1) The author is writing to persuade readers to agree with what main idea? (2) How does the author's word choice influence the reader perceptions about the topic? (3) How does the author's selection of examples and/or facts as supporting evidence influence reader thinking about the topic? And (4) What purpose does the author wish to achieve through the text? Students may find the main idea stated directly, as in a topic sentence found in the text, often somewhere in the first paragraph; or they may need to infer it by carefully reading to identify sentences or paragraphs implying it. Students can assess influences of word choice by identifying words/phrases with positive or negative connotations rather than only objective denotations, emphasis through repetition, etc. Examples/facts should illustrate the main idea/point. Author purpose coincides with point of view.

Analyzing Purpose

These questions will ask the student to determine the purpose of a text or a piece of a text. The pieces of text are typically one particular paragraph of the text.

Author's purpose
An author writes with four main purposes: to inform, to entertain, to describe, or to persuade. These purposes play into an author's motivation to craft a text. If the author wants to entertain, he or she may write a novel or short story that has humorous elements and/or dramatic elements. Remember, entertainment does not have to mean comedy or humor; it can just as easily be drama. To determine an author's motives, think about the author's purpose. If the text is fiction, the author's purpose is most likely to entertain or describe. If the text is nonfiction, the author's purpose is most likely to inform. If the text is an editorial or advertisement, the author's purpose is most likely to persuade. Once you identify the author's purpose, you can determine the author's motives.

Determining author's purpose by looking for context clues
To determine the author's purpose in writing text, students can look for certain words as clues to various purposes. For example, if the author's purpose was to compare similarities between/among ideas, look for "clue words" including "like," "similar(ly)," "same," "in the same way," and "just as." If the author's purpose was to contrast differences between/among ideas, clue words include "but," "however," "on the other hand," "dissimilar(ly)," and "in contrast/contrastingly." If the author's purpose was to criticize an idea, clue words connoting judgment/negative opinion include "poor," "bad," "inadequate," "insufficient," "lacking," "excessive," "wasteful," "harmful," "deleterious," "disservice," "unfair," etc. If the purpose was to paint a picture illustrating an idea, descriptive clue words include "morose," "crestfallen," "lusty," "glittering," "exuberant," etc. Explanatory purposes involve using simpler words to describe or explain more complex/abstract ideas. Identification purposes entail listing series of ideas without much accompanying opinion or description. To intensify an idea, authors add superlative ("-est") adjectives, more specific details; and enlarge concepts. To suggest or propose an idea, authors typically express positive opinions and provide supporting evidence for points to convince readers to agree.

Analyzing Arguments

Students will need to be able to analyze arguments in a text for their structure and content.

Introducing an argument in a persuasive passage
The best way to introduce an argument in a persuasive passage and to structure it is to begin by organizing your thoughts and researching the evidence carefully. You should write everything down in outline format to start. Make sure you put the claim at the beginning of the passage. Then, list the reasons and the evidence that you have to support the claim. It is important that you provide enough evidence. Reasons and evidence should follow each other in a logical order. Write the passage so that you hold the reader's attention; use a strong tone and choose words carefully for maximum effect. If you can get the reader to understand your claim, he or she will be more likely to agree with your argument. Restate your claim in the concluding paragraph to maximize the impact on the reader.

Analyzing Claims and Counterclaims

These questions will ask the student to identify explicitly stated claims and counter claims made in a text. They will also need to be able determine implicit claims and counterclaims made in a text.

Defining and supporting claims

A claim/argument/proposition/thesis is anything a writer asserts in that is not a known/proven/accepted fact. As such, it is the author's opinion or at least includes an element of opinion. The writer usually will, or should, provide evidence to back up this claim. Some writers make claims without supporting them, but these are not as effective in convincing readers to believe or agree with them. Some may attempt to provide evidence but choose it poorly; if they cite evidence that is not related directly enough to the claim, or the "evidence" is information from untrustworthy sources or not verified as accurate, this is also less effective. Writers sometimes state their claims directly and clearly; in other instances, they may discuss a number of related topics from which the reader must infer the claims implied in the discussion. For example, suppose two writers take opposing positions, one that immigration to the USA is bad and the other that it is good. Rather than explicitly stating these claims, both may present information supporting negative/positive aspects/views of immigration. Critical readers can infer these claims from the information's negativity/positivity.

Making claims

A persuasive essay will likely focus on one central argument, but it may make many smaller claims along the way. These are subordinate arguments with which the reader must agree if he or she is going to agree with the central argument. The central argument will only be as strong as the subordinate claims. These claims should be rooted in fact and observation, rather than subjective judgment. The best persuasive essays provide enough supporting detail to justify claims without overwhelming the reader. Remember that a fact must be susceptible to independent verification: that is, it must be something the reader could confirm. Also, statistics are only effective when they take into account possible objections. For instance, a statistic on the number of foreclosed houses would only be useful if it was taken over a defined interval and in a defined area. Most readers are wary of statistics, because they are so often misleading. If possible, a persuasive essay should always include references so that the reader can obtain more information. Of course, this means that the writer's accuracy and fairness may be judged by the inquiring reader.

Compare counterclaims to claims

Whereas a claim represents a text's main argument, a counterclaim represents an argument that opposes that claim. Writers actually use counterclaims to support their claims. They do this by presenting their claim; introducing a counterclaim to it; and then definitively refuting the counterclaim. Rather than only promoting and supporting the claim, which leaves the text open to being refuted or attacked by other writers who present their own counterclaims, authors who present both claim and counterclaim have anticipated opposing arguments before others can raise them; have given a voice to the opposition to their claim, and then discredited that voice; and, when they do this effectively, show that their ability to do so indicates how familiar and competent they are with respect to the topic they are discussing in their text. Words such as "but," "yet," "however," "nevertheless," "nonetheless," "notwithstanding," "despite," "in spite of," "on the contrary," "contrastingly," etc. indicating contrast/difference/disagreement signal counterclaims. If readers/students cannot locate a claim in text, they may identify a counterclaim by signal words and work backwards to discover what claim the counterclaim opposes.

Discrediting a counterclaim

When writers present a claim, i.e., a central argument in text, they may also introduce a counterclaim opposing that claim. When journalists do this, by presenting the other side to their argument they can demonstrate their objectivity. In a different use, writers of argumentative/persuasive text may find that furnishing evidence to support a claim, appealing to various reader responses, and other rhetorical devices may still not lend their claim as much strength as they would like. In such cases, another rhetorical technique they may use is presenting a counterclaim. This enables writers not only to anticipate opposing arguments to their claim, but also to rebut these opposing arguments, which in turn lends additional strength to their original claim. As an example, one might claim that using a dentist-approved mouthwash regularly can prevent gingivitis. A counterclaim might be that in a recent survey, dentists questioned the effectiveness of mouthwash. When the next sentence states that this survey included only three dentists, all of whose dental studies were incomplete, the writer has effectively discredited the counterclaim and opposition, reinforcing the original claim.

Example

While referencing and refuting counterclaims are rhetorical devices we often consider tools of serious argument, they can also be used humorously. In a real-life example, addressing the April 2015 annual White House Correspondents' Association Dinner, President Barack Obama drew many laughs from his audience while rebutting political and journalistic attacks by using the technique of presenting counterclaims and then rejecting them to strengthen his own claims, but with sarcastic humor. A central tactic, replayed repeatedly since on various news programs, was Obama's "bucket" joke. A bucket list is a list of things someone wants to do before he or she dies, i.e., "kicks the bucket," hence its name. The president said he had made a "bucket list" of things he wanted to do before his second term ends in 2017. Taking advantage of the fact that "bucket" rhymes with a profane expression, Obama created a euphemism to address criticisms: "Take executive action on immigration? Bucket. New climate regulations? Bucket. It's the right thing to do," implying what he thought of these criticisms without directly cursing them.

Assessing Reasoning

Assessing a claims soundness

In addition to identifying claims and counterclaims that authors present in their texts, students must be able to evaluate whether those claims and counterclaims are sound. The PSAT, SAT, and other standardized tests ask questions that require students to assess the soundness of an author's reasoning in text. A valid argument is logical, i.e., each premise/statement follows and/or builds upon the previous one. However, test questions are not limited to requiring students to assess text logic/validity; they moreover require students to assess soundness, meaning whether the argument is true. Students will likely not have thorough knowledge of all text content on tests. They should assume the content of unfamiliar text is true, since the test will not try to trick students by providing false material. To assess a text argument, the student must first identify its central claim. The remainder of the argument should both answer why the central claim is true, and also prove or support that claim.

How to approach these types of test questions

Some text-based test questions may ask students not only what central claim or argument an author makes in a passage, but also what the author's reasoning behind that claim is. To help select the correct answer from among multiple choices on such questions, the student will need to follow the reasoning that the author uses in the text and relate it to the answer choices. The student can do this by reading each answer choice and then asking himself/herself whether this choice answers the question of why the author's central claim is true. For the student to be able to assess the author's reasoning for soundness, he or she must have the ability to cite evidence with accuracy to support that assessment of reasoning and its soundness or lack thereof. The best and also easiest way of justifying one's assessment of reasoning and its relative soundness by citing evidence is to ask oneself whether why the author makes the claim; how the author justifies the claim; and whether evidence supports the claim and answers the question of why.

Four levels of critical reading
Experts (cf. Elder and Paul, 2004) identify four levels of critical reading. The first level is paraphrasing the text one sentence at a time, which develops and demonstrates understanding. The second level is identifying and explicating a text paragraph's main idea. The third level is analyzing the author's logic and reasoning, including the main purpose, question, information, inferences, concepts, assumptions, implications, and viewpoints. The fourth level is assessing logic or reasoning. Since text quality varies among authors and texts, readers must assess author reasoning. Paraphrasing author meaning accurately on the first level is a prerequisite. To assess reasoning, consider whether the author states his or her meaning clearly; whether the author's claims are accurate; whether he or she offers specifics and/or details with enough precision when these are relevant; whether the author strays from his or her purpose by introducing irrelevant information; whether the text is written superficially or addresses the topic's inherent complexities; whether the author's perspective is narrow or considers other pertinent perspectives; whether the text has internal contradictions or is consistent; whether the text addresses the topic in a trivial or significant way; and whether the author's attitude is narrow/unilateral or fair.

Analyzing Evidence

For these questions the student will be asked to determine how the author uses evidence to support his claims and counterclaims.

Presenting Evidence
When in a focused discussion, be prepared to present your claims, findings, and supporting evidence in a clear and distinct manner. This means being prepared. When compiling your data, make sure to create an outline that has the main ideas and then the supporting evidence, including graphics that you want to present. Attention to details will result in a successful presentation, one in which the diverse individuals in the group will come away with a feeling of having been part of something meaningful. Facts and examples should be stressed. Repetition creates retention. It is important for the speaker to choose the right words, and to build momentum by gradually building up to the strongest argument(s). Graphics are important, because participants will be more convinced if they can see evidence as well as hear it. By breaking up the flow of the discussion and introducing pauses before and after pertinent arguments, the speaker will make the presentation of facts more interesting.

Identifying evidence
In order to assess claims an author makes in text, the reader must be able to analyze the evidence the author supplies to support those claims and evaluate whether the evidence is convincing or not. Students should ask themselves why the author makes a given claim; how the author justifies that claim; and whether the evidence the author uses to justify the claim convincingly and thoroughly answers the "why" question, which means the evidence is effective. If the student can easily come up with counterclaims to the author's claims, the author's reasoning and/or evidence used to support it may not be as convincing as they could be. When answering text-based multiple-choice questions asking them to identify evidence supporting a central claim, students can determine the

correct choice by identifying and eliminating choices citing text that extends the argument rather than supporting it because it does not answer why; and text that is related but not the main source of support, in addition to completely incorrect choices.

Strategies for supporting evidence

Test questions will not only ask students to identify what evidence an author uses in text to support his or her claims; they will also ask students to evaluate an author's strategy for using evidence to support his or her argument. For example, a passage of text might be an author's review of a book, film, or other work. A review most commonly makes the main point that the work is either good or bad, or sometimes a combination of both. A review might also make, argue, and support the point that a movie or book demonstrates a particular central trait (e.g., a movie identified in the romantic comedy genre is actually "anti-romantic"). In order to support his or her main point, the reviewer could use various tactics, such as comparing the work to others as evidence supporting the claim; stating and then effectively addressing a counterclaim to support the claim; or giving a number of examples from the work which can all be used to serve as support for the claim. Some reviewers combine all of these strategies, which when done well can be most effective.

Essential considerations and questions when analyzing evidence

When analyzing the evidence that an author presents in a text to organize and back up his or her argument, as he or she reads, the student should remember to focus not only on what the author's central claim or point is, but also on what the actual content of that evidence is; how the author uses the evidence to prove the point or claim that he or she is making; and whether or not the evidence that the author provides is effective in supporting that central claim or point. A good way to evaluate whether or not a piece of evidence that an author uses is supportive of that author's central claim is whether or not that evidence answers the question of why the author is making that claim. The reader should also consider the questions of how the author justifies this claim and whether the evidence the author has presented to justify the claim is convincing or not.

Synthesis

The questions in this section will focus on synthesizing across multiple sources of information.

Analyzing Multiple Texts

The student will be required to synthesize information and ideas across multiple texts. This means that they will need to apply all of the other skills above to analyze paired passages.

Define synthesis with respect to analyzing multiple texts

Synthesizing, i.e., understanding and integrating, information from multiple texts can at times be among the most challenging skills for some students to succeed with on tests and in school, and yet it is also among the most important. Students who read at the highest cognitive levels can select related material from different text sources and construct coherent arguments that account for these varied information sources. Synthesizing ideas and information from multiple texts actually combines other reading skills that students should have mastered previously in reading one text at a time, and applies them in the context of reading more than one text. For example, students are required to read texts closely, including identifying explicit and implicit meanings; use critical thinking and reading; draw inferences; assess author reasoning; analyze supporting evidence; and formulate opinions they can justify, based on more passages than one. When two paired texts represent opposing sides of the same argument, students can find analyzing them easier; but this is not always the case.

<u>Similarities in texts</u>
When students are called upon to compare things two texts share in common, the most obvious commonality might be the same subject matter or specific topic. However, two texts need not be about the same thing to compare them. Some other features texts can share include structural characteristics. For example, they may both be written using a sequential format, such as narrating events or giving instructions in chronological order; listing and/or discussing subtopics by order of importance; or describing a place spatially in sequence from each point to the next. They may both use a comparison-contrast structure, identifying similarities and differences between, among, or within topics. They might both organize information by identifying cause-and-effect relationships. Texts can be similar in type, e.g., description, narration, persuasion, or exposition. They can be similar in using technical vocabulary or using formal or informal language. They may share similar tones and/or styles, e.g., humorous, satirical, serious, etc. They can share similar purposes, e.g., to alarm audiences, incite them to action, reassure them, inspire them, provoke strong emotional responses, etc.

<u>Contrasts in texts</u>
When analyzing paired or multiple texts, students might observe differences in tone; for example, one text might take a serious approach while another uses a humorous one. Even within approaches or treatments, style can differ: one text may be humorous in a witty, sophisticated, clever way while another may exercise broad, "lowbrow" humor; another may employ mordant sarcasm; another may use satire, couching outrageous suggestions in a "deadpan" logical voice to lampoon social attitudes and behaviors as Jonathan Swift did in *A Modest Proposal.* Serious writing can range from darkly pessimistic to alarmist to objective and unemotional. Texts might have similar information, yet organize it using different structures. One text may support points or ideas using logical arguments, while another may seek to persuade its audience by appealing to their emotions. A very obvious difference in text is genre: for example, the same mythological or traditional stories have been told as oral folk tales, written dramas, written novels, etc.; and/or set in different times and places (e.g., Shakespeare's *Romeo and Juliet* vs. Laurents, Bernstein, and Sondheim's *West Side Story*).

Analyzing Quantitative Information

These questions will test the student's ability to analyze quantitative information. This information may be presented in graphs, tables, and charts and may relate to other information presented in the text.

<u>Analyzing quantitative information</u>
When students read text, particularly informational text, authors may include graphs, charts, and/or tables to illustrate the written information under discussion. Students need to be able to understand these representations and how they are related to the text they supplement. For example, a line graph can show how some numerical value—like number or percentage of items, people, groups, dollars, births, deaths, cases of specific illnesses, etc. or amount of rainfall, products, waste matter, etc.—has increased, decreased, or stayed the same over designated periods of time. A bar graph may be used like a line graph to show the same chronological change; or to compare different numbers or proportions of things side by side without reference to time. A pie chart visualizes distribution and proportion by depicting percentages or fractions of a whole occupied by different categories, e.g., how much money is allocated or spent for each division among services or

products, what percentages or proportions of a population has certain characteristics, etc. Tables and charts often list numbers by category; students must be able to identify largest and smallest quantities, order by quantity, etc.

Interpreting information from graphics
It is important to be able to interpret information presented in graphics and be able to translate it to text. These graphics can include maps, charts, illustrations, graphs, timelines, and tables. Each of these different graphics is used to present a different type of quantitative or technical information. Maps show a visual representation of a certain area. A map may contain a legend which helps to identify certain geographic features on the map. A graph or chart will usually contain two axes that show the relationship between two variables. A table can also be similar to this but may show the relationship between any number of variables. So no matter how the information is presented it is important to be able to interpret it and explain what it means.

Charts and graphs
An author may organize information in a chart, a graph, in paragraph format, or as a list. Information may also be presented in a picture or a diagram. The information may be arranged according to the order in which it occurred over time, placed in categories, or it may be arranged in a cause-and-effect relationship. Information can also be presented according to where it occurs in a given space (spatial order), or organized through description. The way an author chooses to organize information is often based on the purpose of information that is being presented, the best way to present given information, and the audience that the information is meant to reach.

Sentence Completions

Read each sentence, inserting the answer choices in the blanks. Don't stop at the first answer choice if you think it is right, but read them all. What may seem like the best choice, at first, may not be after you have had time to read all of the choices.

Adjectives Give it Away

Words mean things and are added to the sentence for a reason. Adjectives in particular may be the clue to determining which answer choice is correct.
Example:
　　The brilliant scientist made several _____ discoveries.
　　　　A. dull
　　　　B. dazzling

Look at the adjectives first to help determine what makes sense. A "brilliant" or smart scientist would make dazzling, rather than dull discoveries. Without that simple adjective, no answer choice is clear.

Use logic

Ask yourself questions about each answer choice to see if they are logical.
Example:
　　The deep pounding resonance of the drums could be _____ far off in the distance.
　　A. seen
　　B. heard

Would resonating poundings be "seen"? or Would resonating pounding be "heard"?

Multiple Blanks Are an Opportunity

Some sentence completion questions may have multiple blanks. It may be easier to focus on only one of the blanks and try to determine which answer choices could logically fit. This may allow you to eliminate some of the answer choices and concentrate only upon the ones that remain.

Transitional words

Watch out for key transitional words! This can include however, but, yet, although, so, because, etc. These may change the meaning of a sentence and the context of the missing word.
Example:
> He is an excellent marksman, but surprisingly, he _____ comes home empty handed from a hunting trip.
> > A. often
> > B. never
> > C. rarely

A good shot or marksman would be expected to be a successful hunter. Watch out though for the transition phrase "but surprisingly". It indicates the opposite of what you would expect, which means this particular marksman must not be a successful hunter. A successful hunter would either never or rarely come home empty handed from a hunt, but an unsuccessful hunter would "often" come home empty handed, making "a" the correct answer.

The Trap of Familiarity

Don't just choose a word because you recognize it. On difficult questions, you may only recognize one or two words. PSAT doesn't put "make-believe words" on the test, so don't think that just because you only recognize one word means that word must be correct. If you don't recognize four words, then focus on the one that you do recognize. Is it correct? Try your best to determine if it fits the sentence. If it does, that is great, but if it doesn't, eliminate it.

Reading Passages

Some questions will be concerning sentence insertions. In those cases, do not look for the ones that simply restate what was in the previous sentence. New sentences should contain new information and new insights into the subject of the text. If asked for the paragraph to which a sentence would most naturally be added, find a key noun or word in that new sentence. Then find the paragraph containing exactly or another word closely related to that key noun or word. That is the paragraph that should include the new sentence.

Some questions will ask what purpose a phrase fulfilled in a particular text. It depends upon the subject of the text. If the text is dramatic, then the phrase was probably used to show drama. If the text is comedic, then the phrase was probably to show comedy.

In related cases, you may be asked to provide a sentence that summarizes the text, or to reorganize a paragraph. Simple sentences, without wordy phrases, are usually best. If asked for a succinct answer, then the shorter the answer, the more likely it is correct.

Skimming

Your first task when you begin reading is to answer the question "What is the topic of the selection?" This can best be answered by quickly skimming the passage for the general idea, stopping to read only the first sentence of each paragraph. A paragraph's first is usually the main topic sentence, and it gives you a summary of the content of the paragraph.

Once you've skimmed the passage, stopping to read only the first sentences, you will have a general idea about what it is about, as well as what is the expected topic in each paragraph.

Each question will contain clues as to where to find the answer in the passage. Do not just randomly search through the passage for the correct answer to each question. Search scientifically. Find key word(s) or ideas in the question that are going to either contain or be near the correct answer. These are typically nouns, verbs, numbers, or phrases in the question that will probably be duplicated in the passage. Once you have identified those key word(s) or idea, skim the passage quickly to find where those key word(s) or idea appears. The correct answer choice will be nearby. *Example:*
        What caused Martin to suddenly return to Paris?

The key word is Paris. Skim the passage quickly to find where this word appears. The answer will be close by that word.

However, sometimes key words in the question are not repeated in the passage. In those cases, search for the general idea of the question.
Example:
        Which of the following was the psychological impact of the author's childhood upon the
        remainder of his life?

Key words are "childhood" or "psychology". While searching for those words, be alert for other words or phrases that have similar meaning, such as "emotional effect" or "mentally" which could be used in the passage, rather than the exact word "psychology".

Numbers or years can be particularly good key words to skim for, as they stand out from the rest of the text.
Example:
        Which of the following best describes the influence of Monet's work in the 20th century?

20th contains numbers and will easily stand out from the rest of the text. Use *20th* as the key word to skim for in the passage.

Other good key word(s) may be in quotation marks. These identify a word or phrase that is copied directly from the passage. In those cases, the word(s) in quotation marks are exactly duplicated in the passage.
Example:
        In her college years, what was meant by Margaret's "drive for excellence"?

"Drive for excellence" is a direct quote from the passage and should be easy to find.

Beware of Directly Quoted Answers

Once you've quickly found the correct section of the passage to find the answer, focus upon the answer choices. Sometimes a choice will repeat word for word a portion of the passage near the answer. However, beware of such duplication – it may be a trap! More than likely, the correct choice will paraphrase or summarize the related portion of the passage, rather than being exactly the same wording.

Truth does not equal correctness

For the answers that you think are correct, read them carefully and make sure that they answer the question. An answer can be factually correct, but it MUST answer the question asked. Additionally, two answers can both be seemingly correct, so be sure to read all of the answer choices, and make sure that you get the one that BEST answers the question.

When there's no key word

Some questions will not have a key word.
Example:
> Which of the following would the author of this passage likely agree with?

In these cases, look for key words in the answer choices. Then skim the passage to find where the answer choice occurs. By skimming to find where to look, you can minimize the time required.

Sometimes it may be difficult to identify a good key word in the question to skim for in the passage. In those cases, look for a key word in one of the answer choices to skim for. Often the answer choices can all be found in the same paragraph, which can quickly narrow your search.

Paragraph focus

Focus upon the first sentence of each paragraph, which is the most important. The main topic of the paragraph is usually there.

Once you've read the first sentence in the paragraph, you have a general idea about what each paragraph will be about. As you read the questions, try to determine which paragraph will have the answer. Paragraphs have a concise topic. The answer should either obviously be there or obviously not. It will save time if you can jump straight to the paragraph, so try to remember what you learned from the first sentences.

Example: The first paragraph is about poets; the second is about poetry. If a question asks about poetry, where will the answer be? The second paragraph.

The main idea of a passage is typically spread across all or most of its paragraphs. Whereas the main idea of a paragraph may be completely different than the main idea of the very next paragraph, a main idea for a passage affects all of the paragraphs in one form or another.
Example:
> What is the main idea of the passage?

For each answer choice, try to see how many paragraphs are related. It can help to count how many sentences are affected by each choice, but it is best to see how many paragraphs are affected by the choice. Typically, the answer choices will include incorrect choices that are main ideas of individual paragraphs, but not the entire passage. That is why it is crucial to choose ideas that are supported by the most paragraphs possible.

Eliminate choices

Some choices can quickly be eliminated. "Andy Warhol lived there." Is Andy Warhol even mentioned in the article? If not, quickly eliminate it.

When trying to answer a question such as "the passage indicates all of the following EXCEPT" quickly skim the paragraph searching for references to each choice. If the reference exists, scratch it off as a choice. Similar choices may be crossed off simultaneously if they are close enough.

Watch for answers that are similarly worded. Since only one answer can be correct, if there are two answers that appear to mean the same thing, they must BOTH be incorrect, and can be eliminated.

> Example Answer Choices:
> A.   changing values and attitudes
> B.   a large population of mobile or uprooted people

These answer choices are similar; they both describe a fluid culture. Because of their similarity, they can be linked together. Since the answer can have only one choice, they can also be eliminated together.

Fact/opinion

Remember that answer choices that are facts will typically have no ambiguous words. For example, how long is a long time? What defines an ordinary person? These ambiguous words of "long" and "ordinary" should not be in a factual statement. However, if all of the choices have ambiguous words, go to the context of the passage. Often a factual statement may be set out as a research finding.

Example:
> "The scientist found that the eye reacts quickly to change in light."

Opinions may be set out in the context of words like thought, believed, understood, or wished.
Example:
> "He thought the Yankees should win the World Series."

Time Management

In technical passages, do not get lost on the technical terms. Skip them and move on. You want a general understanding of what is going on, not a mastery of the passage.

When you encounter material in the selection that seems difficult to understand, bracket it. It often may not be necessary and can be skipped. Only spend time trying to understand it if it is going to be relevant for a question. Understand difficult phrases only as a last resort.

Answer general questions before detail questions. A reader with a good understanding of the whole passage can often answer general questions without rereading a word. Get the easier questions out of the way before tackling the more time consuming ones.

Identify each question by type. Usually the wording of a question will tell you whether you can find the answer by referring directly to the passage or by using your reasoning powers. You alone know which question types you customarily handle with ease and which give you trouble and will require more time. Save the difficult questions for last.

Final Warnings

Hedge phrases revisited

Once again, watch out for critical "hedge" phrases, such as likely, may, can, will often, mostly, usually, generally, rarely, sometimes, etc. Question writers insert these hedge phrases, to cover every possibility. Often an answer will be wrong simply because it leaves no room for exception.

Example:
    Animals live longer in cold places than animals in warm places.

This answer choice is wrong, because there are exceptions in which certain warm climate animals live longer. This answer choice leaves no possibility of exception. It states that every animal species in cold places live longer than animal species in warm places. Correct answer choices will typically have a key hedge word to leave room for exceptions.

Example:
    In severe cold, a polar bear cub is likely to survive longer than an adult polar bear.

This answer choice is correct, because not only does the passage imply that younger animals survive better in the cold, it also allows for exceptions to exist. The use of the word "likely" leaves room for cases in which a polar bear cub might not survive longer than the adult polar bear.

Word usage questions

When asked how a word is used in the passage, don't use your existing knowledge of the word. The question is being asked precisely because there is some strange or unusual usage of the word in the passage. Go to the passage and use contextual clues to determine the answer. Don't simply use the popular definition you already know.

Switchback words

Stay alert for "switchbacks". These are the words and phrases frequently used to alert you to shifts in thought. The most common switchback word is "but". Others include although, however, nevertheless, on the other hand, even though, while, in spite of, despite, regardless of.

Avoid "fact traps"

Once you know which paragraph the answer will be in, focus on that paragraph. However, don't get distracted by a choice that is factually true about the paragraph. Your search is for the answer that answers the question, which may be about a tiny aspect in the paragraph. Stay focused and don't fall for an answer that describes the larger picture of the paragraph. Always go back to the question and make sure you're choosing an answer that actually answers the question and is not just a true statement.

Writing and Language Test

The writing and language portion of the PSAT consists of one 35-minute section. It will contain 4 passages and there will be a total of 44 questions relating to these passages. The breakdown of passages and questions is shown in the table below.

Careers	1 passage; 11 questions	25%
History/Social Studies	1 passage; 11 questions	25%
Humanities	1 passage; 11 questions	25%
Science	1 passage; 11 questions	25%

The PSAT Writing and Language Test will contain a range of text complexities from grades 9-10 to post-secondary entry. The passages will cover the subjects from the table above. The test will also contain one or more graphics in one or more sets of questions. These may include tables, graphs, and charts. They will vary in level of difficulty as well as data density, and number of variables.

Expression of Ideas

The questions in this section will focus on the revision of text. They will ask the student to revise for topic development, accuracy, logic, cohesion, rhetorically effective use of language.

Proposition

For these questions the student will add, revise, or retain central ideas, main claims, counterclaims, and topic sentences. These revisions should be made to convey arguments, information, and ideas more clearly and effectively.

Writing propositions

Students need to read and review their own writing critically and make revisions accordingly to ensure it informs its reading/listening audience with clarity and argues points effectively to convince its audience. For example, a short essay needs a topic sentence; longer pieces may need one topic sentence per paragraph. A topic sentence must clearly summarize the main point or idea that the rest of the paragraph or piece addresses. Therefore, a sentence that is overly long and complex is not a good topic sentence; the student must revise it to be shorter, simpler, and clearer. In the same vein as a topic sentence, the main claim in a piece of expository or argumentative writing must also be stated clearly and simply so that the audience both notices and understands it. It should be concise, attention-getting, and unambiguously stated. Any counterclaim, which the writer introduces to present both sides of an argument or to refute as a way of strengthening the original claim that it presumes to oppose, must be stated just as clearly and simply as the claim itself.

Main Idea

The main idea of a passage is what the passage is mostly about. It is the main point of the passage. Sometimes the main idea is stated in a passage by the use of a topic sentence either at the beginning of the passage or elsewhere. Sometimes the main idea may be found in the title of the passage. Oftentimes the main idea is not stated in the passage; the reader needs to determine it from the information or details in the passage. The main idea will become more and more obvious to a reader as detail after detail supports it. Some information in the passage may not be supporting, but most ideas and details will support the main idea. The main idea is filled out by the supporting details in a passage.

Making a claim

When making a claim, it is important to first think about the arguments that support that claim. While researching, try to anticipate what readers might say; this will help you thoroughly develop your claim. It is not enough to research a claim on the Internet, because many sources are dubious at best. Look for sites that are objective. Find authorities that you can quote, and use statistics. Present counterclaims using ample evidence. Mention both the strengths and weaknesses without any prejudice. Divide each counterclaim into a separate paragraph with supporting evidence. Make sure to present everything in a logical manner so that the information will be easily understood by the reader. Most importantly, one needs to separate opinions from facts.

Support

These questions will ask students to add, revise, or retain information and ideas with the intention of supporting claims in the text.

Text evidence

The term text evidence refers to information included in a text that supports the main point of the paper, from which a reader can draw conclusions or generalizations. The author will deliberately include key points that serve as supporting details for the main point of a paper. For example, the main point of a paper may state: The average yearly rainfall in the city has risen by 2 inches per year since 1999. The paper would go on to include the amount of rainfall for each month or season and any contributing factors that may be causing an increase in yearly rainfall. Additional facts, or text evidence to support the point that yearly rainfall is rising in the city would help to prove that the author's main point is correct.

Supporting details

Supporting details are crucial to a story. These details allow the reader to "see" a character or scene in their mind. Supporting details may include descriptions of the weather, the color of a character's eyes or hair, or the sounds that a character hears. All of these details help readers understand the character as a person. Supporting details also add interest to a story. Readers must be able to distinguish between a main idea and supporting details. Supporting details are usually mentioned only once; they help create or develop the main idea.

How supporting information strengthens a text

Anytime a writer wants to convince readers/listeners to believe or agree with his or her opinion or position, he or she should provide factual information that proves or supports it. As an example, by now most people are aware that smoking tobacco can damage health. However, making the written assertion that "Smoking is unhealthy" with no accompanying information does not carry as much weight as saying the same thing and then citing statistics such as how many people die from smoking-related illnesses each year; how many cases of lung and other cancers, emphysema, etc. are caused annually by smoking, etc. Citing a highly reputable source(s) for such statistics lends additional weight to their credibility. This principle can be extended to apply to other assertions that are less obviously true or accepted. In fact, when writers argue opposing sides of some debate or controversy, each can present different facts, statistics, or other details that support one side or the other. Thus, with good supporting evidence and good writing, two authors or students can present equally convincing cases for diametrically opposed arguments about the same subject.

Focus

For these questions students will be asked to add, revise, retain, or delete information for the sake of relevance. These revisions should be made to make the text more relevant and focused.

Maintaining clarity and relevance

One situation wherein students need to add information and ideas to text is if they have stated a main point, but not developed it sufficiently. They may assert a position or opinion—even a fact—in broad and/or simple terms, but not elaborate in enough detail to explain specifically what it means; give examples illustrating it; or anticipate and rebut counterclaims. If the main idea is an abstract concept, providing an analogy with something concrete could illustrate it for better understanding. Students also need to add information if they have asserted some claim without any proof or support. Students especially need to delete text when their writing wanders off topic. If they include too much information that is irrelevant, their topic and main point become unclear and readers become confused. Even when on topic, if sentences discussing it are written unclearly, students must revise them. Feedback from teachers, peers, and/or the actual reading/listening audience is helpful to determine clarity. Students should also develop judgment and conviction and confidence in their writing to retain material they find essential.

Relevant information

Before information is sought, a list of guiding questions should be developed to help determine whether information found is adequate, relevant, and consistent. These questions should be based on the research goals, which should be laid out in an outline or concept map. For example, a student writing a report on Navajo social structure might begin with questions concerning the general lifestyle and location of Navajos, and follow with questions about how Navajo society was organized. While researching his questions, he will come up with pieces of information. This information can be compared to his research questions to determine whether it is relevant to his report. Information from several sources should be compared to determine whether information is consistent. Information that is adequate helps answer specific questions that are part of the research goals. Inadequate information for this particular student might be a statement such as "Navajos had a strong societal structure," because the student is probably seeking more specific information.

Quantitative Information

These questions will ask the student to relate information presented quantitatively to information presented in the text. The quantitative information may be in the form of graphs, charts, and tables.

Quantitative Information

When they include graphs, tables, or charts to illustrate numerical or quantitative information that proves or supports their textual claims; or write text about existing graphical presentations of quantitative information, students should be able to explain clearly how material in a graph/table/chart is related to verbal information in text and vice versa. For example, in a bar graph, higher/taller bars indicate larger numbers/quantities, lower/shorter bars smaller numbers/amounts. These numbers may also be percentages. In a line graph, higher points represent larger numbers; lower points, smaller quantities. If the line connecting points ascends steadily, this depicts some quantity increasing steadily; a descending line indicates an ongoing decrease. Line graphs whose points yo-yo up and down repeatedly indicate instability; flat lines show no change. In pie charts, larger and smaller "slices" or sections equal larger and smaller proportions of the whole, typically percentages. Tables may list numbers in ascending/descending order of quantity, or by order of category without numerical patterns. With the latter, students must be able to read, create, and explain greater/smaller quantities and relationships in tables.

Interpreting information from graphics

It is important to be able to interpret information presented in graphics and be able to translate it to text. These graphics can include maps, charts, illustrations, graphs, timelines, and tables. Each of these different graphics is used to present a different type of quantitative or technical information. Maps show a visual representation of a certain area. A map may contain a legend which helps to identify certain geographic features on the map. A graph or chart will usually contain two axes that show the relationship between two variables. A table can also be similar to this but may show the relationship between any number of variables. So no matter how the information is presented it is important to be able to interpret it and explain what it means.

Organization

These questions will have the student revise the text to improve logic and cohesion at the sentence, paragraph, and whole-text levels.

Transition words

The use of appropriate transition words helps to clarify the relationships between ideas and concepts and creates a more cohesive passage. A good writer knows that such words and phrases serve to indicate the relationship between ideas and concepts. Words or phrases that show causality between ideas include "as a result," "consequently" and "therefore." Words that show a compare-and-contrast relationship include "however," "on the other hand," "in contrast" and "but." When introducing examples of different concepts, words such as "namely," "for example" and "for instance" act as transition words. Transition words such as "foremost," "primarily," "secondly," "former" and "latter" can be used when showing the order of importance of ideas or concepts.

Logical Sequence

For these questions the student should revise the text with the intention of improving the logical order that the information is presented in.

Importance of presenting information logically

Including all of the necessary information in a paragraph is not enough if that information is not presented in the most logical order. The first sentence in the first paragraph of a piece of writing should introduce that paragraph, and sometimes introduce the entire text as well. It should also get the readers' attention and interest and make them want to continue reading. After introducing the main idea, students should present evidence supporting it. They must include transitional language from the first sentence and paragraph to the next, and introduce the evidence by quoting, citing, or paraphrasing. They should then analyze the evidence so readers understand why they chose it and how it connects to their argument. Each sentence should lead to or connect to the next; each succeeding sentence should build upon or extend from the previous one; and all sentences should proceed in a linear fashion to the conclusion. If students write sentences that jump around rather than following a logical sequence, the result will be unclear and confuse readers.

Logical sequence

Students can convince their readers to believe or agree with the points and arguments in their text not only by presenting supportive evidence, but moreover by ordering their ideas in the most compelling sequence. Since writing is a process, any written piece may be regarded as never finite but capable of continually evolving further. If students discover new evidence during their writing process, they may need to assume a different position than they originally had; or use the same argument, but structure it differently; or substitute different transitional language between sentences and/or paragraphs, etc. Some challenges that students face include allowing for complexity in their text while still maintaining clarity and firmness in their textual structure, yet also avoiding having the text read like a "laundry list" or seem mechanical in its execution. Rather than merely repeating their main point, student writers must move their argument and readers forward. Since ideas must follow a logical sequence in text, the transitions or "stitching" connecting them must be transparent to readers.

Revision of text for logic

There are many ways to revise writing. It is important to check for the logic of ideas and make sure the text has cohesion and belongs together. There must also be a progression of ideas that a reader can follow. The ideas should fit naturally with one another. After the writing is done, there are other ways to revise it. Sometimes sentences need to be rearranged or even deleted. Sometimes sentences need to be added to put more information into the text. Sometimes sentences need to be combined so that the sentences are more varied. The best way to revise a text is by rereading it carefully to see if the writing makes sense and flows well and then to make the appropriate changes.

Importance of strong transitions in logical sequence

When they are writing academically, students need to connect their sentences and paragraphs with transitions that make the logical progression of their argument or discussion clear to their readers so they can follow it. Readers should never have to try to figure out why the writer selected certain supporting evidence, what that evidence signifies, or specifically how it backs up the writer's point. Good transitions serve as guides to lead readers from one idea to the next. One element required for strong transitions is using strong verbs. These function as signals to the reader how a new sentence or paragraph (or section or chapter) proceeds logically from the one before. Strong verbs should be active verbs; single words are usually preferable over two-word phrases that combine verbs with prepositions. For example, rather than "set up," students can write "establish." Instead of "go up," they could better write "increase." And rather than writing "help out," they can use a verb like "assist," "aid," or just "help" without the preposition.

Introductions, Conclusions, and Transitions

These questions will have the student revise the beginning or ending of full texts and paragraphs. They should make sure that transition words, phrases, or sentences are used effectively to connect information and ideas.

General guidelines for beginning, transitioning, and concluding a text

Before starting to write, students must ascertain their purposes for writing. Their general purpose might be to inform, convince, or entertain readers; they can determine their specific purpose by finishing the sentence, "After reading my paper (/speech), people will...." While the introduction and conclusion may be shorter than the rest, they are critically important. The introduction gets audience attention; enables readers/listeners to form impressions sooner; and make the impressions they form indelible. To get reader/listener attention, cite a startling opinion/fact; ask a rhetorical question; relate a short anecdote; present a quotation; relate a pertinent joke; or refer to something familiar. State the main idea/proposition/thesis in one clear, direct sentence. Then establish credibility, e.g., by identifying experience with/research into the topic; the reason for topic choice; and/or reasons for writer authority regarding the topic. Briefly preview the main points by listing them in the same order they will be discussed. Connect all discussion ideas and information with transitional words/phrases (e.g., "next," "moreover," "furthermore," "notwithstanding," "however," "for example," "therefore," "similarly/conversely," etc. as applicable), including to the conclusion, which should summarize the main points and restate the main idea differently.

Introduction

An introduction announces the main point of the work. It will usually be a paragraph of 50 to 150 words, opening with a few sentences to engage the reader, and concluding with the essay's main point. The sentence stating the main point is called the thesis sentence. If possible, the sentences leading to the thesis should attract the reader's attention with a provocative question, vivid image, description, paradoxical statement, quotation, or anecdote. The thesis sentence could also appear at the beginning of the introduction. Some types of writing do not lend themselves to stating a thesis in one sentence. Personal narratives and some types of business writing may be better served by conveying an overriding purpose of the text, which may or may not be stated directly. The important point is to impress the audience with the rationale for the writing.

Conclusion

The conclusion of a text is typically found in the last one or two paragraphs of the text. A conclusion wraps-up the text and reminds the reader of the main point of the text. The conclusion is the author's way of leaving the reader with a final note to remember about the paper and comes after all the supporting points of the text have been presented. For example, a paper about the importance of avoiding too much sunlight may have a conclusion that reads: By limiting sun exposure to 15 minutes a day and wearing sunscreen of at least SPF 15, a person can reduce their risk of getting skin cancer later in life.

Transitional words and phrases

A good writer will use transitional words and phrases to guide the reader through the text. You are no doubt familiar with the common transitions, though you may never have considered how they operate. Some transitional phrases (*after, before, during, in the middle of*) give information about time. Some indicate that an example is about to be given (*for example, in fact, for instance*). Writers use them to compare (*also, likewise*) and contrast (*however, but, yet*). Transitional words and phrases can suggest addition (*and, also, furthermore, moreover*) and logical relationships (*if, then, therefore, as a result, since*). Finally, transitional words and phrases can demarcate the steps in a process (*first, second, last*). You should incorporate transitional words and phrases where they will orient your reader and illuminate the structure of your composition.

Effective Language Use

These questions have the student revise the text for the purpose of improving the use of language to accomplish particular rhetorical purposes.

Figure of speech

A figure of speech, sometimes termed a rhetorical figure or device, is a word or phrase that departs from straightforward, literal language. Figures of speech are often used and crafted for emphasis, freshness of expression, or clarity. However, clarity may suffer from their use.

As an example of the figurative use of a word, consider the following sentence: I am going to crown you.

It may mean:

I am going to place a literal crown on your head.

I am going to symbolically exalt you to the place of kingship.

I am going to punch you in the head with my clenched fist.

I am going to put a second checker on top of your checker to signify that it has become a king.

Rhetorical fallacy

A rhetorical fallacy, or a fallacy of argument, does not allow the open, two-way exchange of ideas upon which meaningful conversations exist. They try to distract the reader with various appeals instead of using logic. Examples of a rhetorical fallacy include, ad hominem, exaggeration, stereotyping, and categorical claims. Ad hominem is an attack on a person's character or personal traits in an attempt to undermine their argument. An exaggeration is the representation of something in an obviously excessive manner. Stereotyping is the thought that all people in a certain group have a certain characteristics or tendencies. A categorical claim is a universal statement about a particular type of thing or person. A categorical claim can be thought of as the verbalization of a stereotype.

Figurative language

Figurative language is language that goes beyond the literal meaning of the words. Descriptive language that evokes imagery in the reader's mind is one type of figurative language. Exaggeration is also one type of figurative language. Also, when you compare two things, you are using figurative language. Similes and metaphors are ways of comparing things, and both are types of figurative language commonly found in poetry. An example of figurative language (a simile in this case) is: The child howled like a coyote when her mother told her to pick up the toys. In this example, the child's howling is compared to that of a coyote. Figurative language is descriptive in nature and helps the reader understand the sound being made in this sentence.

Precision

For these questions students will revise the text to improve the exactness or content appropriateness of word choice.

Precise word choice

Consider that a student wants to convey in a text the idea that an innovative composer had deviated from a number of musical traditions (for example, the rhythms that Igor Stravinsky used in *The Firebird*, 1910). The student is looking for a word that means "moved away from" or "left" (tradition) and is most appropriate in the context of the sentence and surrounding text. Using a thesaurus, classmate suggestions, or simply his or her own vocabulary knowledge, the student considers the synonyms "evacuated," "vacated," "retired," and "departed." These words can be synonyms in the sense that they indicate leaving or going away from something. However, they are not all appropriate in this context. "Evacuate" means leaving/going away in the sense of physically exiting/being made to exit a location, as when people must evacuate buildings/towns/cities or a nurse digitally evacuates a patient's bowel. "Vacate" means leaving/going away from a place or role, e.g., vacating the premises or a job position. "Retire" means leaving a job/position/career, or leaving company/waking activity as in going to bed. Only "depart" can mean literally leaving a place OR figuratively diverging from traditions, usual practices, etc.

Examples of strong and precise word choice

Students need to consider whether they choose nouns and verbs that are both strong and accurate. For example, "This book tells about the Civil War" is neither as strong nor as accurate as it could be because the subject noun and verb are not as precise as they could be. If the student instead writes, "This novel describes a Confederate soldier's experiences during the Civil War," the subject noun "novel" specifies what kind of book it is, whereas "book" could mean many different types of books; and the verb "describes" more specifically identifies how the novel communicates its subject matter than "tells," which could mean narrates, informs, entertains, ridicules, etc. rather than—or as well as—describes. Words not mindfully chosen can have unintended connotations, e.g., "We will attack them in their private spots" vs. "We will attack them where they hide." Technical terminology/jargon should only be used as necessary within a discipline, not to impress at the expense of understanding; e.g., "dialogue" is clearer than "dialectical interface."

Examples of poor word choice

Student writers may select words whose precise meaning is inappropriate to the sentence context. The fact that many adults do the same in their speech makes it all too easy for students to fall prey to this type of error. For example, describing a house that she admired, a woman said, "That house positively reeks of charm." Another responded enthusiastically about a performance she had just attended, "Oh, it was horribly good!" (These are both real-life examples.) In both cases, the connotation of a word was inconsistent with sentence meaning and context; word meaning was precise but incorrect. Another type of error is simply lack of precision. Vague, imprecise words/phrases are not descriptive. For instance, contrast the impact of "A bad smell came from the apartment" with "A stench of putrefaction emanated from the apartment." Visual details add precision: contrast "Her pretty dress was shiny" with "Her sequin-encrusted dress sparkled with reflected light." Sensory details evoke emotions: contrast "He was sad" with "His reddened eyes and tear-stained face betrayed him." Precise adjectives and verbs are stronger: contrast "The hungry dog ate the food" with "The famished dog devoured the food."

Concision

For these questions the student will revise the text to improve the economy of word choice. This means they should cut out wordiness and redundancy.

Redundant phrases

In an effort to write as clearly as possible to ensure direct communication and correct reader understanding, student writers may err on the side of excess by using redundant wording. For example, a student might describe something as "the current design of the school building as it stands right now." This is triply redundant: "current," "as it stands," and "right now" all have the same meaning. Therefore the student need not use all three. He or she can write EITHER "the current design of the school building" OR "the design of the school building as it stands" OR "the design of the school building right now." Some common redundancy errors by students and others include "In addition, there is also…"/"adding an additional…"; "advance planning"; "ask the question"; "a brief moment"; "component parts"; "completely destroy," "crisis situation"; "could possibly"; "fellow classmates," etc. Common redundant spoken expressions have become so accepted/taken for granted that these too can invade writing, e.g., "ATM machine" or "PIN number." While calculated repetition can be an effective rhetorical device, redundancy is *unnecessary* repetition. (Classic joke = "Department of Redundancy Department.")

<u>Eliminating wordiness</u>
Edit the following sentence so that it expresses ideas precisely and concisely, and wordiness and redundancy are eliminated.

"If you go to the library on Sunday, you will find the library doors are locked and that the facility is closed on Sunday."

Here is one possible revision:
If you go to the library on Sunday, you will find the library doors are locked and that the facility is closed on Sunday.

Style and Tone

These questions will have the student revise the style and tone of the text. These revisions will be made to ensure consistency of style and tone as well as improve the match of style and tone to purpose.

<u>Style, tone, and mood</u>
An author can vary the feel of a text by changing the style, tone, and mood of each sentence. The style of a text refers to whether the author uses long, flowing sentences, short, choppy sentences, or something in-between. The text may be organized in short lines, short paragraphs, or long paragraphs. The tone of a paper helps to establish the mood of the text. Tone involves the attitude that the author displays in the paper. For example, the author may feel exuberant about a sunny day, but feel down on a gloomy day. The words that the author uses to describe the scene and situation in the story help to define its tone. The mood of a story may be uplifting, down, scared, or excited, again, depending upon the words the author uses. All of these elements: style, tone, and mood, can affect how the reader feels about the story.

<u>Effect on purpose</u>
Authors use language and word choice to convey a certain style, tone, and mood in a piece of literature. When an author writes, he or she uses a style appropriate to the purpose of the text, but also uses language in a way that sets him or her apart. Tone is the author's attitude toward the subject and mood is the feeling the work invokes in the reader. Authors use their own personal style, their attitude toward the subject, and the mood they create to help craft their stories. Style, tone, and mood all contribute to the effect of a text. As readers, we know there is a difference between a serious or humorous piece, for example.

<u>Impact of words on tone</u>
Words can have a large impact on the tone of a passage. Tone is a result of the choice of language. For instance, when talking about or suggesting the mood of a person or a setting, it is vital to choose the right language to describe it. Is a person ecstatic, or is the person simply content? Is a room barren, or is it just empty? Similarly, using strong action verbs can create a tone that is forceful and remembered easily. The verb buttress, for instance, has a much stronger impact than the verb strengthen. Even though both words have basically the same meaning, the first one creates a more

vivid image in the mind of the reader. It is important to use words that will be understood by the audience and will have the desired effect.

<u>Relate style and tone</u>
Although content is what we write and style is how we write it, the two are very closely interrelated because writing style influences reader perception of content. Style encompasses diction (word choice) and tone. Tone reflects how the writing expresses the writer's attitude overall. For example, a writer can use an informative tone, for objectively providing factual information; or an affective tone, for persuading readers to believe or agree with the writing by appealing to their emotions. In addition to objective or subjective, a writer can use a tone that is formal or informal; calm or excited, etc. Just as we behave differently at school, at work, at a party, at a religious service, etc., tone in writing varies with context and purpose. To establish tone, student writers can ask themselves about their purpose and audience, i.e., why they are writing a text; to/for whom they are writing it; and what they want readers to consider, understand, or learn. Developing tone involves as many qualitative as technical factors and is a subjective choice, particularly in creative writing, including literary techniques like metaphor, symbolism, imagery, allusion, etc. as well as usage, grammar and other mechanics.

Syntax

These questions will require the student to use various sentence structures to achieve the needed rhetorical structure.

<u>Syntax</u>
Syntax is the order of the words in a sentence. When writing, it is important to make sure not only that the syntax is correct, but also that it is not repetitive. There is nothing worse than reading a passage that has sentences that are all alike: noun, verb, object. These need to be interspersed with sentences that use a variety of clause constructions. This will lend a musicality to the writing, and will allow for greater flow of language and ideas. Make sure to reread any written material to ensure that the syntax is correct and engaging. Otherwise, you may end up with something that comes off as confused rather than well-written.

Rewrite the following sentences by varying their syntax.

> Marilyn and Rosemary worked together. They were having a party. They had to get all the food done first. They cleaned the house and decorated. They invited about 20 people. The people were all work associates. They were having the party in Marilyn's backyard. This is where she had many similar parties. They were always fun.

This is one way to rewrite the sentences so that the syntax is varied:

Marilyn and Rosemary, who worked together, were going to have a party. But before they could do that, they had to get all the food ready for it, as well as clean the house and decorate. They invited about 20 people, who were all work associates, and were holding the party in Marilyn's backyard, where there had been many other parties that were always fun.

The rewritten sentences provide a greater variety of syntax, and consequently, greater rhythm. The language is more engaging as a result. Remember to make use of clauses to introduce information and create sentences that are complex. In addition, remember to reread any work you rewrite to make sure it makes sense.

<u>Rhetorical devices that use syntax</u>

One way to emphasize an idea is through repetition. For example, **anadiplosis**, a literary/rhetorical device meaning literally to double back, repeats the last word in one sentence, clause, or phrase at the beginning of the next. In *The Caine Mutiny* (1951), author Herman Wouk uses this technique writing Captain Queeg's dialogue, "'Aboard my ship, excellent performance is <u>standard. Standard</u> performance is <u>sub-standard. Sub-standard</u> performance is not permitted to exist.'" Or in a lyric (1979) from Frank Zappa, "Information is not <u>knowledge. Knowledge</u> is not <u>wisdom. Wisdom</u> is not <u>truth. Truth</u> is not <u>beauty. Beauty</u> is not <u>love. Love</u> is not <u>music. Music</u> is the best." Contrasts, particularly subtle ones, can be emphasized or clarified via **antithesis**, i.e., juxtaposition, as in Alexander Pope's famous line from his poem *An Essay on Criticism* (1711), "To err is human; to forgive, divine." While redundancy generally should be avoided, it may be used deliberately to emphasize, as Shakespeare did in *Julius Caesar* (1599): "This was the <u>most unkindest</u> cut of all." The term for this literary device is **pleonasm**.

Standard English Conventions

The questions in this section focus on editing text to make sure that it conforms to the conventions of standard written English. This includes the editing of sentences, usage, and punctuation.

Sentence Structure

These questions will focus on editing text for sentence formation and sentence structure. The main focus will be on inappropriate shifts in construction within and between sentences.

<u>Types of sentence structures</u>

The four major types of sentence structure are:

1. Simple sentences: Simple sentences have one independent clause with no subordinate clauses. A simple sentence may contain compound elements—a compound subject, verb, or object, for example—but does not contain more than one full sentence pattern.

2. Compound sentences: Compound sentences are composed of two or more independent clauses with no subordinate clauses. The independent clauses are usually joined with a comma and a coordinating conjunction or with a semicolon.

3. Complex sentences: A complex sentence is composed of one independent clause with one or more dependent clauses.

4. Compound-complex sentences: A compound-complex sentence contains at least two independent clauses and at least one subordinate clause. Sometimes they contain two full sentence patterns that can stand alone. When each independent clause contains a subordinate clause, this makes the sentence both compound and complex.

Sentence Boundaries

For these questions the student will need to recognize and correct grammatically incorrect sentences. This includes rhetorically inappropriate fragments and run-ons.

<u>Fragments</u>

A fragment is an incomplete sentence or thought that cannot stand on its own. Fragments are missing either nouns or verbs and are very confusing to the reader because the thought is not complete. When revising their writing, the author needs to read carefully to be sure to catch any fragments and revise them, making sure to read each word on the page and only the words on the page. The author will want to identify whether the fragment is missing a noun or verb and replace it. Sometimes, a fragment is the beginning part of the next sentence. In this case, you can combine it with the following sentence in order to make one complete thought.

Run-on

A run-on sentence is a sentence that should be written as two, or more, sentences. It contains too much information for a single sentence. When reading a run-on sentence, a reader would be out of breath, or very confused. When revising their writing, the author needs to read carefully to be sure to catch any run-ons and revise them. Usually, the easiest way to revise a run-on sentence is to split it up into two or more complete sentences. Figure out where to put the period to make the first part a complete sentence, then read the second part. You may have to tweak it a bit to make the second part a complete sentence as well.

Correcting incomplete sentences

Complete sentences need not be long, but require a subject and predicate. For instance, "I see" or "He lives," albeit only two words apiece, are complete sentences. Sentence fragments are missing subject, verb, or both. For example, "While I was walking down the street one day" is a fragment though it seems to have a subject ("I") and predicate ("was walking") because the conjunction "While" makes it a dependent clause needing an independent clause to complete it—e.g., "While I was walking down the street one day, I met a man." The added clause actually contains the subject ("I") and verb ("met"). Run-on sentences lack divisions like punctuation/conjunctions separating clauses and phrases. For example, "We went to the party we had a good time" is a run-on with two independent clauses, which should be separated one of several ways: into two sentences by a period, "We went to the party. We had a good time"; within one sentence by a semicolon, "We went to the party; we had a good time"; by a conjunction, "We went to the party and we had a good time," or "We went to the party, where we had a good time."

Subordination and Coordination

These questions will require the student to recognize and correct problem with coordination and subordination in a sentence.

Subordination vs coordination

Coordination connects clauses that are equal in importance and type, demonstrating relationships between ideas and preventing repetitious writing. According equal importance or emphasis to unrelated or unequal clauses is a coordination error. For example, "This author won the Pulitzer Prize for fiction, and she resides in Columbia, South Carolina." This sentence connects two unrelated clauses. It can be corrected by making one clause dependent, e.g., "This author, who resides in Columbia, South Carolina, won the Pulitzer Prize for fiction"; or by changing one clause to a modifying phrase, e.g., "This author, a Columbia, South Carolina resident, won the Pulitzer Prize for fiction"; or by changing it to an appositive phrase: "This author, a Columbia, South Carolina resident, won the Pulitzer Prize for fiction." Subordination makes one clause less important than/subordinate to another. Reversing their importance is a subordination error. In a piece about American jobs, "American consumers like Japanese cars, though importing them threaten American jobs" emphasizes the wrong clause. Reversing the subordinating clause's position corrects it: "Though American consumers like Japanese cars, importing threatens American jobs."

<u>Subordinating conjunctions</u>
Subordinating conjunctions introduce adverbial clauses. They join a dependent adverb clause to an independent clause.

Cause: as, because, since
Comparison: more than, as...as
Conditional: even if, if, unless
Contrast: although, even though, though
Manner: as, as if, as though
Place: where, wherever
Purpose: in order that, so that
Result: so...that
Time: after, before, since, until, when

<u>Coordinating and correlative conjunctions</u>
Conjunctions join words, phrases, and clauses, showing the relationship between them.

The categories of conjunctions are coordinating, correlative, and subordinating. Conjunctive adverbs or transition words are another type of conjunction.

Coordinating conjunctions join grammatically equal words, phrases, or clauses (two pronouns, two prepositional phrases, two independent clauses, etc.) The coordinating conjunctions are and, but, or, nor.

Correlative conjunctions are used in pairs to join two or more words, phrases, or clauses that are grammatically equal.

Examples:
both...and; not only...but also; either...or; whether...or; neither...no

Parallel Structure

For these questions the student will need to recognize and correct problems dealing with parallel structure in sentences.

<u>Parallel structure</u>
Parallel structure is keeping grammatical elements consistent with one another within the same sentence. As an example, "She likes skiing, skating, and snowboarding" is correct because the three gerunds (i.e., verbs functioning as nouns—in this case, the participial forms of *to ski, to skate,* and *to snowboard*) are all in the same progressive participle ("-ing participle") form of the verbs. However, the sentence "She likes to ski, skate, and snowboarding" is incorrect by mixing two infinitives with one gerund. Similarly, "She likes skiing, skating, and to snowboard" is also wrong. Parts of speech should also not be mixed/inconsistent within the same clause, comparing unlike items. For example, "We have openings in software development, engineering management, sales trainees, and service technicians." Departments and occupations like software development and engineering management are incorrectly equated here with people like sales trainees and service technicians. These can be corrected to "sales and technical services" to make all items consistent/parallel. Or the reverse, i.e., "We have openings for software developers, engineering managers, sales trainees, and service technicians."

Modifier Placement

These questions will require the student to recognize and correct problems with modifier placement such as misplaced or dangling modifiers.

<u>Placing phrases and clauses</u>
Modifying phrases or clauses should be placed as closely as possible to the words they modify to ensure that the meaning of the sentence is clear. A misplaced modifier makes the meaning of a sentence murky. For instance, the meaning of Walt barely missed the dog speeding down the street becomes evident when the phrase is moved: Speeding down the street, Walt barely missed the dog. A dangling modifier doesn't have a word that it is modifying, so a word must be put into the sentence in order to complete its meaning. Having arrived late for assembly, a written excuse was needed. This sentence makes it sound as though the written excuse was late for assembly, so something needs to be added to the sentence. The meaning is clear when the name Jessica is added. Having arrived late for assembly, Jessica needed a written excuse. Here the phrase modifies Jessica.

<u>Misplaced and dangling modifiers</u>
Misplaced and dangling modifiers, especially dangling participles, are among the most common grammatical and syntactic errors made in English writing—and students are not necessarily the primary culprits. A modifier should precede or follow the noun, verb, clause/phrase or other target that it modifies. When separated from its target by intervening words, phrases, or clauses, it will appear to modify those incorrectly instead. For example, in the sentence, "She served him breakfast eggs glistening with mucus," the participial phrase "glistening..." modifies "eggs." However, if the syntax were different, e.g., "Glistening with mucus, she served him breakfast eggs" sounds as if she were glistening with mucus rather than the eggs. When the modifier is not just separated from its target but the target is missing altogether, this creates a dangling modifier—often a participle. An example is, "Walking down the street, the house was on fire." The house was not walking down the street. Correction would add a target in the independent clause: "Walking down the street, <u>we saw that</u> the house was on fire," or in the dependent clause: "<u>As we were</u> walking down the street, the house was on fire."

Word order can give a sentence completely different meanings just by changing the position of one modifier, e.g., an adverb, by one word. For example, consider the meanings of two sentences: (1) "I only ate produce." (2) "I ate only produce." Sentence (1) means I only ATE produce, i.e., I did not plant, grow, harvest, wash, chop, cook, or otherwise prepare the produce; I only ate it. Sentence (2) means I ate nothing other than produce, i.e., I did not eat meat, dairy products, etc.; I only ate PRODUCE. The order of the word "only" changes the meaning. Similarly, (1) "He failed nearly every English class he took" means he passed only one or a few English classes at most because he failed almost all of them; but (2) "He nearly failed every English class he took" means he passed every English class he took, though he came very close to failing all of them. In both sentences, the modifying adverb "nearly" affects the following word—the determiner "every" in (1) and the verb "failed" in (2).

<u>Correct word order</u>
When a modifying phrase, often a participle, begins a sentence and a comma follows it, whatever word(s) that phrase modifies should follow the comma immediately. However, many people frequently misplace such modifiers, following them with an object instead of the subject they modify. For example, this sentence has a misplaced modifier: "Falling down the mountain, Tom was afraid the boulders would hit the campgrounds." This placement means Tom was falling down the mountain. Some correction alternatives include: (1) "Falling down the mountain, the boulders

seemed about to hit the campgrounds, scaring Tom." Or: (2) "Tom was afraid the boulders falling down the mountain would hit the campgrounds." Or: (3) "Tom was afraid the boulders, which were falling down the mountain, would hit the campgrounds." A squinting modifier (sometimes called a two-way modifier) is sandwiched between two words and could modify either, confusing readers. For example, "Children who laugh seldom are shy" could mean children who seldom laugh are shy; or children who laugh are seldom shy. Either corrects it, depending on the meaning.

Inappropriate Shifts in Construction

For these questions the student will need to edit text to correct inappropriate shifts in verb tense, voice, mood, pronoun person, and number.

Verb tense
Verb tenses are ways in which verbs show that an action takes place. Verbs change according to when an action occurs. An action can take place in the present tense, which means the action is happening right now. An action can take place in the past tense, which means the action has already happened and is in the past. An action can take place in the future, which means the action has not yet happened but will do so. A progressive tense shows that the action is ongoing and continuing to go on in the present

Changes in verb tense
Verbs change form to agree with the subject of the action and to indicate the time or tense of the action. Verb tenses can be categorized as simple or perfect. Each of these tenses has a continuous form.

Simple present tense expresses habitual or repeated actions, general truths, future actions, literary or historic present, and states or qualities of being. In statements, do/does expresses emphasis. See examples below:
Susie exercises on Thursdays and Fridays. (habitual action)
Fred is a doctor. (linking verb--state of being)

Simple past tense expresses finished actions. Did in statements expresses emphasis. See examples below.
World War II ended in 1945. (finished action)
Benedict Arnold began as a loyal American, but later he did betray his country. (emphasis)

Future tense expresses actions or conditions occurring in the future. Simple present tense with an adverb of time can indicate future.
She will see it next week. (future tense)
The insurance coverage ends next month. (simple present)

Example of incorrect shift in voice
Read the following sentence and correct it:
When the doctor turned on the instrument, a strange sound was heard.

This sentence is an example of an incorrect shift in the voice of the verb, something that is very common in colloquial English. The sentence starts out with an active verb, "turned on," and then shifts to a passive voice with "was heard." It can be corrected by rewording the second part of the sentence; the correct sentence reads: "When the doctor turned on the instrument, he heard a strange sound." Now both verb forms are in the active voice. The pronoun "he" agrees with its precedent "doctor." The active voice is preferred because it is stronger and more direct than the passive voice.

Noun-pronoun agreement in number
A pronoun must agree with its antecedent in number. If the antecedent is singular, the pronoun referring to it must be singular; if the antecedent is plural, the pronoun referring to it must be plural.

- Use singular pronouns to refer to the singular indefinite pronouns: each, either, neither, one, everyone, everybody, no one, nobody, anyone, anybody, someone, somebody.
Example: Each of the students bought their own lunch. (incorrect)
           Each of the students bought his own lunch. (correct)

- Use plural nouns to refer to the plural indefinite pronouns: both, few, several, many. Example: Both were within their boundaries.

- The indefinite pronouns some, any, none, all, most may be referred to by singular or plural pronouns, depending on the sense of the sentence.
Examples: Some of the children have misplaced their toys. (plural)
          Some of the carpet has lost its nap. (singular)

- Pronouns that refer to compound antecedents joined by and are usually plural. Example: Bill and Joe cook their own meals.

Examples of incorrect shifts
Two verb tenses in one sentence are correct when one event occurs before/after another, e.g., "The class will be tested next week on the lessons they completed last week." However, tense should not shift when describing simultaneous/concurrent events, e.g., "This shirt didn't fit; it is too tight" is incorrect: it still does not fit. It should be, "This shirt doesn't fit; it is too tight." Similarly, "Although I admired her bravery, I cannot stand her rudeness" incorrectly implies I no longer admire her bravery; "admire" is correct. In "The wind abates and the waves rolled gently," coordinating conjunction "and" implies concurrent events; for consistency, it should be either "abated" or "roll." Shifts in voice switch between active and passive voice in one sentence. "After oversleeping, Marshall hurried to class, where it was discovered class was cancelled." The subject, Marshall, hurried in active voice, so the rest of the sentence should maintain this: "...where he discovered class was cancelled." Shifts in mood incorrectly change the conditional in conditional-subjunctive constructions to indicative: "If I was rich..." should be "If I were rich, I would buy you a mansion."

Pronoun person and number

The student will recognize and correct inappropriate shifts in pronoun person and number within and between sentences.

Narrative voice
Narrative voice can be first person "I" or "we"; second person "you"; or third person "he," "she," "it," "one," "anyone"; "they," "people," etc. Students often reproduce person shifts from spoken to written language, e.g., "We should leave early; you never know what could happen" shifts from first to second person. Correction: "We should leave early; we don't know what could happen." "If one reads the book, they will like it better than the movie" should be "If they read the book, they will...." Shifts in pronoun number are often the results when students begin sentences with indefinite

pronouns like "all," "none," or "anyone" as subjects, but then incorrectly switch between singular and plural or vice versa. For example, "Every student is working their hardest" shifts from singular to plural; "All of the students are working their hardest" correctly maintains consistent plural number. "Anyone can be captain since they are well trained" can be corrected to "...since each of them is well trained."

Conventions of Usage

For these questions the student should be able to edit sentences to conform to the conventions of standard written English.

Conventions of written language
The conventions of written language include capitalizing words correctly. Proper names are capitalized. The first word of a sentence is capitalized. Titles are capitalized. The names of countries are capitalized. The names of rivers are capitalized. The conventions also include using proper punctuation. This means using end marks correctly. End marks include periods, question marks, and exclamation marks. It means using commas correctly. It means using apostrophes correctly. Good penmanship is also important. Good penmanship helps a reader to understand what has been written. It means that the handwriting is neat and well formed. Using these conventions will help the author communicate clearly.

Pronouns

These questions will require the student to edit sentences for proper pronoun use. They should be able to recognize and correct pronouns that are unclear or have ambiguous antecedents.

Pronoun use
Pronouns are used to replace nouns. They substitute for a person, place or thing. "Tommy is running home. He is running home." In these sentences the pronoun he takes the place of Tommy. Some pronouns are subject pronouns. They are: *I, you, he, she, it, we,* and *they*. There are also object pronouns. They are: *me, you, him, her, it, us,* and *them*. Possessive pronouns are used to show that someone or something owns something. Some possessive pronouns are used before a noun, such as *my, your, his, her, its, our,* and *their*. Some possessive pronouns stand alone. They are: mine, yours, his, hers, ours, and theirs. Pronouns must always agree with the noun that they refer to. "Peter and Lucy took their seats in the front row." In this sentence, the possessive pronoun *their* refers to the plural subject Peter and Lucy. A reflexive pronoun occurs when the pronoun is after the noun that is in the sentence. Reflexive pronouns are: *myself, herself, ourselves,* and *himself.*

Objective pronoun
An objective pronoun is a pronoun that is the object of a verb. The objective pronouns are: me, you, him, her, it, us, and them. For example, in the sentence, "Monica invited us to her birthday party," *us* is the objective pronoun. It is the object of the verb *invited*. Objective pronouns can be used in compound sentences as well: "Monica invited Jane and us to her birthday party." Here the object of the verb is *Jane and us*. Objective pronouns can be used with a preposition: "His sister pulled the blanket over me." In this case *me* is the object of the preposition *over*.

Pronoun referents
Pronoun referents or antecedents are the word or group of words that a pronoun refers to. All pronouns must agree with their antecedents in number, gender, and person. A pronoun antecedent may be a noun, another pronoun, or a phrase or clause acting as a noun. Read the following

sentence. "Lawyers must research their cases thoroughly." In this example, the pronoun referent or antecedent is the noun lawyers. The pronoun *their* refers to lawyers. It agrees with its antecedent because it is a plural pronoun. "Marian loved her new bicycle." In this sentence the pronoun *her* refers to Marian. It is correct because it agrees with the subject, since it is a singular feminine pronoun.

Pronoun clarity

The student will recognize and correct pronouns with unclear or ambiguous antecedents.

Ambiguous antecedents to pronouns

When sentences describe more than one person, place, or thing, the pronouns referring to each noun must clearly indicate which for reader understanding. Students may write unclearly by using multiple pronouns in one sentence with ambiguous antecedents—i.e., pronouns could refer to more than one antecedent noun. In the sentence "My luggage was in that car, but now it is missing," either the luggage or the car could be missing. Depending on desired meaning, corrections could be either "My luggage was in that car, but now my luggage is missing" or "My luggage was in that car, but now the car is missing." In "The teacher told Helen it would take her a long time to correct all the errors in her essay," "her" could refer to either Helen or the teacher. The first "her" should be either "Helen" or "the teacher" and the second, either "Helen's" or "the teacher's," depending on meaning. Another way antecedents become unclear is by being too far from corresponding pronouns. For example, in "Buford espied Longstreet's troops advancing. Reynolds' unit came quickly to help; soon <u>he</u> was engaged in battle," "he" is unclear and should be the subject, "Buford."

Possessive Determiners

For these questions the student should recognize and correct cases in which possessive determiners, contractions, and adverbs are confused with each other. Examples of possessive determiners are "its, your, their", contractions "it's, you're, they're", and adverbs "there".

Contractions

A contraction is a word formed by combining two other words. Contractions are often used to make writing flow more easily. When the words are formed, letters are left out. An apostrophe is used in place of the letters that were left out. For example, can and not combine to become can't. The apostrophe is put in place of the omitted letter. Some contractions are used often. Learning them is useful. Aren't is a combination of are not; don't is a combination of do not, doesn't is a combination of does not and hasn't is a combination of has not.

Adverbs

An adverb modifies a verb, an adjective, or another adverb by answering such questions as how? how much? how long? when? and where? Adverbs also act as sentence modifiers.
1. He dressed handsomely. how?
2. She knows more than she thinks. how much?
3. He was gone a week. how long?
4. Last month they flew to Hawaii. when?
5. I went home. where?
6. Unfortunately, he revealed the story's surprise ending. Sentence modifier

Other Parts of Speech as Adverbs - Nouns, prepositions and adjectives sometimes act as adverbs.
1. I'll see you Friday. noun when?
2. He came outside. preposition where?
3. My brother Fred runs slow. adjective how?

Adverbs Formed by Adding 'LY' to Adjectives - An adverb is often formed by adding an 'ly' to an adjective

Homophonous possessive determiners and contactors

Common writing errors are confusing "its" with "it's," "your" with "you're," and "their" with "they're" and/or "there." The source of these errors is that in speech, these pairs are homophones, i.e., they sound alike. But in writing, they are spelled differently corresponding to different meanings and grammatical functions. Possessive determiners "its," "your," and "their" do NOT have apostrophes—the same as "hers," "his," and "our." (The fact that possessive pronouns DO use apostrophes, e.g., "Mary's hat," "John's book," "the passenger's ticket," only adds to the confusion.) Contrasting from their homophones, "it's," "you're," and "they're" are all contractions of pronoun and verb—the verb *to be* specifically. Expanded, they mean "it is," "you are," and "they are," not indicating possession. "There" is an adverb indicating place, point, or manner; or an "existential" pronoun as in "There are people inside." The incorrect "This book is missing it's cover" should be "...its cover." "We know your confused" should be "...you're confused." "Sign you're name here" should be "...your name here." "There going their with they're friends" is triply incorrect; "They're going there with their friends" is correct.

Agreement

These questions will require the student to ensure grammatical agreement. This will include agreement between pronoun and antecedent, subject and verb, and noun agreement.

Pronoun-antecedent agreement

The student will recognize and correct lack of agreement between pronoun and antecedent.

Pronoun-antecedent agreement

Pronoun-antecedent agreement means that the pronoun and the antecedent (the word that refers back to the pronoun) need to match in number and gender. A singular pronoun needs a singular antecedent, just as a plural pronoun needs a plural antecedent. Likewise, masculine pronouns need masculine antecedents, and feminine pronouns need feminine antecedents. Here is an example of a sentence with a mistake in pronoun-antecedent agreement: The bike rack is there for everyone to lock up their bikes. This is a very common error and one that people make in speaking and in writing all the time. In the sentence, the pronoun is *their*. This is a plural pronoun. In the sentence, the antecedent is everyone, which is singular. The sentence should have correct pronoun-antecedent agreement. Here is one correct revision of the sentence:
    The bike rack is there for everyone to lock up his bike.

Lack of agreement

Excepting indefinite pronouns, other pronouns need referents, i.e., antecedents. Antecedents and pronouns should agree in number, person, and gender. "Every student must bring their permission slips" is incorrect because "every" and "student" are singular, whereas "their" and "permission slips" are plural. "All students must bring their permission slips" is correct. To correct the antecedent-pronoun number mismatch in "I never eat at that restaurant because they have stale bread," change "they have" to "it has." Differing number, person, and/or gender between antecedent and pronoun can also be called faulty co-reference. For example, "Politics is fun because they are such interesting people" is incorrect because (plural) "they" does not even refer to (singular) "politics." "Politics is fun because politicians are such interesting people" is correct. Faulty co-reference can also involve pronouns not replacing nouns or adverbs not replacing adverbial clauses/phrases. "He should know German well; he lived there for ten years" is incorrect because the second clause refers to the country, not the language from the first clause. "He should know German well; he lived in Germany for ten years" is correct.

Subject-verb agreement

The student will recognize and correct lack of agreement between subject and verb.

Subject-verb agreement
Subject-verb agreement means that the subject and verb in a sentence have to agree in number. A singular subject needs a singular verb, just as a plural subject needs a plural verb. Errors occur when people incorrectly match the number of the subject and the verb. Here is an example of an incorrect sentence: The dogs of the neighborhood was barking loudly. The sentence is incorrect because the subject, dogs, is plural. The sentence is referring to more than one dog. The verb, was, is singular. The subject and verb do not match. Here are two correct versions of the sentence, depending on the meaning the author wants to convey:
    The dog of the neighborhood was barking loudly.
    The dogs of the neighborhood were barking loud.

Subject-verb agreement errors
Common errors in subject-verb agreement involve singular vs. plural number, e.g., students (plural) write; a student (singular) writes. When prepositional phrases intervene between them, subject and verb should still agree regardless. A common error is mistaking the object of the preposition for the sentence subject. "Large <u>amounts</u> of mercury <u>are</u> found in some fish" is correct; "Large amounts of <u>mercury is</u> found in some fish" is incorrect. "<u>Water</u> in your fuel lines <u>makes</u> your car stall" is correct; "Water in your fuel <u>lines make</u> your car stall" is incorrect. Quantitative units, like "ten dollars" or "five miles" are considered singular units, e.g., "Five miles <u>is</u> a long walk" or "The price <u>is</u> ten dollars." Nouns with singular meanings, despite plural forms, take singular verbs: "<u>Mumps is</u> rare today in America." Most compound subjects joined by "and" are plural: "Dogs and cats <u>are</u> popular pets," not "is." Two exceptions are compound subjects that have become units through usage, like "corned beef and cabbage" or "bacon and eggs," which are singular; and compound subjects describing one person/thing: "He is the <u>founder and pioneer</u> of the discipline." Or "This is the <u>cause and solution</u> of our problem."

Noun agreement

The student will recognize and correct lack of agreement between nouns.

Just as verbs must agree with their subject nouns in sentences, and pronouns must agree with the nouns they reference, nouns referring to other nouns must agree in number. For example, "Bert and Ernie both got jobs as <u>a lifeguard</u> over the summer" is incorrect: the noun "jobs" is plural to agree with the compound subject "Bert and Ernie," i.e., two people; but "a lifeguard" is singular. It should be "Bert and Ernie both got jobs <u>as lifeguards</u> over the summer." Related nouns in the same sentence should agree in number, i.e., all singular or all plural. For example, "The teacher said she would give us answers to every question" is incorrect: "answers" is plural but "question" is singular.

- 46 -

Two ways of correcting this sentence are making both nouns singular, e.g., "The teacher said she would give us an answer to every question"; or making both plural, e.g., "The teacher said she would give us answers to all questions." Exceptions include abstract and/or mass nouns that would become awkward if plural: "The <u>courage</u> of the soldiers..." is acceptable because "The <u>courages</u> of the soldiers" is illogical as well as awkward.

Frequently Confused Words

For these questions the student should be able to recognize and correct instances where one word is confused with another. An example would be the words, accept and except.

Contractions
All contractions, such as they're, it's, and who's are actually two words joined together by the use of an apostrophe to replace a missing letter or letters. Whenever a contraction is encountered, it can be broken down into the two distinct words that make it up.

Example:
> I wouldn't eat in the cafeteria. = I would not eat in the cafeteria.

The apostrophe in the contraction is always located where the missing letter or letters should be. In the examples below, the apostrophe replaces the "o" in the word "not". The contraction "doesn't" actually stands for the two words "does not".
> *Incorrect Example*: He does'nt live here.
> *Correct Example*: He doesn't live here.

Whenever there is a contraction in an answer choice, it can always be replaced by the two words that make the contraction up. If necessary, scratch through the contractions in the choices, and replace them with the two words that make up the contraction. Otherwise the choices may be confusing. Alternatively, while reading the answer choices to yourself, instead of reading the contractions as a contraction, read them as the two separate words that make them up. Some contractions are especially confusing.

Its/it's
"It's" is actually a contraction for the two words "it is". Never confuse "it's" for the possessive pronoun "its". "It's" should only be used when the two words "it is" would make sense as a replacement. Use "its" in all other cases.
> *Example 1*: It's going to rain later today. = It is going to rain later today.
> *Example 2*: The dog chewed through its rope and ran away.

They're/their/there
"They're" is actually a contraction for "they are", and those two words should always be used to replace "they're" when it is encountered.
Example:
> They're going to the movie with us. = They are going to the movie with us.

"Their" is an adjective used to show ownership.
> *Example 1*: Their car is a red convertible.
> *Example 2*: The students from each school sat in their own stands.

"There" should be used in all other cases.
>   *Example 1*: There exists an answer to every question.
>   *Example 2*: The man was over there.

Who's/whose
Who's is actually a contraction for "who is", and those two words should always be used to replace who's when it is encountered.
Example:
>   Who's going with me? = Who is going with me?

Whose would be used in all other cases, where "who is" does not fit.
Example:
>   Whose car is this?

Their/his
"Their" is a plural possessive pronoun, referring to multiple people or objects.
Example:
>   The men went to their cars.

"His" is a singular possessive, referring to an individual person or object.
Example:
>   The man went to his car.

Which/that/who
"Which" should be used to refer to things only.
>   John's dog, which was called Max, is large and fierce.

"That" may be used to refer to either persons or things.
>   Is this the only book that Louis L'Amour wrote?
>   Is Louis L'Amour the author that [or who] wrote Western novels?

"Who" should be used to refer to persons only.
>   Mozart was the composer who [or that] wrote those operas.

Who/Whom or Whoever/Whomever
Who/whom will be encountered in two forms, as an interrogative pronoun in a question, or as a relative pronoun not in a question.

Interrogative pronoun in a question: If the answer to the question would include the pronouns he, she, we, or they, then "who" is correct.
Example:
>   Who threw the ball? He threw the ball.

If the answer to the question would include the pronouns him, her, us, or them, then "whom" is correct.
Example:
>   With whom did you play baseball? I played baseball with him.
Relative pronoun NOT in a question: If who/whom is followed by a verb, typically use "who".
Example:
>   Peter Jackson was an obscure director who became a celebrity overnight.

If who/whom is followed by a noun, typically use "whom":
Example:
> Bob, whom we follow throughout his career, rose swiftly up the ladder of success.

However, beware of the insertion of phrases or expressions immediately following the use of who/whom. Sometimes, the phrase can be skipped without the sentence losing its meaning.
Example:
> This is the woman who, we believe, will win the race.

To determine the proper selection of who/whom, skip the phrase "we believe". Thus, "who" would come before "will win", a verb, making the choice of "who" correct.

In other cases, the sentence should be rephrased in order to make the right decision.
Example:
> I can't remember who the author of "War and Peace" is.

To determine the proper selection of who/whom, rephrase the sentence to state, "I can't remember who is the author of 'War and Peace'."

Knowledge of word roots
When words are both homophones, i.e., they sound alike, and *homographs*, i.e., they are spelled alike, students must rely on context to differentiate meaning, e.g., "I cannot <u>bear</u> to think how that <u>bear</u> and others will be unable to <u>bear</u> young because you have destroyed their habitat." However, when homophones are spelled differently, knowing their roots can inform their meaning. For example, the Latin root *cept* means "take" or "receive." Knowing this informs the meaning of "inception"; knowing also that *con* means "with" or "together" informs the meanings of "concept" and "conception." Knowing *ac-* means "to" or "toward" informs the meaning of "accept"; knowing *ex-* means "out of" (as in "exit") or "away from" informs the different meaning of "except." Similarly, knowing *al-* means "to," "toward," or "near" informs the meaning of *allusion;* also knowing *il-* means "not" helps differentiate it from *illusion.* Hence "allusion" means referring TO something whereas "illusion" means something NOT real. In both, the root *lūdere* means "to play." "Allusion" plays TO a referent; "illusion" plays an impression of reality that is false, NOT real.

Logical Comparison

These questions will require the student to recognize and correct cases in which unlike terms are compared.

Incorrect vs correct comparison
To make effective comparisons in written text, writers need to compare terms that are alike rather than unlike ones. For example, if someone writes, "This artist's works have frequently been compared to much earlier portrait artists" or "This artist's works have frequently been compared to portrait painters from earlier historical eras," the writer has incorrectly compared the subject "works" to "artists" and "painters," respectively. To make it correct, the writer would either have to change the sentence to "This artist has frequently been compared to much earlier portrait artists" or "to portrait painters from earlier historical eras," which are both correct but change the meaning slightly; or to "This artist's works have frequently been compared to <u>those of</u> much older portrait artists" or "This artist's works have frequently been compared to portraits painted by much earlier artists" or "to portraits by painters from earlier historical eras," neither of which changes the meaning but both of which compare like nouns, rectifying the error of comparing unlike nouns.

- 49 -

Logically incorrect sentences

Items compared in sentences must be similar to be logically correct. For example, "Living in a city is very different from the country" is logically incorrect by comparing the subject, gerund phrase "Living in a city," to the object of the preposition ("to"), article and noun "the country." In other words, it compares dissimilar terms. "Living in a city is very different from living in the country" is logically correct by comparing like terms. In the same way, "More words in Spanish are pronounced as they are spelled than English" is logically incorrect. It can be corrected by changing the end to "...than words in English," or even "...than in English," to match "...words in Spanish" or "...in Spanish." To avoid always repeating the same/similar word/phrase/clause, writers can simplify sentences by replacing the first term(s) with "that" (singular) or "those" (plural) in the second instance: "The call of the cardinal is much prettier than <u>that of</u> the blue jay" instead of "the call of the blue jay"; "The landforms in Finland are similar to <u>those in</u> eastern Canada" instead of "the landforms in eastern Canada."

Effective comparisons

To make effective comparisons, writers must compare words/phrases representing things/concepts that can legitimately be compared. Some people forget what the sentence subject represents and compare it to something not representing the same kind/class of thing. For example, "Her wedding dress looked as fashionable as a celebrity appearing on the red carpet before an awards show" is a logically incorrect sentence because it compares a dress, the subject of the sentence, to a celebrity, the object of the preposition "as" and of the comparison. A dress is a thing; a celebrity is a person. Hence these are unlike terms. To correct this sentence, one option is to write, "Her wedding dress looked as fashionable as <u>a dress worn by</u> a celebrity appearing on the red carpet before an awards show"—i.e., repeating the noun "dress" on both sides of the comparison. Another way is to refer to the dress, e.g., "as fashionable as <u>that of</u> a celebrity...." Another is to change the sentence subject: "In her wedding dress, <u>she</u> looked as fashionable as a celebrity...."

Conventional Expression

For these questions the student will be required to recognize and correct situations where a given expression is inconsistent with standard written English.

Examples of conventional expressions

Certain expressions have been used so often in speech and writing that speakers and writers may rely upon them as signals of their accepted meanings to clarify audience understanding. However, many people also unwittingly say and write them incorrectly. For example, an English idiomatic expression meaning you can't have it both ways is almost universally stated incorrectly as "You can't have your cake and eat it too." This is backwards; as expert Milton Friedman has pointed out, if you have your cake, of course you can eat it. The original correct saying is "You can't eat your cake and have it too." This means if you eat the cake up, you won't have it anymore; you can either eat it or still have it, not both. Another ubiquitous error involving reversal is "I could care less," literally meaning I care more than possible, i.e., I do care; the correct expression is "I <u>couldn't</u> care less," meaning I care as little as possible, i.e., I don't care.

Common expressions becoming distorted

In typical language development, people learn to listen and speak before learning to read and write. Hence they become acquainted, eventually familiar, with commonly used expressions that have become English conventions. Without seeing correct spelling and exact word choice in print, many people mistake these expressions. Then they become incorrectly used so frequently by so many people that the incorrect form becomes common and taken for granted. Many people incorrectly say—and therefore write—"for all <u>intensive</u> purposes" when they really mean "for all <u>intents and purposes.</u>" The latter means for all practical purposes or for all possible reasons; the former means for purposes that were extremely intense—almost undoubtedly NOT what the writer intended. Another expression is "Nip it in the bud." This metaphor compares a situation to a flower: cutting it while it is a bud will prevent its growing to full bloom. The implied comparison is that eliminating a situation/problem in an early stage will prevent its growing to be bigger/full-blown. The common error, "Nip it in the butt," means bite it in the hindquarters instead, inviting unintended humor.

Knowledge of word roots

Some incorrect usages of Standard English words betray speaker and writer ignorance of the etymologies of words and word parts, and hence of the meanings of those parts. For example, the suffix –*less* means "without," as in speechless, childless, hopeless, reckless, etc. Therefore, the word "regardless" means "without regard." However, many people apparently do not know, pay attention to, or think about this meaning when they use the non-word "irregardless" in writing, which they have transferred from using it in their speech—also incorrectly. There is no such word; it would constitute a double negative, since both *ir-* and –*less* mean "without." Some people may confuse it with "irrespective," which is a correct word because it contains only one negative (*ir-*). But more have likely learned the incorrect usage from others. Another error involves a small yet important difference: instead of "one <u>and</u> the same," an expression meaning exactly alike, many people say/write "one <u>in</u> the same," meaning united inside of something called "the same"—whatever that is.

Conventions of Punctuation

For these questions the student will edit sentences to ensure that they conform to the conventions of standard written English punctuation.

End of sentence punctuation

The student will recognize and correct inappropriate uses of ending punctuation in cases in which the context makes the intent clear.

Most common sentence ending punctuation

Most sentences are declarative, stating facts or opinions, other information, describing or explaining ideas, etc. A declarative sentence is always punctuated with a period at the end. For example: "Technology has advanced very rapidly in the last few years." Questions are not declarative, but interrogative: they do not tell, but ask. Writers and speakers sometimes convert declarative into interrogative by appending a question at the end of a statement; for example, using the sentence above: "Technology has advanced very rapidly in the last few years, am I right?" (In this case the question is rhetorical, emphasizing the preceding statement.) Exclamation points indicate heavy emphasis, excitement, or surprise. They also punctuate spoken, frequently monosyllabic exclamations, as in "Yikes! You scared me!" They can clarify or match meaning: Without additional contextual information, "That test was hard!" expresses a more intense degree of "hard" than "That test was hard." When context indicates intent, as in "I cannot believe how hard that test was!," the exclamation point matches the meaning. Some of these same examples with inappropriate punctuation include: "Technology has advanced very rapidly in the last few years?" "Technology...years, am I right!" "Yikes. You scared me."

Within-sentence punctuation

The student will correctly use and recognize and correct inappropriate uses of colons, semicolons, and dashes to indicate sharp breaks in thought within sentences.

<u>Ways to use colons, semicolons, hyphens, and dashes</u>
Use <u>semicolons</u> to separate two related independent clauses: "People are concerned about the environment; not conserving natural resources endangers our future." Commas, NOT semicolons, separate independent and dependent clauses: "Although he arrived late, Marshall enjoyed the class." Use <u>colons</u> to introduce lists, e.g., "The teacher gave me three choices: do the extra credit report, retake the test, or fail." Introduce new examples/ideas, e.g., "Only one person can remember that war: your grandfather." Separate titles and subtitles, e.g., "The Lord of the Rings: The Return of the King." Hyphenating when adding prefixes to some words avoids confusion; e.g., "I <u>re-sent</u> the message you did not receive" clarifies sending again; "resent" is a verb meaning begrudge/dislike. Use <u>hyphens</u> when creating compound words "up-to-date," "IBM-compatible," etc. Hyphenate spelled-out numbers, e.g., "twenty-four" or "one-hundredth," but NOT "one hundred" "(only hyphenate numbers over 100 as compound adjectives). When interrupting a sentence with a parenthetical but relevant statement, e.g., for clarification; an added comment/dramatic qualification/sudden change in thought, use a dash—singly, e.g., "This is the end of the story—or so we thought"; or paired, enclosing mid-sentence interruption: "Dashes mark an interruption —yes, you guessed it—in the middle of a sentence."

<u>Flow</u>
Commas break the flow of text. To test whether they are necessary, while reading the text to yourself, pause for a moment at each comma. If the pauses seem natural, then the commas are correct. If they are not, then the commas are not correct.

<u>Subjects and verbs</u>
Subjects and verbs must not be separated by commas. However, a pair of commas setting off a nonessential phrase is allowed.
Example:
    The office, which closed today for the festival, was open on Thursday.

"Was" is the verb, while "office" is the subject. The comma pair between them sets off a nonessential phrase, "which is allowed". A single comma between them would not be allowed.
If you are trying to find the subject, first find the verb and use it to fill in the blank in the following sentence. Who or what ____?
Example:
    The boy on the bicycle raced down the hill.

The verb is "raced". If you can find "raced" and identify it as the verb, ask yourself, "Who or what raced down the hill?" The answer to that question is the subject, in this case "boy".

<u>Independent clauses</u>
Use a comma before the words and, but, or, nor, for, yet when they join independent clauses. To determine if two clauses are independent, remove the word that joins them. If the two clauses are capable of being their own sentence by themselves, then they are independent and need a comma between them.
Example:
    He ran down the street, and then he ran over the bridge.

He ran down the street. Then he ran over the bridge. These are both clauses capable of being their own sentence. Therefore, a comma must be used along with the word "and" to join the two clauses together.

If one or more of the clauses would be a fragment if left alone, then it must be joined to another clause and does not need a comma between them.
Example:
> He ran down the street and over the bridge.

He ran down the street. Over the bridge. "Over the bridge" is a sentence fragment and is not capable of existing on its own. No comma is necessary to join it with "He ran down the street".

Note that this does not cover the use of "and" when separating items in a series, such as "red, white, and blue". In these cases, a comma is not always necessary between the last two items in the series, but in general it is best to use one.

Sentence beginnings
Use a comma after words such as so, well, yes, no, and why when they begin a sentence.
> *Example 1*: So, you were there when they visited.
> *Example 2*: Well, I really haven't thought about it.
> *Example 3*: Yes, I heard your question.
> *Example 4*: No, I don't think I'll go to the movie.
> *Example 5*: Why, I can't imagine where I left my keys.

Possessive Nouns and Pronouns

For these questions the student should be able to recognize and correct inappropriate uses of possessive nouns and pronouns. They should also be able to differentiate between possessive and plural forms.

Possessive nouns
Possessive nouns show ownership. They often use apostrophes and the letter "s." For instance, a writer might say, "The house of the Owens is near a lake," but this is awkward so instead ownership is shown by using an apostrophe and the letter "s" to make the name "Owens" into a possessive. The writer would then say, "The Owens' house is near the lake." The apostrophe and "s" take the place of the "of" to show ownership or possession. The writer can check to see if a possessive is correct by inserting the word "of" instead of using the apostrophe and "s" and inverting the order of the words to see if the sentence makes sense.

Correct pronoun usage in combinations
To determine the correct pronoun form in a compound subject, try each subject separately with the verb, adapting the form as necessary. Your ear will tell you which form is correct.
Example:
> Bob and (I, me) will be going.

Restate the sentence twice, using each subject individually. Bob will be going. I will be going.
> "Me will be going" does not make sense.

When a pronoun is used with a noun immediately following (as in "we boys"), say the sentence without the added noun. Your ear will tell you the correct pronoun form.
Example:
>   (We/Us) boys played football last year.

Restate the sentence twice, without the noun. We played football last year. Us played football last year. Clearly "We played football last year" makes more sense.

Apostrophes
If the noun is plural and ends in an "s", the possessive apostrophe would come after the word, without the addition of another "s".
Example:
>   The students' hats were wet from the rain.

In the example above, there are plural or many students, all of whom have wet hats.

If the noun is plural and does not end in an "s", the possessive apostrophe would come after the word, with the addition of an "s".
Example:
>   The mice's feet were wet from the rain.

If the noun is singular, the possessive apostrophe is followed by an "s".
Example:
>   The student's hat was wet from the rain.

In the example above, there is only one student, whose hat is wet.

Errors involving nouns and pronouns
One error some people make when writing is spelling plural pronouns as if they were possessive, e.g., "Writer's need to punctuate correctly." There should be no apostrophe in this or ANY plural noun. Another punctuation error that is more understandable but still incorrect is using an apostrophe in the possessive pronoun "hers," i.e., "her's." This word NEVER has an apostrophe. A way to remember this is to compare it with "his," which also has no apostrophe. Contractions of a noun plus "is," e.g., "she's" contracting "she is" or "she has," require apostrophes; however, "hers" would never be a contraction because "her is" is not a grammatical construction, so it cannot be confused with a contraction needing an apostrophe. Still, the reason this error with a possessive pronoun is more understandable is that possessive nouns, both singular and plural, DO always use apostrophes; for example, "John's shoe," "Meryl's car," "the lady's house," "the company's name," and "the children's toys" indicate possession with apostrophes. Hence some writers confuse possessive pronouns with possessive nouns by equating them. Unlike "children's" above, plural nouns with –s endings take apostrophes after instead of before the –s, e.g., "The cats' fountain needs cleaning."

Items in a Series

For these questions the student should be able to use the correct punctuation (commas and semicolons) to separate items in a series. They should also be able to recognize and correct the inappropriate use of this punctuation.

Semicolons

Semicolons are used to separate 3 or more items in a series that have a comma internally.

Example:

> The club president appointed the following to chair the various committees: John Smith, planning; Jessica Graham, membership; Paul Randolph, financial; and Jerry Short, legal.

Uses for commas and semicolons

Use commas for the following: Within-sentence breaks like appositives, e.g., "Bill Gates, head of Microsoft, developed Windows." List (short) items in a series. Separate adjectives modifying a noun, but NOT following the last adjective: "The sprawling, ramshackle house," NOT "sprawling, ramshackle, house." Separate geographical areas from those containing them, smallest to largest: "Their address is Building #7423, Dhahran Road, Al Mubarraz, Al Ahsa, Saudi Arabia." Also follow the last geographical area with a comma if it is not at the end of the sentence: "Washington, D.C., is the capital of the United States." Separate introductory (typically prepositional) phrases from the main clause: "After dinner, we went for a walk." "At our house, pets are necessities." Separate independent clauses joined by a conjunction ("and," "but," "or," "since," etc.): "He studied hard, but he failed the test." "Since people use air conditioning, electric bills typically increase during the summer." In dialogue, separate names in direct address: "Hugh, would you come here?" Separate direct, full quotations from words introducing them: "Sarah asked, 'Would you like a drink?'"

Separating items in a series by comma or semicolon

Short, easily understandable items listed in a series should be separated by commas. This is an example: "The United States Department of Agriculture divides the food groups into fruits, vegetables, grains, protein foods, dairy products, and oils." However, longer and/or more complex items that include additional explanation, description, or comments should be separated not with commas but with semicolons; for example: "I attended the event with Jennifer, my best friend; her friend, Joe; and his best friend, Rob." Semicolons should also be used to separate clauses in a sentence that contain commas within them to clarify and/or prevent confusion: "Some of these components of foods include saturated fats in meat, poultry, cheese, and butter; unsaturated fats in avocados, beans, nuts, and seeds; and starches in potatoes, corn, and bread." Do NOT use colons to introduce items in a series, as in "In the box were: cookies, candies, and other sweets." This is incorrect.

Nonrestrictive and Parenthetical Elements

These questions will require the student to use punctuation such as commas, parentheses, and dashes to set apart nonrestrictive and parenthetical sentence elements. They also need to be able to recognize and correct when restrictive or essential sentence elements are inappropriately set apart with punctuation.

Nonessential clauses and phrases

A comma should be used to set off nonessential clauses and nonessential participial phrases from the rest of the sentence. To determine if a clause is essential, remove it from the sentence. If the removal of the clause would alter the meaning of the sentence, then it is essential. Otherwise, it is nonessential.

Example:

> John Smith, who was a disciple of Andrew Collins, was a noted archeologist.

In the example above, the sentence describes John Smith's fame in archeology. The fact that he was a disciple of Andrew Collins is not necessary to that meaning. Therefore, separating it from the rest of the sentence with commas, is correct.

Do not use a comma if the clause or phrase is essential to the meaning of the sentence.
Example:

      Anyone who appreciates obscure French poetry will enjoy reading the book.

If the phrase "who appreciates obscure French poetry" is removed, the sentence would indicate that anyone would enjoy reading the book, not just those with an appreciation for obscure French poetry. However, the sentence implies that the book's enjoyment may not be for everyone, so the phrase is essential.

Another perhaps easier way to determine if the clause is essential is to see if it has a comma at its beginning or end. Consistent, parallel punctuation must be used, and so if you can determine a comma exists at one side of the clause, then you can be certain that a comma should exist on the opposite side.

Parenthetical expressions
Commas should separate parenthetical expressions such as the following: after all, by the way, for example, in fact, on the other hand.
Example:

      By the way, she is in my biology class.

If the parenthetical expression is in the middle of the sentence, a comma would be both before and after it.
Example:

      She is, after all, in my biology class.

However, these expressions are not always used parenthetically. In these cases, commas are not used. To determine if an expression is parenthetical, see if it would need a pause if you were reading the text. If it does, then it is parenthetical and needs commas.
Example:

      You can tell by the way she plays the violin that she enjoys its music.

No pause is necessary in reading that example sentence. Therefore, the phrase "by the way" does not need commas around it.

Years
Parentheses should be used around years.
Example:

      The presidency of Franklin Delano Roosevelt (1932-1945) was the longest one in American history.

Nonessential information
Parentheses can be used around information that is added to a sentence but is not essential. Commas or dashes could also be used around these nonessential phrases.
Example: George Eliot (whose real name was Mary Ann Evans) wrote poems and several well-known novels.

<u>Identifying nonrestrictive elements</u>
(1) "Woody Allen's original surname, Konigsberg, originated from two parts: *konig* and *berg,* German for 'king' and 'mountain'." When a teacher dictated this sentence for students to write with correct punctuation, some wrote it this way: (2) "...from two parts, *'konig'* and *'berg'*; German for...." Others wrote: (3) "...from two parts *'konig'* and *'berg'*; German for...." And still others wrote: (4) "...from two parts; *'konig'* and *'berg'* German for...." Version (1) uses the best punctuation. First, the colon following "parts" signals the introduction of what those parts were. Colons in sentences typically introduce or announce information that completes, defines, or explains the preceding thought. Second, the comma following "*'berg'*" correctly separates "*'konig'*" and "*'berg'*" and "German for 'king' and 'mountain'" as nonrestrictive appositives. Version (2) incorrectly connects the independent clause with a phrase by using a semicolon following "*'berg'*." Its comma following "parts" is too weak for the strong sentence break. Version (3) incorrectly connects an independent clause and phrase with a semicolon following "*'berg'*"; and omits punctuation following "parts" for nonrestrictive appositives. Version (4) incorrectly joins the independent clause with phrases using a semicolon following "parts"; and omits punctuation indicating nonrestrictive appositives following "*'berg'*."

Unnecessary punctuation

For these questions the student will need to recognize and correct situations in which unnecessary punctuation was used.

<u>Correct punctuation vs incorrect punctuation</u>
(1) "Students who undertake careers in the hospitality industry can come from a varied range of educational histories." Some students were assigned to identify correct punctuation in this sentence. Some found it needed no change as shown above. Some corrected it to read: (2) "Students, who undertake careers in the hospitality industry, can come from...." Some corrected it to read: (3) "Students who undertake careers, in the hospitality industry, can come from...." Others found it correct punctuated thusly: (4) "Students who undertake careers in the hospitality industry, can come from...." The first group was correct in leaving the sentence as is. The clause "who undertake careers in the hospitality industry" is a restrictive clause, i.e., essential to the sentence meaning, by defining who the "students" are. Restrictive clauses are not punctuated. Version (2) sets this clause off with commas, which are only used with nonrestrictive clauses. Version (3) also incorrectly punctuates "in the hospitality industry" with commas like a nonrestrictive clause when it is essential to meaning, hence restrictive. Version (4) inserts an extraneous comma following "industry," separating the subject from the predicate.

<u>Writing errors involving unnecessary punctuation</u>
Some writers make the mistake of doubling, tripling, quadrupling, or even further multiplying exclamation marks and question marks, thinking they are adding the necessary emphasis they want to convey. While this may be acceptable in more casual formats such as e-mails, it should never be done in formal writing, e.g., "Why did he use so many question marks??? It's really annoying!!!" Another error is inserting a colon following a copula or linking verb (i.e., any form of "to be," "to become," "to seem," "to feel," etc. that connects the subject of a sentence to its complement, e.g., "You are a liar." No colon or other punctuation should be used between a linking verb and a subject complement. Colons should also not follow prepositions, e.g., "This book is by: Stephen King" is incorrect; "This book is by Stephen King" is correct. "This room will be painted yellow" is another construction needing no internal punctuation; some writers incorrectly insert a colon or comma between "painted" and "yellow."

<u>Unnecessary use of commas</u>

There is no need to place a comma between a sentence subject and verb. This includes long subjects, e.g., "The boy who wore a yellow hat and came to the party late spilled the punch" is correct as is. Some writers will incorrectly insert a comma between "late" and "spilled" thinking it clarifies the sentence because of the long subject, but subjects and verbs should not be separated by punctuation marks. When punctuation is needed, though, commas when correct are preferable over parentheses, brackets, dashes, or even semicolons. For example, in this sentence, "The elderly lady (who worked as a server) left at eight" uses unnecessary parentheses. It is more correctly punctuated, "The elderly lady, who worked as a server, left at eight." Commas between the sentence's verb and predicate adjectives or predicate nouns describing the subject are unnecessary. For example, "She was, nervous and anxious" is incorrect. "She was nervous and anxious" is correct. Commas are also unnecessary between two items and should only separate three or more items in a list. "She awoke, washed, dressed, and left" is correct; "She awoke, and left" is incorrect; "She awoke and left" is correct.

Sentence errors

Each question includes a sentence with parts underlined. You must choose which, if any, of those underlined portions contains an error in mechanics, word choice, or structural and grammatical relationships.

Read the text four times, each time replacing the underlined portion with one of the choices. While reading the text, be sure to pause at each comma. If the comma is necessary, the pause will be logical. If the comma is not needed, then the sentence will feel awkward. Transitional words should create smooth, logical transitions and maintain a constant flow of text.

Improving Sentences and Paragraphs

Each question includes a sentence with part or all of it underlined. Your answer choices will offer different ways to reword or rephrase the underlined portion of the sentence. The first answer choice merely repeats the original underlined text, while the others offer different wording.

These questions will test your ability of correct and effective expression. Choose your answer carefully, utilizing the standards of written English, including grammar rules, the proper choice of words and of sentence construction. The correct answer will flow smoothly and be both clear and concise.

Parallelism

Often clues to the best answer are given within the text, if you know where to look for them. The correct answer will always be parallel in grammar type, punctuation, format, and tense as the rest of the sentence.

Grammar type

If a series of nouns is given, then make sure your choice is a noun. If those nouns are plural, then ensure that your choice is plural.
Example:
      Schools, politics, and governments

If a series of verbs is given, then make sure your choice is a verb.
Example:
    eat, sleep, and drink

If a series of infinitives is given, then make sure your choice is an infinitive.
Example:
    to trust, to honor, and to obey

If a series of phrases is given, then make sure your choice is a similar phrase.
Example:
    of controlling, of policing, and of maintaining

Added phrases

Any sentence or phrase added to a paragraph must maintain the same train of thought. This is particularly true when the word "and" is used. The word "and" joins two comments of like nature.
Example:
    These men were tough. They were accustomed to a hard life, and could watch a man die without blinking.

If an added phrase does not maintain a consistent train of thought, it will be set out with a word such as "but", "however", or "although". The new phrase would then be inconsistent to the train of thought and would offer a contrast.
Example:
    These men were tough. They were accustomed to a hard life, but to watch a man die would cause them to faint.

A tough man accustomed to a hard life is not expected to faint. Therefore, the statements are contrasting and must have a contrasting transitional word, such as "but."

Punctuation

If a section of text has an opening dash, parentheses, or comma at the beginning of a phrase, then you can be sure there should be a matching closing dash, parentheses, or comma at the end of the phrase. If items in a series all have commas between them, then any additional items in that series will also gain commas. Do not alternate punctuation. If a dash is at the beginning of a statement, then do not put a parenthesis at the ending of the statement.

Final Tips

Use your ear

Read each sentence carefully, inserting the answer choices in the blanks. Don't stop at the first answer choice if you think it is right, but read them all. What may seem like the best choice, at first, may not be after you have had time to read all of the choices. Allow your ear to determine what sounds right. Often one or two answer choices can be immediately ruled out because it doesn't make sound logical or make sense.

Contextual clues

It bears repeating that contextual clues offer a lot of help in determining the best answer. Key words in the sentence will allow you to determine exactly which answer choice is the best replacement text.

Example:

> Archeology has shown that some of the ruins of the ancient city of Babylon are approximately 500 years <u>as old as any supposed</u> Mesopotamian predecessors.
> A.) as old as their supposed
> B.) older than their supposed

In this example, the key word "supposed" is used. Archaeology would either confirm that the predecessors to Babylon were more ancient or disprove that supposition. Since supposed was used, it would imply that archaeology had disproved the accepted belief, making Babylon actually older, not as old as, and answer choice "B" correct.

Furthermore, because "500 years" is used, answer choice A can be ruled out. Years are used to show either absolute or relative age. If two objects are as old as each other, no years are necessary to describe that relationship, and it would be sufficient to say, "The ancient city of Babylon is approximately as old as their supposed Mesopotamian predecessors," without using the term "500 years."

Simplicity is Bliss

Simplicity cannot be overstated. You should never choose a longer, more complicated, or wordier replacement if a simple one will do. When a point can be made with fewer words, choose that answer. However, never sacrifice the flow of text for simplicity. If an answer is simple, but does not make sense, then it is not correct.

Beware of added phrases that don't add anything of meaning, such as "to be" or "as to them". Often these added phrases will occur just before a colon, which may come before a list of items. However, the colon does not need a lengthy introduction. The phrases "of which [...] are" in the below examples are wordy and unnecessary. They should be removed and the colon placed directly after the words "sport" and "following".

> *Example 1*: There are many advantages to running as a sport, *of which the top advantages are*:
> *Example 2*: The school supplies necessary were the following, *of which a few are*:

Copyright © Mometrix Media. You have been licensed one copy of this document for personal use only. Any other reproduction or redistribution is strictly prohibited. All rights reserved.

Mathematics Test

The math portion of the PSAT consists of a 45-minute section in which a calculator may be used and a 25-minute section in which no calculator may be used. The calculator portion contains 31 questions and the non-calculator portion contains 17 questions.

Concepts covered
PSAT questions fall into four categories:
- Heart of Algebra
- Problem Solving and Data Analysis
- Passport to Advanced Math
- Additional Topics in Math

The table below gives a complete breakdown of questions:

Calculator Portion	Number of Questions	% of Test
Total Questions	**31**	**100%**
Multiple Choice	27	87%
Student-Produced Response	4	13%
Content Categories	**31**	**100%**
Heart of Algebra	8	26%
Problem Solving and Data Analysis	16	52%
Passport to Advanced Math	6	19%
Additional Math Topics	1	3%
No-Calculator Portion		
Total Questions	**17**	**100%**
Multiple Choice	13	76%
Student-Produced Response	4	24%
Content Categories	**17**	**100%**
Heart of Algebra	8	47%
Passport to Advanced Math	8	47%
Additional Math Topics	1	6%

Use the practice tests.
The best thing you can do to prepare for the PSAT is to take several practice tests and review all your wrong answers very carefully. Work back through those problems until you understand how the answer was derived and you're confident you could answer a similar problem on your own.

This guide includes a practice test with answer key and explanations. Examples are also available on the College Board website. If you feel uncertain on a particular concept or problem type, use these tests to practice.

How to Approach PSAT Math Questions

Take an approved calculator you're familiar with. Check its batteries.
If you normally use a scientific or graphic calculator, check the PSAT website to make sure it's one you'll be allowed to use. Use that calculator as you work through the practice tests.

Remember that the test provides all the information you need.
There's even a handy chart of "reference information" in the textbook with geometry formulas you might need, including the Pythagorean Theorem and special right triangles. The chart even tells you that the sum of angles in a triangle equals 180. Don't worry about cramming to memorize the formula for calculating the area of a circle. All you need to know is that A = area, C = circumference, and r = radius.

Read carefully.
Yes, it's a math test, but these questions require careful reading. Look for key words such as "is" (equals), "more than," "less than," "of" (percentage, ratio, or multiplication), and so forth. Ask yourself:
- "What do I know?"
- "What information does the problem provide?"
- "What is the question asking, exactly?"

Remember that you don't always have to solve the whole problem to answer the question.
Especially with algebra problems, answering the question may not actually require solving the entire equation or finding all the variables. This is another example of "read carefully" - be sure you understand what the question is asking for.

Look at the answers before you begin calculating.
What form do the possible answers take? If they're fractions, then work in fractions rather than decimals. Do they include negative numbers? (Negative numbers are an often-forgotten option for many problems involving exponents, roots, and absolute values.)

Take it one step at a time.
If a problem seems overwhelming at first, just look for the first step. Write down what information you know. Break it down. And remember that by just using logic and basic techniques, you can work through even the most complex multi-step problems.

Draw a picture or write down expressions as you read.
Many of the problems require more logic than raw mathematical knowledge. As you read a problem, make a sketch in the margin, draw on the figure in the test book, or write out the

- 62 -

mathematical expression described. (For example, if you read "The area of Circle A is twice the area of Circle B," write down "A = 2B.")

Substitute numbers for variables.
Sometimes the easiest thing to do is pick a value for *x*, *n*, or another variable, and work through the problem using that number. It may be easier to work through that way, especially for geometry problems. (Just remember that the value isn't "true," merely convenient.)

Use elimination.
As with all PSAT questions, the first thing to do is eliminate obviously wrong answers. Are there choices that are clearly too big or too small? In an impossible form? Based on a common error, such as a sign or exponent error?

Check your answers.
When you solve a problem, plug the answer back in to confirm it makes sense. Make sure you haven't made careless mistakes such as skipping a step or making an arithmetic error.

Fill in all the circles, then double-check.
For the "student-produced" responses, where you have to supply the actual number instead of selecting from multiple choices, make sure to fill in all the circles. You get no credit for the number written at the top — those boxes are only there to help you mark the circles accurately. Make sure you've filled in the right spots.

Give an educated guess.
The PSAT no longer penalizes students for wrong answers. This means that you should always narrow down your answer choices by eliminating anything you know is wrong and then give an educated guess at the answer.

Don't get mired down on any one question.
The first, easiest problem on the test is worth the same points as the last, hardest question. If one problem is taking a long time, move on. You can come back to it later if you have time.

Heart of Algebra

The questions in this section will cover a range of topics in algebra. Students will be tested on their ability to analyze and solve linear equations and systems of equations. They will also need to be able to create these equations to represent a relationship between two or more quantities and solve problems. Along with linear equations, students will need to be able to create and solve linear inequalities. Some questions will also require the student to interpret formulas and be able to rearrange them in order to solve the problem.

Solving a linear equation in one variable, where there are infinitely many solutions

When solving a linear equation in one variable, if the process results in a true equation of the form $a = a$ where a is a real number, the equation has infinitely many solutions. This is because the equation is always true, independent of the value of the variable. For example, consider the solution of the equation below:

$$2x - 3(x + 1) = 2 - (x + 5)$$
$$2x - 3x - 3 = 2 - x - 5$$
$$-x - 3 = -x - 3$$
$$-3 = -3$$

For any value of x, each side of the equation evaluates to 3. So the solution is x = any real number, and there are infinitely many solutions.

Solving a linear equation in one variable, where there are no solutions

When solving a linear equation in one variable, if the process results in a false equation of the form $a = b$ where a and b are different (not equal) numbers, the equation has no solution. This is because the equation is always false, independent of the value of the variable. For example, consider the solution of the equation below:

$$2x - 3(x + 1) = 2 - (x + 4)$$
$$2x - 3x - 3 = 2 - x - 4$$
$$-x - 3 = -x - 2$$
$$-3 = -2$$

For any value of x, each side of the equation evaluates to two different values. The equation therefore has no solution.

Types of questions – linear expressions

You should expect to create, solve, or interpret a linear equation in one variable. These equations will have rational coefficients and may require multiple steps to simplify or solve. Linear equations in one variable have just one unknown variable. That variable has an exponent of one. For example, $2m + 3 = 3m + 7$ and $1.2(2.5x + 3.2) = 6.7x$ are linear equations in one variable. Typically, a question asks you to translate a verbal expression into an algebraic expression or a word problem into an equation. Then, you may need to solve the equation or answer another question related to that equation. The problems may include questions about any topic that lends itself to a linear expression or equation in one variable. For instance, you may see a question that says, "Jacob rents a car during his vacation. The rental agency's daily charge is \$49.95, which is taxed at a rate of 7%. Jacob is also charged a one-time nonrefundable rental fee of \$50. Which of the following represents Jacob's total car rental expenses, in dollars, for use of the car for x days?" You would then need to create the expression that computes the total cost for x days.

Mathematical symbols

You must be able to translate verbal expressions or "math words" into math symbols. This chart contains several "math words" and their appropriate symbols:

equal, is, was, will be, has, costs, gets to, is the same as, becomes	=
time, of, multiplied by, product of, twice, doubles, halves, triples	×
divided by, per, ratio of/to, out of	÷
plus, added to, sum, combined, and, more than, totals of	+
subtracted from, less than, decreased by, minus, difference between	-
what, how much, original value, how many, a number, a variable	x, n, etc.

- 64 -

For example, the phrase *four more than twice a number* can be written algebraically as $2x + 4$. The phrase *half a number decreased by six* can be written algebraically as $\frac{1}{2}x - 6$. The phrase *the sum of a number and the product of five and that number* can be written algebraically as $x + 5x$. You may see a test question that says, "Olivia is constructing a bookcase from seven boards. Two of them are for vertical supports and five are for shelves. The height of the bookcase is twice the width of the bookcase. If the seven boards total 36 feet in length, what will be the height of Olivia's bookcase?" You would need to make a sketch and then create the equation to determine the width of the shelves. The height can be represented as double the width. (If x represents the width of the shelves in feet, then the height of the book shelf is $2x$. Since the seven boards total 36 feet, $2x + 2x + x + x + x + x + x = 36$; $9x = 36$; $x = 4$. The height is twice the width, or 8 feet.)

Inequalities

Commonly in algebra and other upper-level fields of math you find yourself working with mathematical expressions that do not equal each other. The statement comparing such expressions with symbols such as < (less than) or > (greater than) is called an *Inequality*. An example of an inequality is $7x > 5$. To solve for x, simply divide both sides by 7 and the solution is shown to be $x > \frac{5}{7}$. Graphs of the solution set of inequalities are represented on a number line. Open circles are used to show that an expression approaches a number but is never quite equal to that number.

> ➤ **Review Video: <u>Inequalities</u>**
> Visit **mometrix.com/academy** and enter **Code: 451494**

Conditional Inequalities are those with certain values for the variable that will make the condition true and other values for the variable where the condition will be false. *Absolute Inequalities* can have any real number as the value for the variable to make the condition true, while there is no real number value for the variable that will make the condition false. Solving inequalities is done by following the same rules as for solving equations with the exception that when multiplying or dividing by a negative number the direction of the inequality sign must be flipped or reversed. *Double Inequalities* are situations where two inequality statements apply to the same variable expression. An example of this is $-c < ax + b < c$.

A *Weighted Mean*, or weighted average, is a mean that uses "weighted" values. The formula is weighted mean $= \frac{w_1 x_1 + w_2 x_2 + w_3 x_3 \ldots + w_n x_n}{w_1 + w_2 + w_3 + \cdots + w_n}$. Weighted values, such as $w_1, w_2, w_3, \ldots w_n$ are assigned to each member of the set $x_1, x_2, x_3, \ldots x_n$. If calculating weighted mean, make sure a weight value for each member of the set is used.

Solving linear inequalities

Solving linear inequalities is very similar to solving linear equations. You must isolate the variable on one side of the inequality by using the inverse, or opposite operations. To undo addition, you use subtraction and vice versa. To undo multiplication, you use division and vice versa. The only difference in solving linear inequalities occurs when you multiply or divide by a negative number. When this is the case, you must flip the inequality symbol. This means that less than becomes greater than, greater than becomes less than, etc. Another type of inequality is called a compound inequality. A compound inequality contains two inequalities separated by an "and" or an "or" statement. An "and" statement can also consist of a variable sandwiched in the middle of two inequality symbols. To solve this type of inequality, simply separate it into two inequalities applying the middle terms to each. Then, follow the steps to isolate the variable.

- 65 -

Types of questions – linear inequalities

You should expect to create, solve, or interpret a linear inequality in one variable. Linear inequalities in one variable are inequalities with just one unknown variable. That variable has an exponent of one. For example, $4x + 2 > 10$ and $100 - 2x \geq 27$ are both linear equalities in one variable. Typically, the questions ask you to translate verbal expressions or word problems into algebraic inequalities. Then, you may be expected to solve the inequality or answer another question related to that inequality. Examples of key words and phrases indicating an inequality include *at least* ($\geq$), *no more than* ($\leq$), *more than* ($>$) and *less than* ($<$). You may see a test question that says, "Emily and Madison sold tickets to the school play. Emily sold 70 more tickets than Madison, but together they sold fewer than 200 tickets. Which of the following represents the number of tickets Madison sold?" You would then need to create an inequality from the given information and simplify that inequality using correct algebraic procedures; afterwards, when solving, remember to flip the inequality symbol if dividing or multiplying both sides by negative numbers.

Types of questions – linear functions

You should expect to build or create a linear function or equation in two variables that models a context. Linear functions or equations in two variables are equations with two unknown variables. Both variables have an exponent of one. You might be required to express the relationship in functional notation. For example, $y = 3x + 12$ and $p = 0.5d + 14.7$ are both linear equations in two variables and can be expressed in functional notation as $f(x) = 3x + 12$ and $f(d) = 0.5d + 14.7$, respectively. You may be expected to simplify your equation or function. You may see a test question that says, "The pressure in a tank which contains an industrial chemical and which is open to the atmosphere increases linearly with the height of the chemical in the tank. The measured pressure is due to the combined hydrostatic pressure of the chemical and the atmospheric pressure. A pressure gauge at a depth of five feet beneath the surface reads 17.2 pounds per square inch (psi), and at a depth of ten feet reads 19.7 psi. Which of the following linear models best describes the pressure p in psi at a depth of d feet?" You must determine the relationship between pressure p and depth d. First, determine the rate at which the pressure changes with depth; then, consider the contribution of the atmospheric pressure to the total pressure.

Modeling linear relationships in two variables

You should expect to build or create a linear function or equation in two variables that models a context. Linear functions or equations in two variables are equations with two unknown variables. Both variables have an exponent of one. You might be required to express the relationship in functional notation. For example, $y = 3x + 12$ and $p = 0.5d + 14.7$ are both linear equations in two variables and can be expressed in functional notation as $f(x) = 3x + 12$ and $f(d) = 0.5d + 14.7$, respectively. You may be expected to simplify your equation or function. You may see a test question that says, "The pressure in a tank which contains an industrial chemical and which is open to the atmosphere increases linearly with the height of the chemical in the tank. The measured pressure is due to the combined hydrostatic pressure of the chemical and the atmospheric pressure. A pressure gauge at a depth of five feet beneath the surface reads 17.2 pounds per square inch (psi), and at a depth of ten feet reads 19.7 psi. Which of the following linear models best describes the pressure p in psi at a depth of d feet?" You must determine the relationship between pressure p and depth d. First, determine the rate at which the pressure changes with depth; then, consider the contribution of the atmospheric pressure to the total pressure.

Types of questions – linear inequalities in two variables

You should expect to create, solve, or interpret systems of linear inequalities in two variables. Linear inequalities in two variables resemble systems of equations except the equal signs are replaced with inequality symbols ($<, >, \leq, \geq$). You may be asked to solve a system of linear equalities. To solve a system of linear inequalities, each inequality must be graphed on the same coordinate plane. If both inequalities are written in slope intercept form, they can be graphed using the slope-intercept method. A dotted line is used when the inequality includes a $<$ or $>$ symbol. A solid line is used when the inequality includes a $\leq$ or $\geq$ symbol. Shade above the line if $y <$ or $\leq mx + b$ and above if $y >$ or $\geq mx + b$. The region where the two shaded areas overlap is the solution to the original system of inequalities; if there is no overlap, there is no solution. You may be asked to determine whether a given point is in the solution set of a system of linear inequalities. If a graph is provided, simply check to see if the given point is located in the region where the regions of the inequalities overlap. If you are not given a graph, see if the point satisfies each of the given inequalities. If the given point satisfies both inequalities, it is in the solution set for the system of inequalities.

Systems of Equations

Systems of Equations are a set of simultaneous equations that all use the same variables. A solution to a system of equations must be true for each equation in the system. *Consistent Systems* are those with at least one solution. *Inconsistent Systems* are systems of equations that have no solution.

> ➢ **Review Video: Systems of Equations**
> Visit **mometrix.com/academy** *and enter* **Code: 658153**

To solve a system of linear equations by *substitution*, start with the easier equation and solve for one of the variables. Express this variable in terms of the other variable. Substitute this expression in the other equation, and solve for the other variable. The solution should be expressed in the form (x, y). Substitute the values into both of the original equations to check your answer. Consider the following problem.

Solve the system using substitution:
$x + 6y = 15$
$3x - 12y = 18$

Solve the first equation for x:
$x = 15 - 6y$

Substitute this value in place of x in the second equation, and solve for y:
$3(15 - 6y) - 12y = 18$
$45 - 18y - 12y = 18$

Plug this value for y back into the first equation to solve for x:
$x = 15 - 6(0.9) = 15 - 5.4 = 9.6$

Check both equations if you have time:
$9.6 + 6(0.9) = 9.6 + 5.4 = 15$
$3(9.6) - 12(0.9) = 28.8 - 10.8 = 18$
Therefore, the solution is $(9.6, 0.9)$.

To solve a system of equations using *elimination*, begin by rewriting both equations in standard form $Ax + By = C$. Check to see if the coefficients of one pair of like variables add to zero. If not, multiply one or both of the equations by a non-zero number to make one set of like variables add to zero. Add the two equations to solve for one of the variables. Substitute this value into one of the original equations to solve for the other variable. Check your work by substituting into the other equation. Next we will solve the same problem as above, but using the addition method.

Solve the system using elimination:
$$x + 6y = 15$$
$$3x - 12y = 18$$

If we multiply the first equation by 2, we can eliminate the y terms:
$$2x + 12y = 30$$
$$3x - 12y = 18$$

Add the equations together and solve for x:
$$5x = 48$$
$$x = \frac{48}{5} = 9.6$$

Plug the value for x back into either of the original equations and solve for y:
$$9.6 + 6y = 15$$
$$y = \frac{15 - 9.6}{6} = 0.9$$

Check both equations if you have time:
$$9.6 + 6(0.9) = 9.6 + 5.4 = 15$$
$$3(9.6) - 12(0.9) = 28.8 - 10.8 = 18$$
Therefore, the solution is $(9.6, 0.9)$.

Solving systems of equations vs solving systems of inequalities

Solving systems of inequalities is very similar to solving systems of equations in that you are looking for a solution or a range of solutions that satisfy all of the equations in the system. Since solutions to inequalities are within a certain interval, it is best to solve this type of system by graphing. Follow the same steps to graph an inequality as you would an equation, but in addition, shade the portion of the graph that represents the solution. Recall that when graphing an inequality on the coordinate plane, you replace the inequality symbol with an equal sign and draw a solid line if the points are included (greater than or equal to or less than or equal to) or a dashed line if the points are not included (greater than or less than). Then replace the inequality symbol and shade the portion of the graph that is included in the solution. Choose a point that is not on the line and test it in the inequality to see if it is makes sense. In a system, you repeat this process for all of the equations and the solution is the region in which the graphs overlap. This is unlike solving a system of equations, in which the solution is a single point where the lines intersect.

Possibilities of a system of 2 linear equations in 2 variables

There are 3 possibilities that can occur graphically for a given system of two linear equations in two variables:
1) The graphs intersect. The point at which they intersect is the solution of the system of equations.
2) The graphs are the same, or coincide with each other. This means that the two equations are actually the same equation. The solution of the system is all points on the line.

3) The graphs do not intersect, and the system has no solution. This occurs when the two equations have the same slope, or the two lines are distinct vertical lines. These lines are parallel.

Types of questions – systems of equations

You should expect to be asked to write and solve a system of linear equations from a word problem. You may see a test question that says, "Alyssa's scout troop is selling tickets for the community fun fair. Adult tickets cost $8.50 each, and child tickets cost $5.50 each. The troop sells a total of 375 tickets and collects $2,512.50 in revenue. Solving which of these systems of equations yields the number of adult tickets, x, and the number of child tickets, y, sold by Alyssa's scout troop? How many of each ticket type are sold?" First, write an equation for the number of tickets sold ($x + y = 375$) and a second equation for revenue generated ($8.50x + 5.50y = 2512.50$). Then, solve the system of equations and answer the question that is asked. The methods used in solving systems of linear equations include elimination (addition), substitution, and graphing. To solve by elimination, write the equations in a way that the like variables line up when one equation is placed above the other. The goal is to add the two equations together to eliminate one of the variables. If necessary, multiply one or both of the equations by a constant to enable such elimination. To solve by substitution, select one of the equations and solve it for one of the variables; then, substitute this into the other equation and solve. To solve by graphing, find the point of intersection of the two lines graphed on the same coordinate plane.

Solving linear equations in one variable

You should expect to be asked to solve linear equations in one variable without the use of a calculator. Linear equations in one variable are equations with just one unknown variable that has an exponent of one. The equation may be complicated with rational coefficients. For example, $\frac{10x-8}{6} = \frac{3x+12}{3}$ and $\frac{x-2}{x+3} = \frac{6}{8}$ are both linear equations in one variable that require several steps to solve. If any of the terms in the given equation has/have a denominator, first clear the equation of fractions by multiplying the entire equation by the least common denominator of all of the fractional terms. Then, simplify each side by collecting like terms. Finally, solve for the unknown variable by isolating the variable on one side.

Solving linear equations in two variables

You should expect to be given a system of linear equations in two variables to solve without a calculator. For example, $\begin{cases} \frac{1}{2}x + \frac{1}{4}y = \frac{-1}{2} \\ 5x + 3y = -3 \end{cases}$ is a system of linear equations which you might be asked to solve. One of the coefficients may be replaced with a variable as shown here: $\begin{cases} \frac{1}{2}x + \frac{1}{4}y = \frac{-1}{2} \\ ax + 3y = -3 \end{cases}$; you may be asked to solve for a. You can solve systems of equations algebraically by elimination or substitution. Systems of equations may have no solution, one solution, or an infinite number of solutions. If when graphed the two lines are parallel, there is no solution. If the lines intersect at one point, there is one solution. If the lines graph as exactly the same line, there are an infinite number of solutions.

Interpreting variables and constants

You should expect to be given a real-world scenario and the linear function associated with that scenario. You may be asked to identify variable terms or constant terms from the given function as well as interpret their meanings in the given real-world situation. You may see a test question like "The school van begins a field trip with 14 gallons of gasoline. After travelling 120 miles, the van has 8 gallons of gasoline. If this relationship is modeled by the linear function $f(x) = -20x + 280$, what does the x represent?" Or you might be asked what -20 and 280 represent in the given function.

Understanding the basic format

Understanding the basic format of a linear function is very helpful. A linear function has an input and an output. The value of the output is determined by substituting the value of the independent variable into the equation. If the function notation is $f(x)$, the x is the input, and the $f(x)$ is the output. Linear functions are just linear equations written with functional notation. For example, the linear equation $y = 4x + 7$ can be written as the function $f(x) = 4x + 7$. You can compare this to the slope-intercept form of a line in which y represents the output, m represents the rate, x represents the input, and b represents a constant. You may see a test question with a word problem that says, "A school play has \$200 in production costs. If tickets are sold at \$5.75, how many tickets must be sold before the play makes a profit?" In addition, you may be given a function $p(x) = 5.75x - 200$ and asked a questions such as, "What does the x represent?" or "Describe why the operator before the 200 is a minus sign."

Helpful knowledge about interpreting variables and constants

Understanding the term *slope* and the various forms of linear equations, such as slope-intercept form, is very useful. Slope indicates the slant of the line. Lines with positive slopes slant up and to the right. Lines with negative slopes slant down and to the right. A horizontal line has a slope of zero, and the slope of a vertical line is undefined. If a linear equation is written in the slope-intercept form $y = mx + b$, the slope of the line is given by m. Slope may be determined from a graph as $m = \frac{\Delta y}{\Delta x}$. This often referred to as "rise over run." Also, the b in the slope-intercept form $y = mx + b$ is the y-intercept of the line. The intercepts are the places where the graphed line crosses the axes. The y-intercept has coordinates $(0, b)$, and the x-intercept has coordinates $(a, 0)$. The two-intercept form of a line is given by $\frac{x}{a} + \frac{y}{b} = 1$, where a is the x-intercept and b is the y-intercept. The point-slope form of a line is given by $y - y_1 = m(x - x_1)$, where m is the slope and (x_1, y_1) is a point on the line. A vertical line has the form $x = a$, and a horizontal line has the form $y = b$.

Assessing understanding of the connection between algebraic and graphical representations

You should expect five types of questions about the connections between algebraic and graphical representations. First, you may be given a linear equation and asked to select from several choices the graph which corresponds to that equation. Key features such as slope and y-intercept provide clues. Second, you may be given the graph of a linear equation and asked to select from several choices the equation which corresponds with that graph. Note the slant of the line, which indicates the slope, and the line's intercepts. Third, you may be given a verbal description of a linear graph and be asked to write the equation that matches the given description. Fourth, you may be given a graph of a linear equation and asked to determine key features such as slope (rate) and intercepts. Fifth, you may be given the graph of a linear equation and asked how a change in the equation impacts the graph. For example, you might be asked how a change in the slope or y-intercept affects the slant or position of the line graphed.

Helpful knowledge about connections between algebraic and graphical representations

Understanding the term *slope* and the various forms of linear equations, such as slope-intercept form, is very useful. Slope indicates the slant of the line. Lines with positive slopes slant up and to the right. Lines with negative slopes slant down and to the right. A horizontal line has a slope of zero, and the slope of a vertical line is undefined. If a linear equation is written in the slope-intercept form $y = mx + b$, the slope of the line is given by m. Slope may be determined from a graph as $m = \frac{\Delta y}{\Delta x}$. This often referred to as "rise over run." Also, the b in the slope-intercept form $y = mx + b$ is the y-intercept of the line. The intercepts are the places where the graphed line crosses the axes. The y-intercept has coordinates $(0, b)$, and the x-intercept has coordinates $(a, 0)$. The two-intercept form of a line is given by $\frac{x}{a} + \frac{y}{b} = 1$, where a is the x-intercept and b is the y-intercept. The point-slope form of a line is given by $y - y_1 = m(x - x_1)$, where m is the slope and (x_1, y_1) is a point on the line. A vertical line has the form $x = a$, and a horizontal line has the form $y = b$.

Problem Solving and Data Analysis

The questions in this section will require students to create and analyze relationships. They will solve single- and multistep problems using ratios, rates, proportions, and percentages. Some questions will also require students to describe relationships that are presented graphically. In addition, students should be able to analyze and summarize both qualitative and quantitative data.

Ratios
A ratio is a comparison of two quantities in a particular order. Example: If there are 14 computers in a lab, and the class has 20 students, there is a student to computer ratio of 20 to 14, commonly written as 20:14. Ratios are normally reduced to their smallest whole number representation, so 20:14 would be reduced to 10:7 by dividing both sides by 2.

Proportions
A proportion is a relationship between two quantities that dictates how one changes when the other changes. A direct proportion describes a relationship in which a quantity increases by a set amount for every increase in the other quantity, or decreases by that same amount for every decrease in the other quantity.
Example: Assuming a constant driving speed, the time required for a car trip increases as the distance of the trip increases. The distance to be traveled and the time required to travel are directly proportional.

Percentages
Percentages can be thought of as fractions that are based on a whole of 100; that is, one whole is equal to 100%. The word percent means "per hundred." Fractions can be expressed as percents by finding equivalent fractions with a denomination of 100. Example: $\frac{7}{10} = \frac{70}{100} = 70\%$; $\frac{1}{4} = \frac{25}{100} = 25\%$.

A percentage problem can be presented three main ways: (1) Find what percentage of some number another number is. Example: What percentage of 40 is 8? (2) Find what number is some percentage of a given number. Example: What number is 20% of 40? (3) Find what number another number is a given percentage of.
Example: What number is 8 20% of? The three components in all of these cases are the same: a whole (W), a part (P), and a percentage (%). These are related by the equation: $P = W \times \%$. This is the form of the equation you would use to solve problems of type (2). To solve types (1) and (3), you would use these two forms: $\% = \frac{P}{W}$ and $W = \frac{P}{\%}$.

The thing that frequently makes percentage problems difficult is that they are most often also word problems, so a large part of solving them is figuring out which quantities are what. Example: In a school cafeteria, 7 students choose pizza, 9 choose hamburgers, and 4 choose tacos. Find the percentage that chooses tacos. To find the whole, you must first add all of the parts: 7 + 9 + 4 = 20. The percentage can then be found by dividing the part by the whole ($\% = \frac{P}{W}$): $\frac{4}{20} = \frac{20}{100} = 20\%$.

Unit rate

Unit rate expresses a quantity of one thing in terms of one unit of another. For example, if you travel 30 miles every two hours, a unit rate expresses this comparison in terms of one hour: in one hour you travel 15 miles, so your unit rate is 15 miles per hour. Other examples are how much one ounce of food costs (price per ounce), or figuring out how much one egg costs out of the dozen (price per 1 egg, instead of price per 12 eggs). The denominator of a unit rate is always 1.

Unit rates are used to compare different situations to solve problems. For example, to make sure you get the best deal when deciding which kind of soda to buy, you can find the unit rate of each. If Soda #1 costs $1.50 for a 1-liter bottle, and soda #2 costs $2.75 for a 2-liter bottle, it would be a better deal to buy Soda #2, because its unit rate is only $1.375 per 1-liter, which is cheaper than Soda #1. Unit rates can also help determine the length of time a given event will take. For example, if you can paint 2 rooms in 4.5 hours, you can determine how long it will take you to paint 5 rooms by solving for the unit rate per room and then multiplying that by 5.

Types of questions – ratios, rates, proportional relationships

You should expect three types of questions in this category. First, you may be asked to use a proportional relationship between two quantities to solve a multistep problem or to find a ratio or rate. Proportional relationships can be direct relationships (as x increases, y increases) or inverse relationships (as x increases, y decreases). Remember, units can be cancelled just like factors. You may be expected to use some basic knowledge such as *distance = rate × time*. Second, you might be asked to calculate a ratio or rate and to use that rate or ratio to solve a multistep problem. Third, you might be given a ratio or rate and be expected to solve a multistep problem. You may see a test question that says, "The ratio of boys to girls in the children's choir is 2:3. If there are eight boys in the choir, how many total children are in the choir?" You may be given a mixture problem in the form of a ratio and be expected to determine how much of a component is needed. You may be asked to determine a ratio associated with a geometric relationship, such as the ratio of a circle's circumference to its radius. You may be given a scale drawing and be expected to find a ratio associated with that drawing.

Types of questions – percentages

Questions involving percentages typically come in three basic forms. For example, "What is 10% of 50?" or "5 is what percent of 50?" or "5 is 10% of what number?" Questions involving percentages may also include percent increase or decrease. These questions may be worded using *percent change*. For example, "If gasoline prices rose from $2.76 to $3.61, what is the percent change?" More complicated questions may be asked, and you will need to have a solid understanding of percentages in order to approach such questions. You may be given a table of values or a pie chart and be expected to calculate percentages from the information given. You may be expected to use these calculations to answer a related question.

Types of questions – units and unit conversion

You should expect to be asked to determine a unit rate and then use that rate to solve another problem. You may see a question that gives a conversion rate for an unfamiliar quantity to a familiar quantity, such as from a foreign currency to US dollars. You may be asked to solve a multistep unit problem using unfamiliar conversion rates along with other concepts, such as finding percentages. You may be asked to solve multistep problems to determine an item's density, or you may be asked to apply the concept of density. You may see a problem that says, "A bar of gold has dimensions of 5.0 cm by 5.0 cm by 10.0 cm. If gold has a density of 19,300 kg/m³, what is the mass of the gold bar in grams?"

Scatter plot

Scatter plots show the relationship between two sets of data. The first step in creating a scatter plot is to collect data. Suppose you are analyzing the relationship between age and hours of sleep. You would collect a representative sample of the population using a list or chart to organize your data. Next, you would arrange the data in a table with the independent variable on the left-hand side and the dependent variable on the right-hand side. To graph your data, look at the range in the values. In this situation, the independent variable, or x-values, and the dependent variable, or y-values, all are positive so you only need to draw and label Quadrant I on the coordinate grid. Look at the data and find the most appropriate intervals to label the axes. Plot the points using (x,y), moving over x units on the horizontal axis and up y units on the vertical axis to see the relationship between the two data sets.

Types of questions – scatter plot

You should expect to be given a scatterplot in a real-world context. The scatterplot may already include a line of best fit, or you may be expected to select the equation of a line or curve of best fit. You may be expected to interpret the relationship between two variables based on the scatterplot. This relationship may be linear, quadratic, or exponential. You may be expected to use the line or curve of best fit to make a prediction about the situation. You may be given a scatter plot and asked, "Based on the line of best fit to the data shown, which of the following values is closest to the average yearly increase?." You must determine the slope of the line of best fit to answer the question. It is important to understand correlations shown by scatterplots. Make sure you do not try to apply a line of best fit to data that show no correlation. Make sure you do not try to apply a line to a curvilinear model. You probably will not have to actually find the equation of the line of best fit. You just need to be able to interpret the information that is given.

Correlations

A scatter plot is a way to represent the relationship between two data sets. The data can have one of three types of relationships, or correlations: a positive correlation, a negative correlation, or no correlation. A positive correlation is one in which the points increase from left to right. A negative correlation is one in which the points decrease from left to right. A scatter plot with no correlation is one in which the points show no relationship and neither rise nor fall. The correlation can help to determine the line of best fit. The line of best fit is a line drawn to best represent the data values. The line usually falls in the middle of the group of points and contains as many points as possible. When a graph has a positive or negative correlation, a line of regression can be drawn to determine an equation based on the relationship. When a graph has no correlation, a regression line cannot be drawn.

Summarize data in two-way frequency table

A two-way frequency table is a table that shows the number of data points falling into each combination of two categories in the form of a table, with one category on each axis. Creating a two-way frequency table is simply a matter of drawing a table with each axis labeled with the possibilities for the corresponding category, and then filling in the numbers in the appropriate cells. For instance, suppose you're told that at a given school, 30 male students take Spanish, 20 take French, and 25 German, while 26 female students take Spanish, 28 French, and 21 German. These data can be represented by the following two-way frequency table:

# of students	SPANISH	FRENCH	GERMAN
MALE	30	20	25

FEMALE	26	28	21

You should expect to see questions with categorical data summarized in two-way tables. You need to make comparisons among the data contained in the columns and rows of data. You may need to use proportions or calculate percentages. Two-way frequency tables typically include cells which total the data contained in the columns and rows, as well as an overall sum of data. These sums are used when calculating proportions and percentages. You may be asked to determine the relative frequencies of the data included in the rows or the columns. You may need to determine conditional probability, which is the probability of one event given the occurrence of another; additionally, you may be asked to compare conditional probabilities to determine the association between events. For example, consider a table with a row of data showing the number of students who study for a test more than and less than four hours a week and a row of data showing the number of students whose test grades are above and below 80%. The probability of a student making above 80% is calculated given a study time of more than four hours, and the probability of a student making below a 80% given a study time of more than four hours; if the probability of a student making above an 80% is much greater than the probability of making below an 80% given the same study time, there may be a correlation between study time and test score; alternatively, if the probabilities are approximately the same, there would appear to be no correlation.

Types of questions – inferences about population parameters
You may be asked to estimate a population parameter given the results from a random sample of a population. A question might say, "In the survey of a random sample of 1,200 cell phone users aged 18-25 from a particular region, 420 used their phones exclusively to do their banking. If the region had 160,000 residents aged 18-25, approximately how many of those residents could be expected to use their cell phones exclusively to do their banking?" You are also expected to understand any confidence intervals and measurement errors included in the problem. You may see a question that says, "A researcher collected information from 1,000 randomly selected public high school science teachers in the United States and concluded that the median annual salary was between $52,400 and $63,800 with a 99% confidence level. Which of the following could represent the median annual salary for the same sample with a 95% confidence level?"

Estimating a conditional probability from a two-way frequency table
If we have a two-way frequency table, it is generally a straightforward matter to read off the probabilities of any two events A and B, as well as the joint probability of both events occurring, $P(A \cap B)$. We can then find the conditional probability P(A|B) by calculating $P(A|B) = \frac{P(A \cap B)}{P(B)}$.

For example, a certain store's recent T-shirt sales:

		Size			
		Small	Medium	Large	Total
Color	Blue	25	40	35	100
	White	27	25	22	74
	Black	8	23	15	26
	Total	60	88	72	220

- 74 -

Suppose we want to find the conditional probability that a customer buys a black shirt (event A), given that the shirt he buys is size small (event B). From the table, the probability P(A) that a customer buys a small shirt is $\frac{60}{220} = \frac{3}{11}$. The probability $P(A \cap B)$ that he buys a small, black shirt is $\frac{8}{220} = \frac{2}{55}$. The conditional probability P(A|B) that he buys a black shirt, given that he buys a small shirt, is therefore $P(A|B) = \frac{2/55}{3/11} = \frac{2}{15}$.

Probability
Probability is a branch of statistics that deals with the likelihood of something taking place. One classic example is a coin toss. There are only two possible results: heads or tails. The likelihood, or probability, that the coin will land as heads is 1 out of 2 (1/2, 0.5, 50%). Tails has the same probability. Another common example is a 6-sided die roll. There are six possible results from rolling a single die, each with an equal chance of happening, so the probability of any given number coming up is 1 out of 6.

Terms frequently used in probability:
- Event – a situation that produces results of some sort (a coin toss)
- Compound event – event that involves two or more independent events (rolling a pair of dice; taking the sum)
- Outcome – a possible result in an experiment or event (heads, tails)
- Desired outcome (or success) – an outcome that meets a particular set of criteria (a roll of 1 or 2 if we are looking for numbers less than 3)
- Independent events – two or more events whose outcomes do not affect one another (two coins tossed at the same time)
- Dependent events – two or more events whose outcomes affect one another (two cards drawn consecutively from the same deck)
- Certain outcome – probability of outcome is 100% or 1
- Impossible outcome – probability of outcome is 0% or 0
- Mutually exclusive outcomes – two or more outcomes whose criteria cannot all be satisfied in a single event (a coin coming up heads and tails on the same toss)

➤ **Review Video: Simple Probability**
Visit ***mometrix.com/academy*** *and enter* ***Code: 212374***

Probability is the likelihood of a certain outcome occurring for a given event. The theoretical probability can usually be determined without actually performing the event. The likelihood of a outcome occurring, or the probability of an outcome occurring, is given by the formula

$$P(A) = \frac{\text{Number of acceptable outcomes}}{\text{Number of possible outcomes}}$$

where P(A) is the probability of an outcome A occurring, and each outcome is just as likely to occur as any other outcome. If each outcome has the same probability of occurring as every other possible outcome, the outcomes are said to be equally likely to occur. The total number of acceptable outcomes must be less than or equal to the total number of possible outcomes. If the two are equal, then the outcome is certain to occur and the probability is 1. If the number of acceptable outcomes is zero, then the outcome is impossible and the probability is 0.

Example:
There are 20 marbles in a bag and 5 are red. The theoretical probability of randomly selecting a red marble is 5 out of 20, (5/20 = 1/4, 0.25, or 25%).

When trying to calculate the probability of an event using the $\frac{desired\ outcomes}{total\ outcomes}$ formula, you may frequently find that there are too many outcomes to individually count them. Permutation and combination formulas offer a shortcut to counting outcomes. A permutation is an arrangement of a specific number of a set of objects in a specific order. The number of permutations of r items given a set of n items can be calculated as $_nP_r = \frac{n!}{(n-r)!}$. Combinations are similar to permutations, except there are no restrictions regarding the order of the elements. While ABC is considered a different permutation than BCA, ABC and BCA are considered the same combination. The number of **combinations** of r items given a set of n items can be calculated as $_nC_r = \frac{n!}{r!(n-r)!}$ or $_nC_r = \frac{_nP_r}{r!}$.

Example: Suppose you want to calculate how many different 5-card hands can be drawn from a deck of 52 cards. This is a combination since the order of the cards in a hand does not matter. There are 52 cards available, and 5 to be selected. Thus, the number of different hands is $_{52}C_5 = \frac{52!}{5! \times 47!} = 2{,}598{,}960$.

Sometimes it may be easier to calculate the possibility of something not happening, or the complement of an event. Represented by the symbol $\bar{A}$, the complement of A is the probability that event A does not happen. When you know the probability of event A occurring, you can use the formula $P(\bar{A}) = 1 - P(A)$, where $P(\bar{A})$ is the probability of event A not occurring, and $P(A)$ is the probability of event A occurring.

The addition rule for probability is used for finding the probability of a compound event. Use the formula $P(A \text{ or } B) = P(A) + P(B) - P(A \text{ and } B)$, where $P(A \text{ and } B)$ is the probability of both events occurring to find the probability of a compound event. The probability of both events occurring at the same time must be subtracted to eliminate any overlap in the first two probabilities.

Conditional Probability

Conditional probability is the probability of an event occurring once another event has already occurred. Given event A and dependent event B, the probability of event B occurring when event A has already occurred is represented by the notation $P(A|B)$. To find the probability of event B occurring, take into account the fact that event A has already occurred and adjust the total number of possible outcomes. For example, suppose you have ten balls numbered 1–10 and you want ball number 7 to be pulled in two pulls. On the first pull, the probability of getting the 7 is $\frac{1}{10}$ because there is one ball with a 7 on it and 10 balls to choose from. Assuming the first pull did not yield a 7, the probability of pulling a 7 on the second pull is now $\frac{1}{9}$ because there are only 9 balls remaining for the second pull.

The multiplication rule can be used to find the probability of two independent events occurring using the formula $P(A \text{ and } B) = P(A) \times P(B)$, where $P(A \text{ and } B)$ is the probability of two independent events occurring, $P(A)$ is the probability of the first event occurring, and $P(B)$ is the probability of the second event occurring.

The multiplication rule can also be used to find the probability of two dependent events occurring using the formula $P(A \text{ and } B) = P(A) \times P(B|A)$, where $P(A \text{ and } B)$ is the probability of two dependent events occurring and $P(B|A)$ is the probability of the second event occurring after the first event has already occurred.

Before using the multiplication rule, you MUST first determine whether the two events are dependent or independent.

Use a combination of the multiplication rule and the rule of complements to find the probability that at least one outcome of the element will occur. This given by the general formula P(at least one event occurring) $= 1 - P$(no outcomes occurring). For example, to find the probability that at least one even number will show when a pair of dice is rolled, find the probability that two odd numbers will be rolled (no even numbers) and subtract from one. You can always use a tree diagram or make a chart to list the possible outcomes when the sample space is small, such as in the dice-rolling example, but in most cases it will be much faster to use the multiplication and complement formulas.

Expected Value

Expected value is a method of determining expected outcome in a random situation. It is really a sum of the weighted probabilities of the possible outcomes. Multiply the probability of an event occurring by the weight assigned to that probability (such as the amount of money won or lost). A practical application of the expected value is to determine whether a game of chance is really fair. If the sum of the weighted probabilities is equal to zero, the game is generally considered fair because the player has a fair chance to at least to break even. If the expected value is less than zero, then players lose more than they win. For example, a lottery drawing might allow the player to choose any three-digit number, 000–999. The probability of choosing the winning number is 1:1000. If it costs \$1 to play, and a winning number receives \$500, the expected value is $\left(-\$1 \cdot \frac{999}{1,000}\right) +$ $\left(\$500 \cdot \frac{1}{1,000}\right) = -0.499$ or $-\$0.50$. You can expect to lose on average 50 cents for every dollar you spend.

Empirical Probability

Most of the time, when we talk about probability, we mean theoretical probability. Empirical probability, or experimental probability or relative frequency, is the number of times an outcome occurs in a particular experiment or a certain number of observed events. While theoretical probability is based on what *should* happen, experimental probability is based on what *has* happened. Experimental probability is calculated in the same way as theoretical, except that actual outcomes are used instead of possible outcomes.

Theoretical and experimental probability do not always line up with one another. Theoretical probability says that out of 20 coin tosses, 10 should be heads. However, if we were actually to toss 20 coins, we might record just 5 heads. This doesn't mean that our theoretical probability is incorrect; it just means that this particular experiment had results that were different from what was predicted. A practical application of empirical probability is the insurance industry. There are no set functions that define life span, health, or safety. Insurance companies look at factors from hundreds of thousands of individuals to find patterns that they then use to set the formulas for insurance premiums.

Measures of Central Tendency

The quantities of mean, median, and mode are all referred to as measures of central tendency. They can each give a picture of what the whole set of data looks like with just a single number. Knowing what each of these values represents is vital to making use of the information they provide.

The mean, also known as the arithmetic mean or average, of a data set is calculated by summing all of the values in the set and dividing that sum by the number of values. For example, if a data set has 6 numbers and the sum of those 6 numbers is 30, the mean is calculated as 30/6 = 5.

The median is the middle value of a data set. The median can be found by putting the data set in numerical order, and locating the middle value. In the data set (1, 2, 3, 4, 5), the median is 3. If there is an even number of values in the set, the median is calculated by taking the average of the two middle values. In the data set, (1, 2, 3, 4, 5, 6), the median would be (3 + 4)/2 = 3.5.

The mode is the value that appears most frequently in the data set. In the data set (1, 2, 3, 4, 5, 5, 5), the mode would be 5 since the value 5 appears three times. If multiple values appear the same number of times, there are multiple values for the mode. If the data set were (1, 2, 2, 3, 4, 4, 5, 5), the modes would be 2, 4, and 5. If no value appears more than any other value in the data set, then there is no mode.

Confidence interval

A confidence interval gives a range of a values that is likely to include the parameter of interest. After a random sample, suppose a parameter, such as a median is estimated to be within a certain range with a 99% confidence level. This essentially means one time out of 100 times, the median value will not be in the specified interval. (You will not be asked to actually calculate the confidence levels; they will be given with the question.) For example, you may see a question that says, "A researcher collected information from 1,000 randomly selected public high school science teachers in the United States and concluded that the median annual salary was between $52,400 and $63,800 with a 99% confidence level. Which of the following could represent the median annual salary for the same sample with a 95% confidence level?" The key to answering this is to understand that a 95% confidence means that five out of 100 times the median value will not be in the specified interval. That means you are less confident that the median will be in that range. The range of salaries in the 95% confidence interval would be a subset of the range of salaries within the 99% confidence interval. The correct answer choice would show a narrower range of salaries, such as $55,000 to $60,000. This type of question can be answered without performing any calculations. You simply need to understand the meaning of confidence levels.

Standard deviation

The standard deviation of a data set is a measurement of how much the data points vary from the mean. More precisely, it is equal to the square root of the average of the squares of the differences between each point and the mean: $s_x = \sqrt{\frac{\sum(X - \bar{X})^2}{N-1}}$.

The standard deviation is useful for determining the spread, or dispersion, of the data, or how far they vary from the mean. The smaller the standard deviation, the closer the values tend to be to the mean; the larger the standard deviation, the more they tend to be scattered far from the mean.

Types of questions – center, shape, and spread of data

You may be given a data set and asked to calculate measures of center such as mean, median, and mode. You might be asked to determine spread, or range, for a given set of data. You may be asked to use given statistics to compare two separate sets of data. This comparison may involve mean, median, mode, range, and standard deviation, which are key topics in these types of questions. The mean is the numerical average of the data set. The median is the data point (or the average of two data points if there are an even number of data) when the data are ranked from least to greatest. The mode is the data point which occurs most often; there may be one mode, or there may be no mode or multiple modes. The range is the difference between the highest and lowest data points. The standard deviation is a measure of how much the data points differ from the mean. Basically, it describes how closely the data is clustered around the mean.

Types of questions – evaluate reports to make inferences

You should expect to be given tables, graphs, and/or text summaries and to be asked to make inferences, justify conclusions, and determine the appropriateness of the data collection methods. Data is often collected from a subset of a large population in order to draw conclusions about the population as a whole; the subset must be sufficiently large and randomly selected in order for the statistics to be reliable. Sometimes, data is collected over a period of time in order to determine possible trends, such as "x increases over time." Two variables may be compared and conclusions such as "As one variable increases, the other decreases," or "When one variable increases, the other variable increases" may be drawn. While you can make a statistical association, you cannot determine causal relationships. That means you cannot say that one variable increased or decreased as a result of the other variable increasing or decreasing. Another way to say this is that correlation does not imply causation. Correlation tells how strongly two variables are associated. However, just because two variables are strongly correlated does not mean that one causes the other.

Drawing conclusions from data trends

You will be asked to determine if there is a correlation between two variables, but you cannot conclude that a change in one variable causes a change in the other. Ask yourself questions like, "Do both variables increase or decrease?" or "Does one increase as the other decreases?" Then, find the answer choice that makes the best statement explaining that correlation. If there is no correlation, look for a statement that reflects that. Avoid answer choices that say, "The increase of ___ caused the increase of ___" or "The increase of ___ caused the decrease of ___." Again, correlation does not imply causation. You may simply have to choose between answer choices that say, "There is a correlation between ___," or "There is no correlation between ___."

Types of questions – relating equations to graphs

You need to be able to match a given graph to the type of equation it represents, whether it be linear, quadratic, or exponential. Questions about bacteria cultures and radioactive isotopes are modeled with exponential equations. Questions about initial fees plus rates associated with a variable are modeled with linear equations. The projectiles of arrows, rocks, balls, missiles or anything that is shot or thrown are modeled with quadratic equations. You should know the general shapes for linear equations (line), quadratic equations (parabola), and exponential equations (steep curve). Also, you should have a firm grasp of the slope-intercept from of a line. When you are working with a linear equation, it is important to avoid making quick, erroneous conclusions about the line. Often, the equation of the line will be written in a form to "hide" the true nature of the line. For example, you may be given an equation like $y - x = k(x + y)$ and asked to determine which is necessarily true of its graph: the graph is a line passing through the origin; the graph is a parabola; the graph is a line with a positive slope; or the graph is a line with a slope of k. At first glance, you might think this is a factored quadratic equation, or you might think it is a linear equation in point-slope form with a slope of k. However, if you rearrange the equation into the slope-intercept form $y = \frac{1+k}{1-k}x$, you can see that the graph of the equation is a line with a y-intercept of zero, which means that the line passes through the origin. Depending on the value of k, the slope of the line can be positive, negative, zero, or undefined.

Types of questions – relating two variables on a graph

You need to be able to match a given graph to the type of equation it represents, whether it be linear, quadratic, or exponential. Questions about bacteria cultures and radioactive isotopes are modeled with exponential equations. Questions about initial fees plus rates associated with a variable are modeled with linear equations. The projectiles of arrows, rocks, balls, missiles or anything that is shot or thrown are modeled with quadratic equations. You should know the general shapes for linear equations (line), quadratic equations (parabola), and exponential equations (steep curve). Also, you should have a firm grasp of the slope-intercept from of a line. When you are working with a linear equation, it is important to avoid making quick, erroneous conclusions about the line. Often, the equation of the line will be written in a form to "hide" the true nature of the line. For example, you may be given an equation like $y - x = k(x + y)$ and asked to determine which is necessarily true of its graph: the graph is a line passing through the origin; the graph is a parabola; the graph is a line with a positive slope; or the graph is a line with a slope of k. At first glance, you might think this is a factored quadratic equation, or you might think it is a linear equation in point-slope form with a slope of k. However, if you rearrange the equation into the slope-intercept form $y = \frac{1+k}{1-k}x$, you can see that the graph of the equation is a line with a y-intercept of zero, which means that the line passes through the origin. Depending on the value of k, the slope of the line can be positive, negative, zero, or undefined.

Linear growth vs. exponential growth

Linear growth has a constant rate of growth. The growth over each interval is exactly the same. Linear growth is modeled by a line which has the growth rate as its slope. Exponential growth has a rate of growth that increases over time. The growth over each interval is not constant. This rate of growth is modeled by a steep curve. Linear growth can be modeled by an equation in the form slope-intercept form $y = mx + b$, in which m is the slope and b is the y-intercept. Exponential growth is modeled by an equation in the form $y = a(b^{kx}) + c$ in which b is the base such that $b > 0$ and $b \neq 1$. Exponential functions are used to model growth and decay. The values of b and k determine if the function models growth or decay. If you are given a table of values, linear growth is shown as an arithmetic sequence. The value of y increases (by addition) by a constant value over equal intervals of x. Exponential growth is shown as a geometric sequence. The value of y is multiplied by a fixed value over a set interval. Comparing tables for the linear equation $y = 2x$ and the exponential function $y = 2^x$ shows that y-values for the exponential function quickly surpasses those of the linear function.

x	-3	-2	-1	0	1	2	3	4
$y = 2x$	-6	-4	-2	0	2	4	6	8

x	-3	-2	-1	0	1	2	3	4
$y = 2^x$	$\frac{1}{8}$	$\frac{1}{4}$	$\frac{1}{2}$	1	2	4	8	16

Passport to Advanced Math

In this section the questions will deal with more advanced equations and expressions. Students need to be able to create quadratic and exponential equations that model a context. They also need to be able to solve these equations. Students should also be able to create equivalent expressions that involve radicals and rational exponents. Like the Heart of Algebra section this section will test systems of equations. These systems however will involve one linear and one quadratic equation in two variables. Finally, students should be able to perform operations such as addition, subtraction, and multiplication on polynomials.

Solving Quadratic Equations

The *Quadratic Formula* is used to solve quadratic equations when other methods are more difficult. To use the quadratic formula to solve a quadratic equation, begin by rewriting the equation in standard form $ax^2 + bx + c = 0$, where a, b, and c are coefficients. Once you have identified the values of the coefficients, substitute those values into the quadratic formula $= \frac{-b \pm \sqrt{b^2 - 4ac}}{2a}$. Evaluate the equation and simplify the expression. Again, check each root by substituting into the original equation. In the quadratic formula, the portion of the formula under the radical ($b^2 - 4ac$) is called the *Discriminant*. If the discriminant is zero, there is only one root: zero. If the discriminant is positive, there are two different real roots. If the discriminant is negative, there are no real roots.

To solve a quadratic equation by *Factoring*, begin by rewriting the equation in standard form, if necessary. Factor the side with the variable then set each of the factors equal to zero and solve the resulting linear equations. Check your answers by substituting the roots you found into the original equation. If, when writing the equation in standard form, you have an equation in the form $x^2 + c = 0$ or $x^2 - c = 0$, set $x^2 = -c$ or $x^2 = c$ and take the square root of c. If $c = 0$, the only real root is zero. If c is positive, there are two real roots—the positive and negative square root values. If c is negative, there are no real roots because you cannot take the square root of a negative number.

> ➤ **Review Video: <u>Factoring Quadratic Equations</u>**
> *Visit **mometrix.com/academy** and enter **Code**: 336566*

To solve a quadratic equation by *Completing the Square*, rewrite the equation so that all terms containing the variable are on the left side of the equal sign, and all the constants are on the right side of the equal sign. Make sure the coefficient of the squared term is 1. If there is a coefficient with the squared term, divide each term on both sides of the equal side by that number. Next, work with the coefficient of the single-variable term. Square half of this coefficient, and add that value to both sides. Now you can factor the left side (the side containing the variable) as the square of a binomial. $x^2 + 2ax + a^2 = C \Rightarrow (x + a)^2 = C$, where x is the variable, and a and C are constants. Take the square root of both sides and solve for the variable. Substitute the value of the variable in the original problem to check your work.

Types of questions – quadratic function with rational coefficients

A quadratic function is a second degree equation that graphs as a parabola. The general form for a quadratic function is $f(x) = ax^2 + bx + c$, where $f(x) = y$. If $a > 0$, the parabola is concave up. If $a < 0$, the parabola is concave down. The axis of symmetry for the parabola is given by $x = \frac{-b}{2a}$. The turning point of the parabola (the minimum value for a concave down and maximum for a concave up parabola) is given by $\left(\frac{-b}{2a}, f\left(\frac{-b}{2a}\right)\right)$. Quadratic functions are often used to model projectile motion. A rocket or other projectile launched from the ground will follow a parabolic trajectory. You may be given a graph of a trajectory and asked to choose the function that best models that parabola. You must use the concavity, axis of symmetry, and turning point to work backwards to find the equation for the parabola.

Exponential function with rational coefficients

An exponential function has the general form of $f(x) = a(b^{kx}) + c$, in which b is the base and $b > 0$ and $b \neq 1$. Exponential functions are used to model growth and decay. The values of b and k determine if the function models exponential growth or exponential decay. When graphed, an exponential function has a horizontal asymptote at $y = c$. The y-intercept of an exponential function is located at $(0, a + c)$.

Type	Values of b	Values of k	Example
Exponential Growth	$b > 1$	$k > 0$	$f(x) = 2^x$
Exponential Growth	$b < 1$	$k < 0$	$f(x) = \left(\dfrac{1}{2}\right)^{-x}$
Exponential Decay	$b > 1$	$k < 0$	$f(x) = 2^{-x}$
Exponential Decay	$b < 1$	$k > 0$	$f(x) = \left(\dfrac{1}{2}\right)^{x}$

You may be given the graph of an exponential function and asked to choose the correct equation. If y increases rapidly as x increases, the function models exponential growth. If y decreases rapidly as x increases, the function models exponential decay. You can determine c from the horizontal asymptote. Then, you can determine a from the y-intercept.

Types of questions – Writing expressions
You must be able to translate verbal expressions into mathematical language. These may be simple or complex algebraic expressions (linear, quadratic, or exponential); you must be able to simplify these expressions using order of operations. You may be asked to determine an algebraic model involving costs or interest and then use that model to perform a calculation. You may be given a geometric situation involving area or perimeter in which you have to write and simplify an expression. These problems may be complex and require sketches in order to choose or produce a correct answer.

Produce expressions or equations given a context
Often, complex geometry problems involve writing a system of equations. For example, if the problem gives the area and perimeter of a rectangular garden and asks for its length and width, you can use the formulas $A = lw$ and $p = 2l + 2w$ to write a system of equations. Sometimes, geometry problems involve two shapes, one of which is inside another. For example, you may be given the inner dimensions of a picture frame and asked to find the outer dimensions; in this case, if you designate the length and width of frame's inner rectangle as l and w, respectively, then the length and width of the outer rectangle are respectively represented by $l + 2x$ and $w + 2x$, where x is the width of the picture frame.

Consistent, inconsistent, or dependent systems
If a system of equations set up to represent a real-world problem turns out to be consistent (having exactly one solution), that solution is the solution to the problem.

If the system turns out to be dependent (having infinitely many solutions), that means that the original information given was redundant, and was therefore not enough information to solve the problem. Practically speaking, this may mean that any of that infinite set of solutions will do, or it may mean that more information is needed.

If the system turns out to be inconsistent (having no solutions), that means the real-world situation described cannot be true. If the situation described was a hypothetical desired outcome, we now know that it is not possible to achieve that outcome; if the situation described was supposed to have really occurred, we can only conclude that it must have been described inaccurately.

Solve the rational equation: $\frac{2}{x} - 2 = x - 1$

To solve the rational equation, multiply each side of the equation by the LCD, which is x. This will transform the rational equation into a quadratic equation that can be solved by factoring:

$$\frac{2}{x} - 2 = x - 1$$
$$x\left(\frac{2}{x} - 2\right) = x(x - 1)$$
$$2 - 2x = x^2 - x$$
$$x^2 + x - 2 = 0$$
$$(x + 2)(x - 1) = 0$$
$$x = -2, x = 1$$

Both $x = -2$ and $x = 1$ check out in the original equation. The solution is $x = \{-2, 1\}$.

Solve the radical equation: $\sqrt{x - 1} + 3 = x$

To solve the radical equation, isolate the radical $\sqrt{x - 1}$ on one side of the equation. Then square both sides and solve the resulting quadratic equation:

$$\sqrt{x - 1} + 3 = x$$
$$\sqrt{x - 1} = x - 3$$
$$\left(\sqrt{x - 1}\right)^2 = (x - 3)^2$$
$$x - 1 = x^2 - 6x + 9$$
$$x^2 - 7x + 10 = 0$$
$$(x - 5)(x - 2) = 0$$
$$x = 2, x = 5$$

Only $x = 5$ checks out in the original equation; $\sqrt{2 - 1} + 3 \overset{?}{\Leftrightarrow} 2 \xrightarrow{yields} \sqrt{1} + 3 = 4 \neq 2$!

The solution, then, is just $x = \{5\}$.

Extraneous solution to rational and radical equation
An extraneous solution is the solution of an equation that arises during the process of solving an equation, which is not a solution of the original equation. When solving a rational equation, each side is often multiplied by x or an expression containing x. Since the value of x is unknown, this may mean multiplying by zero, which will make any equation the true statement 0 = 0. Similarly, when solving a radical expression, each side of the equation is often squared, or raised to some power. This can also change the sign of unknown expressions. For example, the equation 3 = –3 is false, but squaring each side gives 9 = 9, which is true.

Rewriting radical expressions
Radical expressions can be rewritten as equivalent expressions with rational exponents. In general $\sqrt[b]{n^a}$ is equivalent to $n^{\frac{a}{b}}$ and $\sqrt[b]{m^c n^a}$ is equivalent to $m^{\frac{c}{b}} n^{\frac{a}{b}}$. For example, $\sqrt{x}$ is equivalent to $x^{\frac{1}{2}}$ and $\sqrt[3]{x^2}$ is equivalent to $x^{\frac{2}{3}}$. The radical $\sqrt[5]{x - 1}$ is equivalent to $(x - 1)^{\frac{1}{5}}$. Another point to remember is

- 83 -

that, while $n^{\frac{a}{b}}$ can be rewritten as $\sqrt[b]{n^a}$, it can also be rewritten as $(\sqrt[b]{n})^a$. It is also important to understand the concept of negative exponents. A negative exponent basically flips a term from the numerator to the denominator or from the denominator to the numerator. You may see a question that says, "Rewrite the expression $2x^{-\frac{3}{4}}$ in radical form" or "Rewrite the expression $(\sqrt[3]{2xy})^2$ with rational exponents."

Equivalent expressions with radical and rational exponents
You may see questions asking you to simplify a radical expression or perform operations with radicals. You may see a question that says, "Simplify $\sqrt[3]{-27x^6y^{15}}$," or "Simplify the expression $\sqrt{2}(3\sqrt{5} + \sqrt{20})$." You many see a question that says, "Which of the following expressions is equivalent to $\sqrt{(20)(4) + (12)(16)}$?" You should expect to be asked to simplify rational expressions. You may need to factor the numerator and the denominator and then cancel like factors, as in this example: "Simplify $\frac{x^2-4}{x^2-x-2}$." You may also be asked to change a rational expression from one form into another. For example, you may see a question that says, "If the expression $\frac{6x^2-5}{x-1}$ is written in the equivalent form $\frac{1}{x-1} + B$, what is B in terms of x?" You could equate the two expressions and solve for B, or you could use long division to simplify the first expression and compare the result to the equivalent expression to determine B.

Situations modeled by statements that use function notation
A statement using function notation can model any situation in which one quantity depends uniquely on one or more other quantities. For example, the area of a rectangle can be expressed as a function of its width and height. The maximum vertical distance a projectile travels can be expressed as a function of its initial vertical speed. An object's position, the amount of money in a bank account, or any other quantity that changes over time can be expressed as a function of time.

A relationship cannot be modeled with a function, however, if it involves two quantities neither of which is uniquely determined by the other—that is, if each quantity may have multiple values corresponding to the same value of the other. For example, we could not write a function to represent the relationship between peoples' height in inches and their weight in pounds. There are people of the same height with different weights, and people of the same weight but different heights.

Using structure and mathematical operations
You might be given an algebraic expression and asked which, if any, of several other expressions is equivalent, or you might be given several pairs of algebraic expressions and be asked to determine which pairs are equivalent. For example, you may see a question that says, "Which of following pairs of algebraic expressions are equivalent" and an answer choice such as "$(2x + 3)(3x - 4)$ and $6x^2 + x + 12$." You would determine that is an incorrect choice since these are not equivalent expressions. You might see a question that says, "Which of the following rational expressions is equivalent to $\frac{x+3}{x-5}$?" You may be given choices in which the numerators and denominators can factored and some of the factors canceled.

Determining if two equations are equivalent
One way to check for equivalence is to evaluate each expression at a chosen value, say $x = 0$ or $x = 1$, and see if the results agree. If the expressions do not yield the same result, then they are not equivalent, but it is important to note that yielding the same result does not necessarily mean the

expressions are equivalent. This is only a method to eliminate incorrect answers; as the choices are narrowed, you may continue to try other values until all but the correct choice have been eliminated. Another way to determine whether two algebraic expressions are equivalent is to choose the most complex expression and simplify it algebraically to see if you can produce the second expression. This may involve factoring and canceling like factors or distributing and combining like terms.

Methods to solve quadratic equations

Quadratic equations may be solved by graphing, factoring, completing the square, or using the quadratic formula. Since these types of questions are in the no calculator section of the test, graphing is not your best choice due to time constraints. Set the equation equal to zero; if the quadratic expression is easily factored, factor it, and then solve the equation by setting each factor equal to zero. If the expression is not factorable and $a = 1$ when the equation is written in the general form $ax^2 + bx + c = 0$, you may choose to complete the square. Remember, if $a \neq 1$, you must divide the entire equation by a and work with resulting fractions. In these situations, it is easier to solve the equation using the quadratic formula $x = \frac{-b \pm \sqrt{b^2 - 4ac}}{2a}$. You may simply be asked to find the roots of a quadratic equation, or you may be asked to perform some operation with one of the roots once you have found the roots. Be careful to answer the question that is asked. For example, you may see a question that says, "If $3x^2 + 4x = 4$ and $x > 0$, what is the value of $x + \frac{1}{3}$?" First, you would write the equation in the form $3x^2 + 4x - 4 = 0$ and solve by factoring or by using the quadratic formula; then, you would use the positive root to find $x + \frac{1}{3}$.

Performing arithmetic operations on polynomials

You should expect to add, subtract, and multiply polynomial expressions and simplify the results. These expressions will have rational coefficients. You may see a question that says, "Add $(2x^2 + 4y + 5xy)$, $(3x^2 - 3xy - x)$, and $(xy + 1)$" or "Subtract $(6x^2 + 6y - xy + 1)$ from $(2x^2 + 3xy - 2)$." You may see a question that says, "If $p = 3x^3 - 2x^2 + 5x - 7$ and $q = 2x^3 - 7x^2 - x + 3$, what is $p - 2q$?" You may see a question that says, "Multiply $(x + 2y)(4x - 3y + 1)$" or "What is the product of $(2x + 1)$, $(2x - 1)$, and $(2x^2 + 1)$?" In each of these types of questions, you should perform the operation, collecting like terms to simplify the result.

Adding and subtracting polynomials

When adding or subtracting two polynomials, you should first identify the like terms. Like terms have the same base and the same exponent but not necessarily the same coefficient. When adding or subtracting polynomials, only like terms can be combined. For example, $2xy$ and $3xy$ are like terms, but $2x^2$ and $2x^3$ are not like terms. When finding a difference, make sure you have the polynomials written in the correct order. When removing parentheses from an expression which follows a minus sign, remember to change the sign of every term inside the parentheses. For example, when subtracting $(2x - y)$ from $(5x + 3y)$, the problem is written as $(5x + 3y) - (2x - y)$. Removing the parentheses yields $5x + 3y - 2x + y$, which is further simplified to $3x + 4y$. When multiplying two polynomials, you should multiply each term of one polynomial by each term of the other and then simplify the result when necessary. Remember, when multiplying monomial terms, you should multiply coefficients but add the exponents of like bases.

Single- variable equation with radicals

To solve an equation with radicals, first, isolate the radical on one side of the equation. If there is more than one radical, isolate the most complex radical. Then, raise the equation to the appropriate power. For example, if the radical is a square root, you should square both sides. If there is still a radical in the equation, isolate the radical and repeat. Once the radicals are removed, solve for the unknown variable. Be sure to check every solution to determine if any are extraneous ones. You may see a question such as "What is one possible solution to the equation $\sqrt{x-1} = x - 7$?" You would need to solve for x and substitute each solution back into the original equation to see if the resulting statement is true. If the resulting statement is false, the solution is extraneous. (Note: if=f you are given choices for this type of question, you may simply plug each possible solution into the equation until you find one that works.) To solve an equation with a variable in the denominator of a fraction, multiply the equation by the least common denominator of every fraction included in the equation. This will clear the equation of fractions. Then, solve normally. Remember to check all solutions by substituting them back to the original equations. If any substituted value does not result in a true statement, it is an extraneous solution.

Types of questions – solving systems of equations
You may see a question with a graph of a line intersecting a circle or parabola. The question may ask about the number of solutions (which would be the number of times the line and circle or parabola intersect) or about the actual solutions (which would be the points of those intersections).

You may see a question with the equation of a line and the equation of a circle or parabola. In this case, you need to solve the linear equation for one variable and then substitute for that variable in the quadratic equation. If the question simply asks for the number of solutions, you may choose to make a quick sketch of the line and circle or parabola to see if you can see if they intersect and, if so, how many times.

One method to solve a system of equations is by graphing. A line with slope m and y-intercept b has the general form $y = mx + b$. A circle with radius r and center (h, k) has the general form $(x - h)^2 + (y - k)^2 = r^2$. A parabola has the general form $y = ax^2 + bx + c$. A line may intersect a circle or parabola at no point, one point, or two points. For example, if you are asked for the solutions to the system $\begin{cases} y = -x + 5 \\ x^2 + y^2 = 25 \end{cases}$, you would graph a line with a slope of -1 and a y-intercept of 5 and a circle centered at the origin with a radius of 5 units. You should be able to see even from a simple sketch that line intersects the circle at $(0, 5)$ and $(5, 0)$. More complicated systems of equations can be solved by substitution. For example, if you are asked for the solutions to the system $\begin{cases} 2x + 3y = 7 \\ (x - 4)^2 + y^2 = 10 \end{cases}$, it would be difficult to find the coordinates of the intersection points with a quick sketch. The quickest option is to solve the linear equation for one of the variables and then substitute the result for the corresponding variable in the quadratic equation.

Adding or subtracting rational exponents
You should expect questions asking you to add or subtract rational expressions. You may see a question that says, "Add $\frac{2a+3}{3ab} + \frac{3a-2}{2bc}$," or "Subtract $\frac{m-2}{m-3} - \frac{m-1}{m-2}$." The questions may have more than two terms and may combine addition and subtraction, such as "Simplify $\frac{1}{x} + \frac{2}{y} - \frac{3}{z}$." In order to be able to add or subtract rational expressions, the expressions must have the same denominator. Find the least common denominator (LCD) of the terms in the expression. Then, multiply each term of the expression by the ratio $\frac{LCD}{LCD}$. Simplify where possible and present your answer as one term over the LCD. Since these are rational expressions, not equations, you cannot clear the fractions as you do in an equation.

- 86 -

Multiplying and dividing rational expressions

You should expect questions asking you to multiply or divide rational expressions. You may see a question that says, "Multiply $\frac{n^2+n-6}{4} \cdot \frac{8}{2n+6}$" or "Divide $\frac{m^2+6m+5}{m^2-2m-3} \div \frac{m^2+8m+15}{3m^2-9m}$." In order to multiply rational expressions, the numerators and the denominators of each expression must be factored. Always check for a common monomial factor first. Then, check for differences of squares or a perfect square trinomials. A difference of squares $a^2 - b^2$ factors to $(a + b)(a - b)$. A perfect square trinomial factors to a binomial squared: $a^2 + 2ab + b^2$ factors to $(a + b)^2$, and $a^2 - 2ab + b^2$ factors to $(a - b)^2$. Also, check for other factorable trinomials. After factoring the numerators and denominators, cancel like factors and then multiply. To divide a rational expression, change the problem to a multiplication problem by multiplying the dividend by the reciprocal of the divisor, just like you would do if you were asked to divide two fractions containing no variables.

Types of questions – Interpreting nonlinear expressions

You should to be given a nonlinear expression that represents a real-life context. These nonlinear expressions may be rational expressions with a variable in the denominator. They may be exponential expressions or quadratic expressions or any other type of expression that is not linear. You should also expect to interpret non-linear functions. For example, if the nonlinear function is a quadratic function that models a projectile's trajectory, you may be given the equation and asked, "What are the values of x for which y is minimum?" You may be given a nonlinear function that models a scientific concept. For example, Newton's Universal Law of Gravitation states that the gravitational force (F) in Newtons is inversely proportional to the square of the distance (r) in meters between the centers of those two objects; this is represented by the relationship $F \propto \frac{1}{r^2}$. You may be asked a question like, "If the distance between two objects is doubled, what happens to the strength of the force between them?"

Modeling a projectile's trajectory

Since quadratic equations graph as parabolas, they are often used to model trajectories. To find the values of x for which a quadratic equation is equal to zero, you should set the equation equal to zero and then solve by factoring or by using the quadratic equation. For a trajectory problem, usually one zero is at $x = 0$, representing the launch of the projectile, and the other zero represents the landing. Inverse square relationships model scientific concepts, such as the relationship between gravitational force and the distance between two objects, the electric force between two charges, and the magnetic force between two poles. In each of these laws, the force increases as the distance between the objects decreases, and the force decreases as the distance between the objects increase. More specifically, if the distance is doubled, the force is reduced to one fourth of the original value; if the distance is halved, the force quadruples. When working with exponential relationships, a common mistake is to handle the exponent incorrectly. If you are given an equation and values to plug into that equation, be sure to apply the exponent to every factor inside the parenthesis under the exponent. Remember, when raising a power to a power, you should multiply exponents.

Zeros and factors of polynomials

Zeros are roots or solutions of polynomials when the polynomials are set equal to zero. These zeros are the locations where the graph of the polynomial intersects the x-axis. If the polynomials are set equal to zero and then factored, each individual factor is set equal to zero and solved; this gives the root or zero associated with that factor. If a polynomial equation has a zero of -2, the polynomial has a factor of $(x + 2)$. The Factor Theorem can be used to determine whether a given value is a zero. The polynomial is divided (using synthetic division) by the value, and if there is no remainder, the given value is a zero of the polynomial; if remainder is not zero, the value is not a root. If you are given one or more factors or roots of a polynomial function, you can use these factors or roots to determine the remaining factors and roots of the polynomial by dividing the polynomial by the given factor.

Types of questions – zeros and factors of polynomials

You may be expected to factor a polynomial, or you may be given the factored form of a polynomial and asked to select the appropriate graph from a set of given graphs. You may see a question that says, "Which of the following graphs represents the polynomial $f(x) = (x-1)(x+2)(x+5)$?" or "Which of the following graphs represents the quadratic equation $y = x^2 + 4x - 5$?" You may be given a polynomial function with the ordered pairs of its zeros and be asked to solve for a missing coefficient or a missing coordinate. You may be given a function such as $f(x) = 2x^4 + 3x^2 - 5x + 7$ and be expected to use the Factor Theorem to find zeros or verify zeros. You may be given the zeros of a quadratic or cubic function and asked to write the function. You might see a question that says, "If the zeros of a cubic function are -2, 3, and 5 and the graph of that function passes through $(1, 8)$, what is the equation of the function?"

Types of questions – nonlinear relationships between two variables

You may be asked to select a graph for a given nonlinear equation. You may be asked to select an equation given a nonlinear graph. You may be given a system of equations with both algebraic and graphical representations. You may be given a verbal description of the curve of a nonlinear relationship and asked to determine the equation of the function. You may be asked to determine key features of the graph of a nonlinear function from its equation. For example, you may see a question in which you are given a graph containing an intersecting circle, parabola, and line as well as the equations associated with them which says. "A system of equations and their graphs are shown above. How many solutions does the system have?" You may be given the equations of two exponential functions and asked if the graphs (which are not given) show that they are increasing or decreasing. You may see a question that says, "The functions $y_1 = 2\left(\frac{1}{2}\right)^x$ and $y_2 = 2\left(\frac{3}{2}\right)^x$ are graphed in the xy plane. Which of the following statements correctly describes whether each function is increasing or decreasing?"

Finding a solution to a system of three equations

This test typically has one problem with a system of three equations. Usually the graphs as well as the equations are given. The key point is that the only solutions to this graph are the points at which all three graphs coincide or intersect. For example, the graph might include a circle, a parabola, and a line. There are no solutions to the given system if all three graphs do not intersect at one or more points. If the three graphs intersect at one point, then there is one solution to the given system, and that solution is the point of intersection. If the line intersects the circle at two points, and the line also intersects the parabola at the same exact two points, there are two solutions to the given system, and those solutions are the points of intersection. This system has at most two solutions.

Types of questions – using function notation

You may be asked to evaluate a given function. For example, you may see a question that says, "If $f(x) = x^3 - 4x^2 + 3x - 1$, find $f(2)$." You should expect to be given two functions such as $f(x)$ and $g(x)$ and be asked to find $f(g(x))$ or $g(f(x))$. For example, you may see a question that says, "Let $f(x) = x^2 - 1$ and $g(x) = x + 1$. Which of the following describes $f(g(x))$?" Or you may be asked to work a similar problem given $f(x)$ and $g(f(x))$ and be asked to find $g(x)$. For example, you may see a question that says, "Let $f(x) = x^2 - 3$. If $g(f(x)) = \sqrt{x^2 + 1}$, which of the following describes

$g(x)$?" You may be asked to evaluate composite functions, as in this example: "Two functions are defined as $f(t) = 4t^2 - t$ and $g(x) = -3x^2 - 2x - 1$. Find the value of $g(f(2))$."

<u>Types of questions – isolate or identify</u>
You will be given a literal equation and be asked to be solve for one of the unknowns. Literal equations are equations often referred to as formulas. For example, in geometry, the formula for the area of a trapezoid is $A = \frac{h(b_1 + b_2)}{2}$, and in physics, the mirror equation is $\frac{1}{f} = \frac{1}{d_o} + \frac{1}{d_i}$. You may see a question that says, "The area of a trapezoid with bases b_1 and b_2 and height h can be found by $A = \frac{h(b_1 + b_2)}{2}$. Which of the following is the correct expression to find the height of a trapezoid given the area and lengths of the bases?" You may see a question that says, "The focal length f of a mirror can be determined from the object distance d_o and image distance d_i by the equation $\frac{1}{f} = \frac{1}{d_o} + \frac{1}{d_i}$. Which of the following is the correct expression to find the image distance of an image formed by a lens with a given object distance and focal length?"

Solving $A = \frac{h(b_1 + b_2)}{2}$
Literal equations can be solved for one of the unknown variables using basic algebraic operations. To solve $A = \frac{h(b_1 + b_2)}{2}$ for b_2, first multiply both sides of the equation by 2: $2A = h(b_1 + b_2)$. Then, divide by h: $\frac{2A}{h} = b_1 + b_2$. Then, subtract b_1: $\frac{2A}{h} - b_1 = b_2$. To solve $\frac{1}{f} = \frac{1}{d_o} + \frac{1}{d_i}$ for d_i, first subtract $\frac{1}{d_o}$ from both sides of the equation: $\frac{1}{f} - \frac{1}{d_o} = \frac{1}{d_i}$. Then, find a common denominator to combine the terms on the left-hand side of the equation: $\frac{d_o - f}{f d_o} = \frac{1}{d_i}$. Then, solve by taking the reciprocal of both sides: $\frac{f d_o}{d_o - f} = d_i$.

Additional Topics in Math

Questions in this section will test geometric and trigonometric concepts and the Pythagorean Theorem. The student should be familiar with geometric concepts such as volume, radius, diameter, chord length, angle, arc, and sector area. The questions will give certain information about a figure and require the student to solve for some missing information. Any required volume formulas will be provided on the test. The trigonometry questions will require students to use trigonometric ratios and the Pythagorean Theorem to solve problems dealing with right triangles. The student should be able to use these ratios and the Pythagorean Theorem to solve for missing lengths and angle measures in right triangles.

<u>Volume formulas</u>
The formula for a prism or a cylinder is $V = Bh$, where B is the area of the base and h is the height of the solid. For a cylinder, the area of the circular base is determined by the formula $B = \pi r^2$. For a prism, the area of the base depends on the shape of the base; for example, a triangular base would have area $\frac{1}{2}bh$, while a rectangular base would have area bh.

For a pyramid or cone, the volume is $V = \frac{1}{3}Bh$, where B once again is the area of the base and h is the height. In other words, the volume of a pyramid or cone is one-third the volume of a prism or cylinder with the same base and the same height.

Pythagorean Theorem

The side of a triangle opposite the right angle is called the hypotenuse. The other two sides are called the legs. The Pythagorean Theorem states a relationship among the legs and hypotenuse of a right triangle: $a^2 + b^2 = c^2$, where a and b are the lengths of the legs of a right triangle, and c is the length of the hypotenuse. Note that this formula will only work with right triangles.

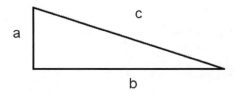

Types of questions – volume formulas

You should expect to be asked questions concerning volumes of figures such as rectangular prisms and cylinders. You may be asked to use information such as length of a side, area of a face, or volume of a solid to calculate missing information. Area formulas for circles, rectangles, and triangles and volume formulas for rectangular prisms and cylinders are provided with the test. It is important to understand that the volume calculations may be more complicated than simply applying basic formulas. For example, you may be asked to find the volume of a hexagonal nut and given that the volume of a prism is $V = Bh$, where B is the area of the base and h is the height of the prism. Since you are not given the area formula for a regular hexagon, however, you must find the area by adding the areas of the six equilateral triangles which comprise the hexagon. Once you calculate the area of the base, you can find the volume of a hexagonal prism by multiplying the area of the base and the height; afterward, you must subtract the volume of the cylindrical hole from the volume of the hexagonal prism in order to find the volume of the hexagonal nut.

Types of questions – applied problems with right triangles

You should expect questions requiring you to use the Pythagorean Theorem and trigonometric ratios to find missing side lengths and angles of right triangles. The Pythagorean Theorem as well as the 30°-60°-90° and 45°-45°-90° special right triangles are provided on the test. You should be able to recognize situations in which the Pythagorean Theorem, trigonometry, and special right triangles can be applied. For example, a square can be divided by a diagonal into two 45°-45°-90° triangles. An equilateral triangle can be divided by an altitude into two 30°-60°-90° right triangles. Hexagons can be divided into six equilateral triangles, each of which can be further divided into two 30°-60°-90° triangles. You need to be able to apply the special right triangles to given triangles. For example, if you are given a 45°-45°-90° triangle with a side length of 5 cm, you should be able to determine that the hypotenuse has a length of $5\sqrt{2}$ cm. If you are given a 30°-60°-90° triangle with a short leg of length 3 inches, you should be able to determine that the hypotenuse has a length of 6 inches.

Trigonometric ratio sine for an acute angle using ratios of sides in similar right triangles

Similar triangles have three pairs of congruent angles and three pairs of proportional sides. The proportion has the same value for all pairs of sides, so $\frac{a}{d} = \frac{c}{f}$ or (using cross multiplication and division to reorganize) $\frac{a}{c} = \frac{d}{f}$. The trigonometric ratio sine is opposite over hypotenuse. In $\triangle ABC$, $\sin A = \frac{a}{c}$ and in $\triangle DEF$, $\sin D = \frac{d}{f}$. So since $\frac{a}{c} = \frac{d}{f}$, $\sin A = \sin D$. This shows that the trigonometric ratio sine is a property of the angle because the ratio is the same in both triangles even though the triangles are different sizes.

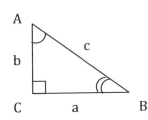
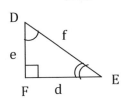

Trigonometric ratio cosine for an acute angle using ratios of sides in similar right triangles

Similar triangles have three pairs of congruent angles and three pairs of proportional sides. The proportion has the same value for all pairs of sides, so $\frac{b}{e} = \frac{c}{f}$ or (using cross multiplication and division to reorganize) $\frac{b}{c} = \frac{e}{f}$. The trigonometric ratio cosine is adjacent over hypotenuse. In $\triangle ABC$, $\cos A = \frac{b}{c}$ and in $\triangle DEF$, $\cos D = \frac{e}{f}$. So since $\frac{b}{c} = \frac{e}{f}$, $\cos A = \cos D$. This shows that the trigonometric ratio cosine is a property of the angle because the ratio is the same in both triangles even though the triangles are different sizes.

Trigonometric ratio tangent for an acute angle using ratios of sides in similar right triangles

Similar triangles have three pairs of congruent angles and three pairs of proportional sides. The proportion has the same value for all pairs of sides, so $\frac{a}{d} = \frac{b}{e}$ or (using cross multiplication and division to reorganize) $\frac{a}{b} = \frac{d}{e}$. The trigonometric ratio tangent is opposite over adjacent. In $\triangle ABC$, $\tan A = \frac{a}{b}$ and in $\triangle DEF$, $\tan D = \frac{d}{e}$. So since $\frac{a}{b} = \frac{d}{e}$, $\tan A = \tan D$. This shows that the trigonometric ratio tangent is a property of the angle because the ratio is the same in both triangles even though the triangles are different sizes.

Complex numbers

Complex numbers consist of a real component and an imaginary component. Complex numbers are expressed in the form $a + bi$ with real component a and imaginary component bi. The imaginary unit i is equal to $\sqrt{-1}$. That means $i^2 = -1$. The imaginary unit provides a way to find the square root of a negative number. For example, $\sqrt{-25}$ is $5i$. You should expect questions asking you to add, subtract, multiply, divide, and simplify complex numbers. You may see a question that says, "Add $3 + 2i$ and $5 - 7i$" or "Subtract $4 + i\sqrt{5}$ from $2 + i\sqrt{5}$." Or you may see a question that says, "Multiply $6 + 2i$ by $8 - 4i$" or "Divide $1 - 3i$ by $9 - 7i$."

Perform operations on complex numbers

Operations with complex numbers resemble operations with variables in algebra. Complex numbers are expressed in the form $a + bi$ with real component a and imaginary component bi. When adding or subtracting complex numbers, you can only combine like terms — real terms with real terms and imaginary terms with imaginary terms. For example, if you are asked to simplify $-2 + 4i - (-3 + 7i) - 5i$, you should first remove the parentheses to yield $-2 + 4i + 3 - 7i - 5i$. Combining likes terms yields $1 - 8i$. One interesting aspect with imaginary number is that if i has an exponent greater than 1, it can be simplified. For example, $i^2 = -1$, $i^3 = -i$, and $i^4 = 1$. When multiplying complex numbers, remember to simplify each i with an exponent greater than 1. For example, you might see a question that says, "Simplify $(2 - i)(3 + 2i)$." You need to distribute and multiply to get $6 + 4i - 3i - 2i^2$. This is further simplified to $6 + i - 2(-1)$, or $8 + i$.

Simplifying with i in the denominator

If an expression contains an i in the denominator, it must be simplified. Remember, roots cannot be left in the denominator of a fraction. Since i is equivalent to $\sqrt{-1}$, i cannot be left in the denominator of a fraction. You must rationalize the denominator of a fraction that contains a complex denominator by multiplying the numerator and denominator by the conjugate of the denominator. The conjugate of the complex number $a + bi$ is $a - bi$. You can simplify $\frac{2}{5i}$ by simply multiplying $\frac{2}{5i} \cdot \frac{i}{i}$, which yields $-\frac{2}{5}i$. And you can simplify $\frac{5+3i}{2-4i}$ by multiplying $\frac{5+3i}{2-4i} \cdot \frac{2+4i}{2+4i}$. This yields $\frac{10+20i+6i-12}{4-8i+8i+16}$ which simplifies to $\frac{-2+26i}{20}$ or $\frac{-1+13i}{10}$, which can also be written as $-\frac{1}{10} + \frac{13}{10}i$.

Converting between degrees and radians

To convert from degrees to radians, multiply by $\frac{\pi \text{ rad}}{180°}$. For example $60° \cdot \frac{\pi \text{ rad}}{180°}$ is $\frac{\pi}{3}$ radians. To convert from radians to degrees, multiply by $\frac{180°}{\pi \text{ rad}}$. For example, $\frac{\pi}{4}$ radians $\frac{180°}{\pi \text{ rad}}$ is $45°$. The equation to determine are length is $s = r\theta$, in which s is the arc length, r is the radius of the circle, and θ is the angular displacement or the angle subtended in radians. For example, if you are asked to find the length of the arc that subtends a $60°$ central angle in a circle with a radius of 10 cm, you would solve $s = (10 \text{ cm})(60°)\left(\frac{\pi \text{ rad}}{180°}\right)$ to obtain an arc length in centimeters. You also need to be able to evaluate trigonometric functions of angles in radian measure without your calculator. You may see a question that involves finding the $\sin x$ in which $\frac{\pi}{2} < x < \pi$. It is important to be able recognize given intervals which indicate angle-containing quadrants, which are bound by $0, \frac{\pi}{2}, \pi, \frac{3\pi}{2}$, and 2π. The statement "all students take calculus" or ASTC can help you to remember the signs of $\sin x$, $\cos x$, and $\tan x$ for an angle measuring $x°$ or x radians. In Quadrant I, the values of $\sin x$, $\cos x$, and $\tan x$ are all positive. In Quadrant II, only $\underline{\sin x}$ is positive. In Quadrant III, only $\underline{\tan x}$ is positive. In Quadrant IV, only $\underline{\cos x}$ is positive.

Area of a sector of a circle and arc length of a sector of a circle

The area of a sector of a circle is found by the formula, $A = \theta r^2$, where A is the area, θ is the measure of the central angle in radians, and r is the radius. To find the area when the central angle is in degrees, use the formula, $A = \theta \pi r^2$, where θ is the measure of the central angle in degrees and r is the radius. The arc length of a sector of a circle is found by the formula: arc length$=r\theta$, where r is the radius and θ is the measure of the central angle in radians. To find the arc length when the central angle is given in degrees, use the formula: arc length$=\theta 2\pi r$, where θ is the measure of the central angle in degrees and r is the radius.

Circles

The center is the single point inside the circle that is equidistant from every point on the circle. (Point O in the diagram below.)

> ➢ **Review Video: <u>Points of a Circle</u>**
> Visit **mometrix.com/academy** and enter **Code: 420746**

The radius is a line segment that joins the center of the circle and any one point on the circle. All radii of a circle are equal. (Segments OX, OY, and OZ in the diagram below.)

The diameter is a line segment that passes through the center of the circle and has both endpoints on the circle. The length of the diameter is exactly twice the length of the radius. (Segment XZ in the diagram below.)

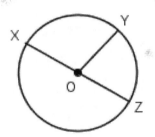

The area of a circle is found by the formula $A = \pi r^2$, where r is the length of the radius. If the diameter of the circle is given, remember to divide it in half to get the length of the radius before proceeding.

The circumference of a circle is found by the formula $C = 2\pi r$, where r is the radius. Again, remember to convert the diameter if you are given that measure rather than the radius.

Concentric circles are circles that have the same center, but not the same length of radii. A bulls-eye target is an example of concentric circles.

An arc is a portion of a circle. Specifically, an arc is the set of points between and including two points on a circle. An arc does not contain any points inside the circle. When a segment is drawn from the endpoints of an arc to the center of the circle, a sector is formed.

A central angle is an angle whose vertex is the center of a circle and whose legs intercept an arc of the circle. Angle *XOY* in the diagram above is a central angle. A minor arc is an arc that has a measure less than 180°. The measure of a central angle is equal to the measure of the minor arc it intercepts. A major arc is an arc having a measure of at least 180°. The measure of the major arc can be found by subtracting the measure of the central angle from 360°.

A semicircle is an arc whose endpoints are the endpoints of the diameter of a circle. A semicircle is exactly half of a circle.

An inscribed angle is an angle whose vertex lies on a circle and whose legs contain chords of that circle. The portion of the circle intercepted by the legs of the angle is called the intercepted arc. The measure of the intercepted arc is exactly twice the measure of the inscribed angle. In the following diagram, angle *ABC* is an inscribed angle. $\overset{\frown}{AC} = 2(m\angle ABC)$

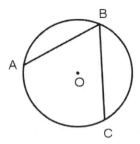

Any angle inscribed in a semicircle is a right angle. The intercepted arc is 180°, making the inscribed angle half that, or 90°. In the diagram below, angle *ABC* is inscribed in semicircle *ABC*, making angle *ABC* equal to 90°.

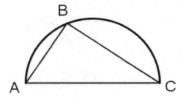

A chord is a line segment that has both endpoints on a circle. In the diagram below, $\overline{EB}$ is a chord. Secant: A line that passes through a circle and contains a chord of that circle. In the diagram below, $\overleftrightarrow{EB}$ is a secant and contains chord $\overline{EB}$.

A tangent is a line in the same plane as a circle that touches the circle in exactly one point. While a line segment can be tangent to a circle as part of a line that is tangent, it is improper to say a tangent can be simply a line segment that touches the circle in exactly one point. In the diagram below, $\overleftrightarrow{CD}$ is tangent to circle A. Notice that $\overline{FB}$ is not tangent to the circle. $\overline{FB}$ is a line segment that touches the circle in exactly one point, but if the segment were extended, it would touch the circle in a second point. The point at which a tangent touches a circle is called the point of tangency. In the diagram below, point B is the point of tangency.

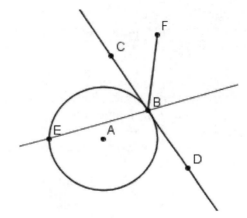

A secant is a line that intersects a circle in two points. Two secants may intersect inside the circle, on the circle, or outside the circle. When the two secants intersect on the circle, an inscribed angle is formed.

When two secants intersect inside a circle, the measure of each of two vertical angles is equal to half the sum of the two intercepted arcs. In the diagram below, $m\angle AEB = \frac{1}{2}(\widehat{AB} + \widehat{CD})$ and $m\angle BEC = \frac{1}{2}(\widehat{BC} + \widehat{AD})$.

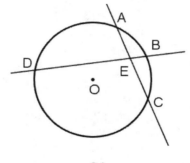

When two secants intersect outside a circle, the measure of the angle formed is equal to half the difference of the two arcs that lie between the two secants. In the diagram below, $m\angle E = \frac{1}{2}(\widehat{AB} - \widehat{CD})$.

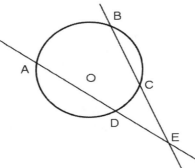

The arc length is the length of that portion of the circumference between two points on the circle. The formula for arc length is $s = \frac{\pi r \theta}{180°}$ where s is the arc length, r is the length of the radius, and θ is the angular measure of the arc in degrees, or $s = r\theta$, where θ is the angular measure of the arc in radians (2π radians = 360 degrees).

A sector is the portion of a circle formed by two radii and their intercepted arc. While the arc length is exclusively the points that are also on the circumference of the circle, the sector is the entire area bounded by the arc and the two radii.

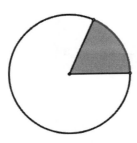

The area of a sector of a circle is found by the formula, $A = \frac{\theta r^2}{2}$, where A is the area, θ is the measure of the central angle in radians, and r is the radius. To find the area when the central angle is in degrees, use the formula, $A = \frac{\theta \pi r^2}{360}$, where θ is the measure of the central angle in degrees and r is the radius.

Formulas for circles

One formula for arc length is $s = r\theta$, in which s is the arc length, r is the radius of the circle, and θ is the angular displacement or the angle subtended in radians. Another formula for arc length

- 95 -

involving the circumference is given by C is $\frac{s}{C} = \frac{\theta}{360°}$ when central angle θ is measured in degrees or $\frac{s}{C} = \frac{\theta}{2\pi}$ when θ is measured in radians. These formulas can be rearranged to solve for s, C, or θ; of course, if you know a circle's circumference, you can also determine its diameter d or radius r using the formula $C = \pi d$ or $C = 2\pi r$. The area of a sector is given by $\frac{A_{Sector}}{A_{Circle}} = \frac{\theta}{360°}$ when θ is measured in degrees or $\frac{A_{Sector}}{A_{Circle}} = \frac{\theta}{2\pi}$ when θ is measured in radians. Chord lengths are often found by drawing the perpendicular bisector of the chord through the center of the circle and then drawing line segments from the center of the circle to each of the chord's endpoints. This forms two congruent right triangles. The length of the chord can be found using a trigonometric function or the Pythagorean Theorem. On some questions, you may be expected to combine your knowledge of circles with your knowledge of other geometric concepts, such as properties of parallel lines. The formulas for the area and circumference of a circle and the Pythagorean Theorem are provided with the test.

Similarity and Congruence Rules
Similar triangles are triangles whose corresponding angles are equal and whose corresponding sides are proportional. Represented by AA. Similar triangles whose corresponding sides are congruent are also congruent triangles.

> ➤ **Review Video: Similar Triangles**
> Visit *mometrix.com/academy* and enter **Code: 398538**

Three sides of one triangle are congruent to the three corresponding sides of the second triangle. Represented as SSS.

Two sides and the included angle (the angle formed by those two sides) of one triangle are congruent to the corresponding two sides and included angle of the second triangle. Represented by SAS.

Two angles and the included side (the side that joins the two angles) of one triangle are congruent to the corresponding two angles and included side of the second triangle. Represented by ASA.

Two angles and a non-included side of one triangle are congruent to the corresponding two angles and non-included side of the second triangle. Represented by AAS.

Note that AAA is not a form for congruent triangles. This would say that the three angles are congruent, but says nothing about the sides. This meets the requirements for similar triangles, but not congruent triangles.

Solving problems with similarity and congruence
Congruent figures have the same size and same shape. Similar figures have the same shape but not the same size; their corresponding angles are congruent and their sides are proportional. All circles are similar. All squares are similar; likewise, all regular n-gons are similar to other regular n-gons. These concepts may appear in different types of test questions. For example, if a line is drawn through that triangle such that it is parallel to one side, a triangle similar to the original triangle is formed. The corresponding angles are congruent, and proportional relationships can be used to determine missing side lengths from the given information. Also, if parallel lines are cut by two transversals which intersect between or outside of parallel lines, two similar triangles are formed.

If an altitude is drawn from the vertex of an isosceles triangle, two congruent triangles are formed. If an altitude is drawn from the vertex of the right angle to the hypotenuse of a right triangle, the two triangles that are formed are similar to each other and to the original right triangle.

Relationship between similarity, right triangles, and trigonometric ratios

An interesting relationship exists between similarity, right triangles, and the trigonometric ratios. If a line that is parallel to one of the legs of a right triangle is drawn through the right triangle, a right triangle is formed which is similar to the original triangle since the triangles share one acute angle and both contain a right angle. Therefore, the trigonometric ratios of similar right triangles are equal.

Complementary angles have a sum of 90°. The acute angles in a right triangle are complementary. In a right triangle, the sine of one of the acute angles equals the cosine of the other acute angle.

If an altitude is drawn from the vertex of the right angle to the hypotenuse of a right triangle as shown, the two triangles that are formed are similar to each other and to the original right triangle: $\triangle ACH \sim \triangle CBH$, $\triangle ACH \sim \triangle ABC$, and $\triangle CBH \sim \triangle ABC$.

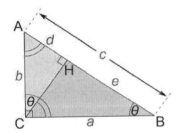

Equation of a circle

A circle with radius r centered at the origin on the coordinate plane can be represented by the equation $x^2 + y^2 = r^2$. A circle with radius r and center (h, k) is represented by the equation $(x-h)^2 + (y-k)^2 = r^2$. For example, a circle at the origin with a radius of 5 units is represented by the equation $x^2 + y^2 = 25$. If this circle is shifted three units right and two units down, the translated circle is represented by the equation $(x-3)^2 + (y+2)^2 = 25$.

<u>Integrating information from a circle into more complex questions</u>
A single question on this test may require knowledge of multiple geometric concepts. You may see a question about concentric circles or two intersecting circles; you might need to use information given about one circle to find information about the other. A question may provide the points of intersection of a line and a circle, and you may be asked to write and solve the system of equations, which would include both an equation for the line and an equation for the circle. You may be asked to convert between polar coordinates (r, θ) and rectangular (or Cartesian) coordinates (x, y). The relationship between polar and rectangular coordinates is shown below.

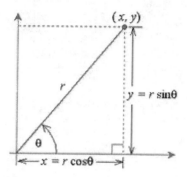

<u>Angles</u>
An angle is formed when two lines or line segments meet at a common point. It may be a common starting point for a pair of segments or rays, or it may be the intersection of lines. Angles are represented by the symbol $\angle$.

The vertex is the point at which two segments or rays meet to form an angle. If the angle is formed by intersecting rays, lines, and/or line segments, the vertex is the point at which four angles are formed. The pairs of angles opposite one another are called vertical angles, and their measures are equal.

An acute angle is an angle with a degree measure less than 90°.
A right angle is an angle with a degree measure of exactly 90°.
An obtuse angle is an angle with a degree measure greater than 90° but less than 180°.
A straight angle is an angle with a degree measure of exactly 180°. This is also a semicircle.
A reflex angle is an angle with a degree measure greater than 180° but less than 360°.
A full angle is an angle with a degree measure of exactly 360°.

> ➤ **Review Video: <u>Geometric Symbols: Angles</u>**
> *Visit **mometrix.com/academy** and enter **Code**: 452738*

Two angles whose sum is exactly 90° are said to be complementary. The two angles may or may not be adjacent. In a right triangle, the two acute angles are complementary.

Two angles whose sum is exactly 180° are said to be supplementary. The two angles may or may not be adjacent. Two intersecting lines always form two pairs of supplementary angles. Adjacent supplementary angles will always form a straight line.

Two angles that have the same vertex and share a side are said to be adjacent. Vertical angles are not adjacent because they share a vertex but no common side.

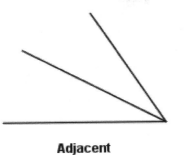

Adjacent

Share vertex and side

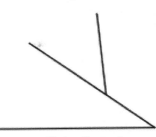

Not adjacent

Share part of side, but not vertex

When two parallel lines are cut by a transversal, the angles that are between the two parallel lines are interior angles. In the diagram below, angles 3, 4, 5, and 6 are interior angles.

When two parallel lines are cut by a transversal, the angles that are outside the parallel lines are exterior angles. In the diagram below, angles 1, 2, 7, and 8 are exterior angles.

When two parallel lines are cut by a transversal, the angles that are in the same position relative to the transversal and a parallel line are corresponding angles. The diagram below has four pairs of corresponding angles: angles 1 and 5; angles 2 and 6; angles 3 and 7; and angles 4 and 8. Corresponding angles formed by parallel lines are congruent.

When two parallel lines are cut by a transversal, the two interior angles that are on opposite sides of the transversal are called alternate interior angles. In the diagram below, there are two pairs of alternate interior angles: angles 3 and 6, and angles 4 and 5. Alternate interior angles formed by parallel lines are congruent.

When two parallel lines are cut by a transversal, the two exterior angles that are on opposite sides of the transversal are called alternate exterior angles.

In the diagram below, there are two pairs of alternate exterior angles: angles 1 and 8, and angles 2 and 7. Alternate exterior angles formed by parallel lines are congruent.

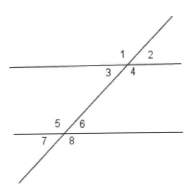

When two lines intersect, four angles are formed. The non-adjacent angles at this vertex are called vertical angles. Vertical angles are congruent. In the diagram, $\angle ABD \cong \angle CBE$ and $\angle ABC \cong \angle DBE$.

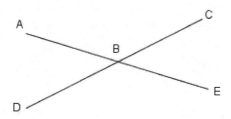

Triangles

An equilateral triangle is a triangle with three congruent sides. An equilateral triangle will also have three congruent angles, each 60°. All equilateral triangles are also acute triangles.

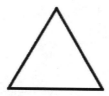

An isosceles triangle is a triangle with two congruent sides. An isosceles triangle will also have two congruent angles opposite the two congruent sides.

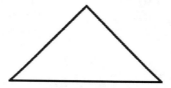

A scalene triangle is a triangle with no congruent sides. A scalene triangle will also have three angles of different measures. The angle with the largest measure is opposite the longest side, and the angle with the smallest measure is opposite the shortest side.

An acute triangle is a triangle whose three angles are all less than 90°. If two of the angles are equal, the acute triangle is also an isosceles triangle. If the three angles are all equal, the acute triangle is also an equilateral triangle.

A right triangle is a triangle with exactly one angle equal to 90°. All right triangles follow the Pythagorean Theorem. A right triangle can never be acute or obtuse.

An obtuse triangle is a triangle with exactly one angle greater than 90°. The other two angles may or may not be equal. If the two remaining angles are equal, the obtuse triangle is also an isosceles triangle.

Terminology

Altitude of a Triangle: A line segment drawn from one vertex perpendicular to the opposite side. In the diagram below, $\overline{BE}$, $\overline{AD}$, and $\overline{CF}$ are altitudes. The three altitudes in a triangle are always concurrent.

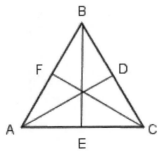

Height of a Triangle: The length of the altitude, although the two terms are often used interchangeably.

Orthocenter of a Triangle: The point of concurrency of the altitudes of a triangle. Note that in an obtuse triangle, the orthocenter will be outside the circle, and in a right triangle, the orthocenter is the vertex of the right angle.

Median of a Triangle: A line segment drawn from one vertex to the midpoint of the opposite side. This is not the same as the altitude, except the altitude to the base of an isosceles triangle and all three altitudes of an equilateral triangle.

Centroid of a Triangle: The point of concurrency of the medians of a triangle. This is the same point as the orthocenter only in an equilateral triangle. Unlike the orthocenter, the centroid is always inside the triangle. The centroid can also be considered the exact center of the triangle. Any shape triangle can be perfectly balanced on a tip placed at the centroid. The centroid is also the point that is two-thirds the distance from the vertex to the opposite side.

Other Useful Math Concepts

Numbers and Operations
Numbers are the basic building blocks of mathematics. Specific features of numbers are identified by the following terms:

- Integers – The set of whole positive and negative numbers, including zero. Integers do not include fractions ($\frac{1}{3}$), decimals (0.56), or mixed numbers ($7\frac{3}{4}$).
- Prime number – A whole number greater than 1 that has only two factors, itself and 1; that is, a number that can be divided evenly only by 1 and itself.
- Composite number – A whole number greater than 1 that has more than two different factors; in other words, any whole number that is not a prime number. For example: The composite number 8 has the factors of 1, 2, 4, and 8.
- Even number – Any integer that can be divided by 2 without leaving a remainder. For example: 2, 4, 6, 8, and so on.
- Odd number – Any integer that cannot be divided evenly by 2. For example: 3, 5, 7, 9, and so on.
- Decimal number – a number that uses a decimal point to show the part of the number that is less than one. Example: 1.234.

- Decimal point – a symbol used to separate the ones place from the tenths place in decimals or dollars from cents in currency.
- Decimal place – the position of a number to the right of the decimal point. In the decimal 0.123, the 1 is in the first place to the right of the decimal point, indicating tenths; the 2 is in the second place, indicating hundredths; and the 3 is in the third place, indicating thousandths.

The decimal, or base 10, system is a number system that uses ten different digits $(0, 1, 2, 3, 4, 5, 6, 7, 8, 9)$. An example of a number system that uses something other than ten digits is the binary, or base 2, number system, used by computers, which uses only the numbers 0 and 1. It is thought that the decimal system originated because people had only their 10 fingers for counting.

Rational, irrational, and real numbers can be described as follows:
- Rational numbers include all integers, decimals, and fractions. Any terminating or repeating decimal number is a rational number.
- Irrational numbers cannot be written as fractions or decimals because the number of decimal places is infinite and there is no recurring pattern of digits within the number. For example, pi (π) begins with 3.141592 and continues without terminating or repeating, so pi is an irrational number.
- Real numbers are the set of all rational and irrational numbers.

Operations

There are four basic mathematical operations:
- Addition increases the value of one quantity by the value of another quantity. Example: $2 + 4 = 6; 8 + 9 = 17$. The result is called the sum. With addition, the order does not matter. $4 + 2 = 2 + 4$.
- Subtraction is the opposite operation to addition; it decreases the value of one quantity by the value of another quantity. Example: $6 - 4 = 2; 17 - 8 = 9$. The result is called the difference. Note that with subtraction, the order does matter. $6 - 4 \neq 4 - 6$.
- Multiplication can be thought of as repeated addition. One number tells how many times to add the other number to itself. Example: 3×2 (three times two) $= 2 + 2 + 2 = 6$. With multiplication, the order does not matter. $2 \times 3 = 3 \times 2$ or $3 + 3 = 2 + 2 + 2$.
- Division is the opposite operation to multiplication; one number tells us how many parts to divide the other number into. Example: $20 \div 4 = 5$; if 20 is split into 4 equal parts, each part is 5. With division, the order of the numbers does matter. $20 \div 4 \neq 4 \div 20$.

An exponent is a superscript number placed next to another number at the top right. It indicates how many times the base number is to be multiplied by itself. Exponents provide a shorthand way to write what would be a longer mathematical expression. Example: $a^2 = a \times a$; $2^4 = 2 \times 2 \times 2 \times 2$. A number with an exponent of 2 is said to be "squared," while a number with an exponent of 3 is said to be "cubed." The value of a number raised to an exponent is called its power. So, 8^4 is read as "8 to the 4th power," or "8 raised to the power of 4." A negative exponent is the same as the reciprocal of a positive exponent. Example: $a^{-2} = \frac{1}{a^2}$.

> ➤ **Review Video: Exponents**
> Visit *mometrix.com/academy* and enter *Code*: **600998**

Parentheses are used to designate which operations should be done first when there are multiple operations. Example: 4 – (2 + 1) = 1; the parentheses tell us that we must add 2 and 1, and then subtract the sum from 4, rather than subtracting 2 from 4 and then adding 1 (this would give us an answer of 3).

Order of Operations is a set of rules that dictates the order in which we must perform each operation in an expression so that we will evaluate at accurately. If we have an expression that includes multiple different operations, Order of Operations tells us which operations to do first. The most common mnemonic for Order of Operations is PEMDAS, or "Please Excuse My Dear Aunt Sally." PEMDAS stands for Parentheses, Exponents, Multiplication, Division, Addition, Subtraction. It is important to understand that multiplication and division have equal precedence, as do addition and subtraction, so those pairs of operations are simply worked from left to right in order.

> **Review Video: <u>Order of Operations</u>**
> *Visit mometrix.com/academy and enter Code:* **259675**

Example: Evaluate the expression $5 + 20 \div 4 \times (2 + 3)^2 - 6$ using the correct order of operations.
P: Perform the operations inside the parentheses, $(2 + 3) = 5$.
E: Simplify the exponents, $(5)^2 = 25$.
The equation now looks like this: $5 + 20 \div 4 \times 25 - 6$.
MD: Perform multiplication and division from left to right, $20 \div 4 = 5$; then $5 \times 25 = 125$.
The equation now looks like this: $5 + 125 - 6$.
AS: Perform addition and subtraction from left to right, $5 + 125 = 130$; then $130 - 6 = 124$.

The laws of exponents are as follows:
1) Any number to the power of 1 is equal to itself: $a^1 = a$.
2) The number 1 raised to any power is equal to 1: $1^n = 1$.
3) Any number raised to the power of 0 is equal to 1: $a^0 = 1$.
4) Add exponents to multiply powers of the same base number:$a^n \times a^m = a^{n+m}$.
5) Subtract exponents to divide powers of the same number; that is $a^n \div a^m = a^{n-m}$.
6) Multiply exponents to raise a power to a power: $(a^n)^m = a^{n \times m}$.
7) If multiplied or divided numbers inside parentheses are collectively raised to a power, this is the same as each individual term being raised to that power: $(a \times b)^n = a^n \times b^n$; $(a \div b)^n = a^n \div b^n$.
Note: Exponents do not have to be integers. Fractional or decimal exponents follow all the rules above as well. Example: $5^{\frac{1}{4}} \times 5^{\frac{3}{4}} = 5^{\frac{1}{4}+\frac{3}{4}} = 5^1 = 5$.

A root, such as a square root, is another way of writing a fractional exponent. Instead of using a superscript, roots use the radical symbol ($\sqrt{}$) to indicate the operation. A radical will have a number underneath the bar, and may sometimes have a number in the upper left: $\sqrt[n]{a}$, read as "the nth root of a." The relationship between radical notation and exponent notation can be described by this equation: $\sqrt[n]{a} = a^{\frac{1}{n}}$. The two special cases of $n = 2$ and $n = 3$ are called square roots and cube roots. If there is no number to the upper left, it is understood to be a square root ($n = 2$). Nearly all of the roots you encounter will be square roots. A square root is the same as a number raised to the one-half power. When we say that a is the square root of b ($a = \sqrt{b}$), we mean that a multiplied by itself equals b: ($a \times a = b$).

> **Review Video: <u>Square Root and Perfect Square</u>**
> *Visit mometrix.com/academy and enter Code:* **648063**

A perfect square is a number that has an integer for its square root. There are 10 perfect squares from 1 to 100: 1, 4, 9, 16, 25, 36, 49, 64, 81, 100 (the squares of integers 1 through 10).

Scientific notation is a way of writing large numbers in a shorter form. The form $a \times 10^n$ is used in scientific notation, where a is greater than or equal to 1, but less than 10, and n is the number of places the decimal must move to get from the original number to a.

Example: The number 230,400,000 is cumbersome to write. To write the value in scientific notation, place a decimal point between the first and second numbers, and include all digits through the last non-zero digit ($a = 2.304$). To find the appropriate power of 10, count the number of places the decimal point had to move ($n = 8$). The number is positive if the decimal moved to the left, and negative if it moved to the right. We can then write 230,400,000 as 2.304×10^8. If we look instead at the number 0.00002304, we have the same value for a, but this time the decimal moved 5 places to the right ($n = -5$). Thus, 0.00002304 can be written as 2.304×10^{-5}. Using this notation makes it simple to compare very large or very small numbers. By comparing exponents, it is easy to see that 3.28×10^4 is smaller than 1.51×10^5, because 4 is less than 5.

> ➤ **Review Video: <u>Scientific Notation</u>**
> Visit *mometrix.com/academy* and enter *Code*: **976454**

Positive and Negative Numbers

A precursor to working with negative numbers is understanding what absolute values are. A number's *Absolute Value* is simply the distance away from zero a number is on the number line. The absolute value of a number is always positive and is written $|x|$.

When adding signed numbers, if the signs are the same simply add the absolute values of the addends and apply the original sign to the sum. For example, $(+4) + (+8) = +12$ and $(-4) + (-8) = -12$. When the original signs are different, take the absolute values of the addends and subtract the smaller value from the larger value, then apply the original sign of the larger value to the difference. For instance, $(+4) + (-8) = -4$ and $(-4) + (+8) = +4$.

For subtracting signed numbers, change the sign of the number after the minus symbol and then follow the same rules used for addition. For example, $(+4) - (+8) = (+4) + (-8) = -4$.

If the signs are the same the product is positive when multiplying signed numbers. For example, $(+4) \times (+8) = +32$ and $(-4) \times (-8) = +32$. If the signs are opposite, the product is negative. For example, $(+4) \times (-8) = -32$ and $(-4) \times (+8) = -32$. When more than two factors are multiplied together, the sign of the product is determined by how many negative factors are present. If there are an odd number of negative factors then the product is negative, whereas an even number of negative factors indicates a positive product. For instance, $(+4) \times (-8) \times (-2) = +64$ and $(-4) \times (-8) \times (-2) = -64$.

The rules for dividing signed numbers are similar to multiplying signed numbers. If the dividend and divisor have the same sign, the quotient is positive. If the dividend and divisor have opposite signs, the quotient is negative. For example, $(-4) \div (+8) = -0.5$.

Factors and Multiples

Factors are numbers that are multiplied together to obtain a product. For example, in the equation $2 \times 3 = 6$, the numbers 2 and 3 are factors. A prime number has only two factors (1 and itself), but other numbers can have many factors.

A common factor is a number that divides exactly into two or more other numbers. For example, the factors of 12 are 1, 2, 3, 4, 6, and 12, while the factors of 15 are 1, 3, 5, and 15. The common factors of 12 and 15 are 1 and 3.

A prime factor is also a prime number. Therefore, the prime factors of 12 are 2 and 3. For 15, the prime factors are 3 and 5.

The greatest common factor (GCF) is the largest number that is a factor of two or more numbers. For example, the factors of 15 are 1, 3, 5, and 15; the factors of 35 are 1, 5, 7, and 35. Therefore, the greatest common factor of 15 and 35 is 5.

> ➢ **Review Video: <u>Greatest Common Factor (GCF)</u>**
> *Visit **mometrix.com/academy** and enter **Code**: 838699*

The least common multiple (LCM) is the smallest number that is a multiple of two or more numbers. For example, the multiples of 3 include 3, 6, 9, 12, 15, etc.; the multiples of 5 include 5, 10, 15, 20, etc. Therefore, the least common multiple of 3 and 5 is 15.

Fractions, Percentages, and Related Concepts

A fraction is a number that is expressed as one integer written above another integer, with a dividing line between them $(\frac{x}{y})$. It represents the quotient of the two numbers "*x* divided by *y*." It can also be thought of as *x* out of *y* equal parts.

The top number of a fraction is called the numerator, and it represents the number of parts under consideration. The 1 in $\frac{1}{4}$ means that 1 part out of the whole is being considered in the calculation. The bottom number of a fraction is called the denominator, and it represents the total number of equal parts. The 4 in $\frac{1}{4}$ means that the whole consists of 4 equal parts. A fraction cannot have a denominator of zero; this is referred to as "undefined."

> ➢ **Review Video: <u>Fractions</u>**
> *Visit **mometrix.com/academy** and enter **Code**: 262335*

Fractions can be manipulated, without changing the value of the fraction, by multiplying or dividing (but not adding or subtracting) both the numerator and denominator by the same number. If you divide both numbers by a common factor, you are reducing or simplifying the fraction. Two fractions that have the same value, but are expressed differently are known as equivalent fractions. For example, $\frac{2}{10}, \frac{3}{15}, \frac{4}{20}$, and $\frac{5}{25}$ are all equivalent fractions. They can also all be reduced or simplified to $\frac{1}{5}$.

When two fractions are manipulated so that they have the same denominator, this is known as finding a common denominator. The number chosen to be that common denominator should be the least common multiple of the two original denominators. Example: $\frac{3}{4}$ and $\frac{5}{6}$; the least common multiple of 4 and 6 is 12. Manipulating to achieve the common denominator: $\frac{3}{4} = \frac{9}{12}$; $\frac{5}{6} = \frac{10}{12}$.

If two fractions have a common denominator, they can be added or subtracted simply by adding or subtracting the two numerators and retaining the same denominator. Example: $\frac{1}{2} + \frac{1}{4} = \frac{2}{4} + \frac{1}{4} = \frac{3}{4}$. If the two fractions do not already have the same denominator, one or both of them must be manipulated to achieve a common denominator before they can be added or subtracted.

Two fractions can be multiplied by multiplying the two numerators to find the new numerator and the two denominators to find the new denominator.
Example: $\frac{1}{3} \times \frac{2}{3} = \frac{1 \times 2}{3 \times 3} = \frac{2}{9}$.

> **Review Video: <u>Multiplying Fractions</u>**
> *Visit **mometrix.com/academy** and enter **Code**: 638849*

Two fractions can be divided flipping the numerator and denominator of the second fraction and then proceeding as though it were a multiplication. Example: $\frac{2}{3} \div \frac{3}{4} = \frac{2}{3} \times \frac{4}{3} = \frac{8}{9}$.

> **Review Video: <u>Dividing Fractions</u>**
> *Visit **mometrix.com/academy** and enter **Code**: 300874*

A fraction whose denominator is greater than its numerator is known as a proper fraction, while a fraction whose numerator is greater than its denominator is known as an improper fraction. Proper fractions have values less than one and improper fractions have values greater than one.

A mixed number is a number that contains both an integer and a fraction. Any improper fraction can be rewritten as a mixed number. Example: $\frac{8}{3} = \frac{6}{3} + \frac{2}{3} = 2 + \frac{2}{3} = 2\frac{2}{3}$. Similarly, any mixed number can be rewritten as an improper fraction. Example: $1\frac{3}{5} = 1 + \frac{3}{5} = \frac{5}{5} + \frac{3}{5} = \frac{8}{5}$.

> **Review Video: <u>Improper Fractions and Mixed Numbers</u>**
> *Visit **mometrix.com/academy** and enter **Code**: 731507*

Percentages can be thought of as fractions that are based on a whole of 100; that is, one whole is equal to 100%. The word percent means "per hundred." Fractions can be expressed as percents by finding equivalent fractions with a denomination of 100. Example: $\frac{7}{10} = \frac{70}{100} = 70\%$; $\frac{1}{4} = \frac{25}{100} = 25\%$. To express a percentage as a fraction, divide the percentage number by 100 and reduce the fraction to its simplest possible terms. Example: $60\% = \frac{60}{100} = \frac{3}{5}$; $96\% = \frac{96}{100} = \frac{24}{25}$.

Converting decimals to percentages and percentages to decimals is as simple as moving the decimal point. To convert from a decimal to a percent, move the decimal point two places to the right. To convert from a percent to a decimal, move it two places to the left. Example: 0.23 = 23%; 5.34 = 534%; 0.007 = 0.7%; 700% = 7.00; 86% = 0.86; 0.15% = 0.0015.It may be helpful to remember that the percentage number will always be larger than the equivalent decimal number.

A percentage problem can be presented three main ways: (1) Find what percentage of some number another number is. Example: What percentage of 40 is 8? (2) Find what number is some percentage of a given number. Example: What number is 20% of 40? (3) Find what number another number is a given percentage of. Example: What number is 8 20% of? The three components in all of these cases are the same: a whole (W), a part (P), and a percentage (%). These are related by the equation: $P = W \times \%$. This is the form of the equation you would use to solve problems of type (2). To solve types (1) and (3), you would use these two forms: $\% = \frac{P}{W}$ and $W = \frac{P}{\%}$.

> **Review Video: <u>Percentages</u>**
> Visit *mometrix.com/academy* and enter *Code*: **141911**

The thing that frequently makes percentage problems difficult is that they are most often also word problems, so a large part of solving them is figuring out which quantities are what. Example: In a school cafeteria, 7 students choose pizza, 9 choose hamburgers, and 4 choose tacos. Find the percentage that chooses tacos. To find the whole, you must first add all of the parts: 7 + 9 + 4 = 20. The percentage can then be found by dividing the part by the whole ($\% = \frac{P}{W}$): $\frac{4}{20} = \frac{20}{100} = 20\%$.

A ratio is a comparison of two quantities in a particular order. Example: If there are 14 computers in a lab, and the class has 20 students, there is a student to computer ratio of 20 to 14, commonly written as 20:14. Ratios are normally reduced to their smallest whole number representation, so 20:14 would be reduced to 10:7 by dividing both sides by 2.

A proportion is a relationship between two quantities that dictates how one changes when the other changes. A direct proportion describes a relationship in which a quantity increases by a set amount for every increase in the other quantity, or decreases by that same amount for every decrease in the other quantity. Example: Assuming a constant driving speed, the time required for a car trip increases as the distance of the trip increases. The distance to be traveled and the time required to travel are directly proportional.

Inverse proportion is a relationship in which an increase in one quantity is accompanied by a decrease in the other, or vice versa. Example: the time required for a car trip decreases as the speed increases, and increases as the speed decreases, so the time required is inversely proportional to the speed of the car.

Algebra, Functions, and Graphs

Polynomial Algebra

To multiply two binomials, follow the *FOIL* method. FOIL stands for:
- First: Multiply the first term of each binomial
- Outer: Multiply the outer terms of each binomial
- Inner: Multiply the inner terms of each binomial
- Last: Multiply the last term of each binomial

Using FOIL $(Ax + By)(Cx + Dy) = ACx^2 + ADxy + BCxy + BDy^2$.

> **Review Video: <u>Multiplying Terms Using the FOIL Method</u>**
> Visit *mometrix.com/academy* and enter *Code*: **854792**

Equations and Graphing

When algebraic functions and equations are shown graphically, they are usually shown on a *Cartesian Coordinate Plane*. The Cartesian coordinate plane consists of two number lines placed perpendicular to each other, and intersecting at the zero point, also known as the origin. The horizontal number line is known as the *x*-axis, with positive values to the right of the origin, and negative values to the left of the origin. The vertical number line is known as the *y*-axis, with positive values above the origin, and negative values below the origin. Any point on the plane can be identified by an ordered pair in the form (x,y), called coordinates. The *x*-value of the coordinate is called the abscissa, and the *y*-value of the coordinate is called the ordinate. The two number lines divide the plane into four quadrants: I, II, III, and IV.

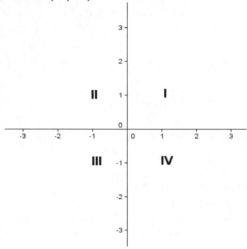

Before learning the different forms equations can be written in, it is important to understand some terminology. A ratio of the change in the vertical distance to the change in horizontal distance is called the *Slope*. On a graph with two points, (x_1, y_1) and (x_2, y_2), the slope is represented by the formula $= \frac{y_2 - y_1}{x_2 - x_1}$; $x_1 \neq x_2$. If the value of the slope is positive, the line slopes upward from left to right. If the value of the slope is negative, the line slopes downward from left to right. If the *y*-coordinates are the same for both points, the slope is 0 and the line is a *Horizontal Line*. If the *x*-coordinates are the same for both points, there is no slope and the line is a *Vertical Line*. Two or more lines that have equal slopes are *Parallel Lines*. *Perpendicular Lines* have slopes that are negative reciprocals of each other, such as $\frac{a}{b}$ and $\frac{-b}{a}$.

Equations are made up of monomials and polynomials. A *Monomial* is a single variable or product of constants and variables, such as x, $2x$, or $\frac{2}{x}$. There will never be addition or subtraction symbols in a monomial. Like monomials have like variables, but they may have different coefficients. *Polynomials* are algebraic expressions which use addition and subtraction to combine two or more monomials. Two terms make a binomial; three terms make a trinomial; etc.. The *Degree of a Monomial* is the sum of the exponents of the variables. The *Degree of a Polynomial* is the highest degree of any individual term.

As mentioned previously, equations can be written many ways. Below is a list of the many forms equations can take.
- *Standard Form*: $Ax + By = C$; the slope is $\frac{-A}{B}$ and the *y*-intercept is $\frac{C}{B}$

- *Slope Intercept Form*: $y = mx + b$, where m is the slope and b is the y-intercept
- *Point-Slope Form*: $y - y_1 = m(x - x_1)$, where m is the slope and (x_1, y_1) is a point on the line
- *Two-Point Form*: $\frac{y - y_1}{x - x_1} = \frac{y_2 - y_1}{x_2 - x_1}$, where (x_1, y_1) and (x_2, y_2) are two points on the given line
- *Intercept Form*: $\frac{x}{x_1} + \frac{y}{y_1} = 1$, where $(x_1, 0)$ is the point at which a line intersects the x-axis, and $(0, y_1)$ is the point at which the same line intersects the y-axis

> ➢ **Review Video: <u>Slope Intercept and Point-Slope Forms</u>**
> Visit *mometrix.com/academy* and enter *Code*: 113216

Equations can also be written as $ax + b = 0$, where $a \neq 0$. These are referred to as *One Variable Linear Equations*. A solution to such an equation is called a *Root*. In the case where we have the equation $5x + 10 = 0$, if we solve for x we get a solution of $x = -2$. In other words, the root of the equation is -2. This is found by first subtracting 10 from both sides, which gives $5x = -10$. Next, simply divide both sides by the coefficient of the variable, in this case 5, to get $x = -2$. This can be checked by plugging -2 back into the original equation $(5)(-2) + 10 = -10 + 10 = 0$.

The *Solution Set* is the set of all solutions of an equation. In our example, the solution set would simply be -2. If there were more solutions (there usually are in multivariable equations) then they would also be included in the solution set. When an equation has no true solutions, this is referred to as an *Empty Set*. Equations with identical solution sets are *Equivalent Equations*. An *Identity* is a term whose value or determinant is equal to 1.

Calculations Using Points

Sometimes you need to perform calculations using only points on a graph as input data. Using points, you can determine what the midpoint and distance are. If you know the equation for a line you can calculate the distance between the line and the point.

To find the *Midpoint* of two points (x_1, y_1) and (x_2, y_2), average the x-coordinates to get the x-coordinate of the midpoint, and average the y-coordinates to get the y-coordinate of the midpoint. The formula is Midpoint $= \left(\frac{x_1 + x_2}{2}, \frac{y_1 + y_2}{2} \right)$.

The *Distance* between two points is the same as the length of the hypotenuse of a right triangle with the two given points as endpoints, and the two sides of the right triangle parallel to the x-axis and y-axis, respectively. The length of the segment parallel to the x-axis is the difference between the x-coordinates of the two points. The length of the segment parallel to the y-axis is the difference between the y-coordinates of the two points. Use the Pythagorean Theorem $a^2 + b^2 = c^2$ or $c = \sqrt{a^2 + b^2}$ to find the distance. The formula is Distance $= \sqrt{(x_2 - x_1)^2 + (y_2 - y_1)^2}$.

When a line is in the format $Ax + By + C = 0$, where A, B, and C are coefficients, you can use a point (x_1, y_1) not on the line and apply the formula $d = \frac{|Ax_1 + By_1 + C|}{\sqrt{A^2 + B^2}}$ to find the distance between the line and the point (x_1, y_1).

Geometry

Lines and Planes

A point is a fixed location in space; has no size or dimensions; commonly represented by a dot.

A line is a set of points that extends infinitely in two opposite directions. It has length, but no width or depth. A line can be defined by any two distinct points that it contains. A line segment is a portion of a line that has definite endpoints. A ray is a portion of a line that extends from a single point on that line in one direction along the line. It has a definite beginning, but no ending.

A plane is a two-dimensional flat surface defined by three non-collinear points. A plane extends an infinite distance in all directions in those two dimensions. It contains an infinite number of points, parallel lines and segments, intersecting lines and segments, as well as parallel or intersecting rays. A plane will never contain a three-dimensional figure or skew lines. Two given planes will either be parallel or they will intersect to form a line. A plane may intersect a circular conic surface, such as a cone, to form conic sections, such as the parabola, hyperbola, circle or ellipse.

Perpendicular lines are lines that intersect at right angles. They are represented by the symbol ⊥. The shortest distance from a line to a point not on the line is a perpendicular segment from the point to the line.

Parallel lines are lines in the same plane that have no points in common and never meet. It is possible for lines to be in different planes, have no points in common, and never meet, but they are not parallel because they are in different planes.

A bisector is a line or line segment that divides another line segment into two equal lengths. A perpendicular bisector of a line segment is composed of points that are equidistant from the endpoints of the segment it is dividing.

Intersecting lines are lines that have exactly one point in common. Concurrent lines are multiple lines that intersect at a single point.

A transversal is a line that intersects at least two other lines, which may or may not be parallel to one another. A transversal that intersects parallel lines is a common occurrence in geometry.

General Rules

The Triangle Inequality Theorem states that the sum of the measures of any two sides of a triangle is always greater than the measure of the third side. If the sum of the measures of two sides were equal to the third side, a triangle would be impossible because the two sides would lie flat across the third side and there would be no vertex. If the sum of the measures of two of the sides was less than the third side, a closed figure would be impossible because the two shortest sides would never meet.

The sum of the measures of the interior angles of a triangle is always 180°. Therefore, a triangle can never have more than one angle greater than or equal to 90°.

In any triangle, the angles opposite congruent sides are congruent, and the sides opposite congruent angles are congruent. The largest angle is always opposite the longest side, and the smallest angle is always opposite the shortest side.

The line segment that joins the midpoints of any two sides of a triangle is always parallel to the third side and exactly half the length of the third side.

Area and Perimeter Formulas

The perimeter of any triangle is found by summing the three side lengths; $P = a + b + c$. For an equilateral triangle, this is the same as $P = 3s$, where s is any side length, since all three sides are the same length.

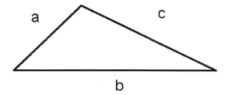

The area of any triangle can be found by taking half the product of one side length (base or b) and the perpendicular distance from that side to the opposite vertex (height or h). In equation form, $A = \frac{1}{2}bh$. For many triangles, it may be difficult to calculate h, so using one of the other formulas given here may be easier.

Another formula that works for any triangle is $A = \sqrt{s(s-a)(s-b)(s-c)}$, where A is the area, s is the semiperimeter $s = \frac{a+b+c}{2}$, and a, b, and c are the lengths of the three sides.

The area of an equilateral triangle can found by the formula $A = \frac{\sqrt{3}}{4}s^2$, where A is the area and s is the length of a side. You could use the $30° - 60° - 90°$ ratios to find the height of the triangle and then use the standard triangle area formula, but this is faster.

The area of an isosceles triangle can found by the formula, $A = \frac{1}{2}b\sqrt{a^2 - \frac{b^2}{4}}$, where A is the area, b is the base (the unique side), and a is the length of one of the two congruent sides. If you do not remember this formula, you can use the Pythagorean Theorem to find the height so you can use the standard formula for the area of a triangle.

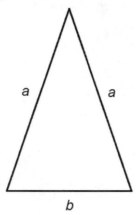

Congruent figures are geometric figures that have the same size and shape. All corresponding angles are equal, and all corresponding sides are equal. It is indicated by the symbol ≅.

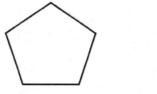 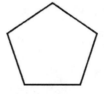

Congruent polygons

Similar figures are geometric figures that have the same shape, but do not necessarily have the same size. All corresponding angles are equal, and all corresponding sides are proportional, but they do not have to be equal. It is indicated by the symbol ~.

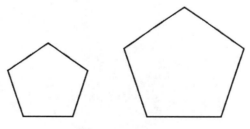

Similar polygons

Note that all congruent figures are also similar, but not all similar figures are congruent.

Line of Symmetry: The line that divides a figure or object into two symmetric parts. Each symmetric half is congruent to the other. An object may have no lines of symmetry, one line of symmetry, or more than one line of symmetry.

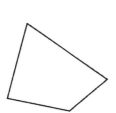

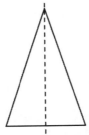

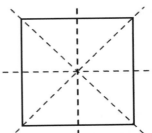

No lines of symmetry   One line of symmetry   Multiple lines of symmetry

Quadrilateral: A closed two-dimensional geometric figure composed of exactly four straight sides. The sum of the interior angles of any quadrilateral is 360°.

Parallelogram: A quadrilateral that has exactly two pairs of opposite parallel sides. The sides that are parallel are also congruent. The opposite interior angles are always congruent, and the consecutive interior angles are supplementary. The diagonals of a parallelogram bisect each other. Each diagonal divides the parallelogram into two congruent triangles.

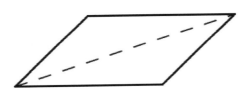

Trapezoid: Traditionally, a quadrilateral that has exactly one pair of parallel sides. Some math texts define trapezoid as a quadrilateral that has at least one pair of parallel sides. Because there are no rules governing the second pair of sides, there are no rules that apply to the properties of the diagonals of a trapezoid.

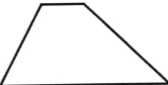

Rectangles, rhombuses, and squares are all special forms of parallelograms.

Rectangle: A parallelogram with four right angles. All rectangles are parallelograms, but not all parallelograms are rectangles. The diagonals of a rectangle are congruent.

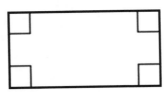

Rhombus: A parallelogram with four congruent sides. All rhombuses are parallelograms, but not all parallelograms are rhombuses. The diagonals of a rhombus are perpendicular to each other.

Square: A parallelogram with four right angles and four congruent sides. All squares are also parallelograms, rhombuses, and rectangles. The diagonals of a square are congruent and perpendicular to each other.

A quadrilateral whose diagonals bisect each other is a parallelogram. A quadrilateral whose opposite sides are parallel (2 pairs of parallel sides) is a parallelogram.

A quadrilateral whose diagonals are perpendicular bisectors of each other is a rhombus. A quadrilateral whose opposite sides (both pairs) are parallel and congruent is a rhombus.

A parallelogram that has a right angle is a rectangle. (Consecutive angles of a parallelogram are supplementary. Therefore if there is one right angle in a parallelogram, there are four right angles in that parallelogram.)

A rhombus with one right angle is a square. Because the rhombus is a special form of a parallelogram, the rules about the angles of a parallelogram also apply to the rhombus.

Area and Perimeter Formulas

The area of a square is found by using the formula $A = s^2$, where and s is the length of one side.

The perimeter of a square is found by using the formula $P = 4s$, where s is the length of one side. Because all four sides are equal in a square, it is faster to multiply the length of one side by 4 than to add the same number four times. You could use the formulas for rectangles and get the same answer.

The area of a rectangle is found by the formula $A = lw$, where A is the area of the rectangle, l is the length (usually considered to be the longer side) and w is the width (usually considered to be the shorter side). The numbers for l and w are interchangeable.

The perimeter of a rectangle is found by the formula $P = 2l + 2w$ or $P = 2(l + w)$, where l is the length, and w is the width. It may be easier to add the length and width first and then double the result, as in the second formula.

The area of a parallelogram is found by the formula $A = bh$, where b is the length of the base, and h is the height. Note that the base and height correspond to the length and width in a rectangle, so this formula would apply to rectangles as well. Do not confuse the height of a parallelogram with the length of the second side. The two are only the same measure in the case of a rectangle.

> ➤ **Review Video: <u>Finding Areas in Geometry</u>**
> *Visit **mometrix.com/academy** and enter **Code**: **663492***

The perimeter of a parallelogram is found by the formula $P = 2a + 2b$ or $P = 2(a + b)$, where a and b are the lengths of the two sides.

The area of a trapezoid is found by the formula $A = \frac{1}{2}h(b_1 + b_2)$, where h is the height (segment joining and perpendicular to the parallel bases), and b_1 and b_2 are the two parallel sides (bases). Do not use one of the other two sides as the height unless that side is also perpendicular to the parallel bases.

The perimeter of a trapezoid is found by the formula $P = a + b_1 + c + b_2$, where a, b_1, c, and b_2 are the four sides of the trapezoid.

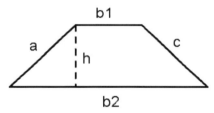

Data Analysis, Statistics, and Probability

Statistics

Statistics is the branch of mathematics that deals with collecting, recording, interpreting, illustrating, and analyzing large amounts of data. The following terms are often used in the discussion of data and statistics:
- Data – the collective name for pieces of information (singular is datum).
- Quantitative data – measurements (such as length, mass, and speed) that provide information about quantities in numbers
- Qualitative data – information (such as colors, scents, tastes, and shapes) that cannot be measured using numbers
- Discrete data – information that can be expressed only by a specific value, such as whole or half numbers; For example, since people can be counted only in whole numbers, a population count would be discrete data.
- Continuous data – information (such as time and temperature) that can be expressed by any value within a given range

- Primary data – information that has been collected directly from a survey, investigation, or experiment, such as a questionnaire or the recording of daily temperatures; Primary data that has not yet been organized or analyzed is called raw data.
- Secondary data – information that has been collected, sorted, and processed by the researcher
- Ordinal data – information that can be placed in numerical order, such as age or weight
- Nominal data – information that cannot be placed in numerical order, such as names or places

Displaying data

A bar graph is a graph that uses bars to compare data, as if each bar were a ruler being used to measure the data. The graph includes a scale that identifies the units being measured.

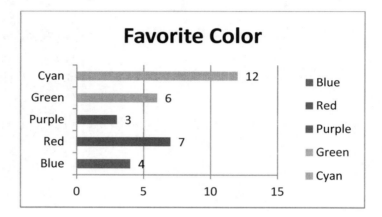

A line graph is a graph that connects points to show how data increases or decreases over time. The time line is the horizontal axis. The connecting lines between data points on the graph are a way to more clearly show how the data changes.

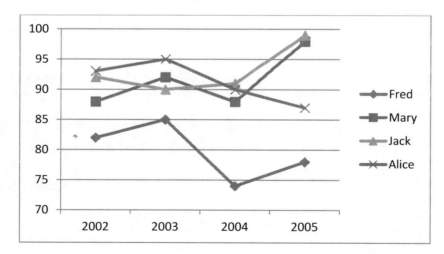

A pictograph is a graph that uses pictures or symbols to show data. The pictograph will have a key to identify what each symbol represents. Generally, each symbol stands for one or more objects.

A pie chart or circle graph is a diagram used to compare parts of a whole. The full pie represents the whole, and it is divided into sectors that each represent something that is a part of the whole. Each sector or slice of the pie is either labeled to indicate what it represents, or explained on a key associated with the chart. The size of each slice is determined by the percentage of the whole that the associated quantity represents. Numerically, the angle measurement of each sector can be computed by solving the proportion: x/360 = part/whole.

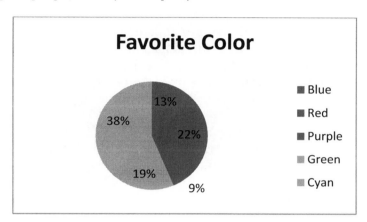

A histogram is a special type of bar graph where the data are grouped in intervals (for example 20-29, 30-39, 40-49, etc.). The frequency, or number of times a value occurs in each interval, is indicated by the height of the bar. The intervals do not have to be the same amount but usually are (all data in ranges of 10 or all in ranges of 5, for example). The smaller the intervals, the more detailed the information.

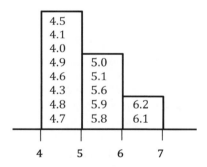

A stem-and-leaf plot is a way to organize data visually so that the information is easy to understand. A stem-and-leaf plot is simple to construct because a simple line separates the stem (the part of the plot listing the tens digit, if displaying two-digit data) from the leaf (the part that shows the ones digit). Thus, the number 45 would appear as 4 | 5. The stem-and-leaf plot for test scores of a group of 11 students might look like the following:

9 | 5
8 | 1, 3, 8
7 | 0, 2, 4, 6, 7
6 | 2, 8

A stem-and-leaf plot is similar to a histogram or other frequency plot, but with a stem-and-leaf plot, all the original data is preserved. In this example, it can be seen at a glance that nearly half the students scored in the 70's, yet all the data has been maintained. These plots can be used for larger numbers as well, but they tend to work better for small sets of data as they can become unwieldy with larger sets.

Student-Produced Response

The PSAT test includes 8 questions that are not multiple choice. Instead, they require you to solve the problem, then fill the exact number into a grid very similar to the one you used to enter your name and address on the form. The grid has a row of four boxes on top, with a column of numbers 0–9, a slash, and a decimal beneath each box.

To fill in the grid, write your answer in the boxes on top, then fill in the corresponding circle underneath. Use the slash to indicate fractions. It's a machine-scored test, so you don't get any credit for the number you write on top — that's strictly to help you fill in the circles correctly. If your answer doesn't fill up all four columns, that's okay. And it doesn't matter whether you left-justify or right-justify your answers. What *does* matter is that the circles be filled in correctly.

If you can't write it using the characters provided, it's not right.
No student-produced response will be a negative number or a percent. If you get a negative number, you've made a mistake. Percentages should be expressed as a ratio or decimal; for example, 50% can be written as .50.

Start on the left.
There are a few reasons to start with the first box every time. For one thing, it's faster. It will also help you be as precise as possible. If your answer is <1, though, don't use a leading 0 before the decimal. The PSAT omits the 0 from column one to help you be as precise as possible. For decimals, use as many columns as you can. Don't round or truncate answers. If you calculate an answer to be .125, enter the full number, not .13.

Repeat a repeating decimal.
Repeating decimals such as .666666 are only counted correct if you fill all the available columns. Either .666 or .667 will get credit. However, .66 will be counted as wrong.

Don't use mixed numbers.
If you try to write 2 ½, the computer will think you've written 21/2 and count it wrong. Instead, use the improper fraction form of such numbers; for example, 2 ½ = 5/2.

Use your calculator.
You brought a calculator; use it. Work the problem twice to make sure you entered all the numbers correctly.

Check your work.
More than any other questions in the math section, student-produced responses need to be double-checked. Try working the problem backward, plugging answers back into the original equation.

It's okay to get multiple answers.
Some questions may have more than one answer. In that case, any correct answer will do.

In general:
Approach the problem systematically. Take time to understand what is being asked for. In many cases there is a drawing or graph that you can write on. Draw lines, jot notes, do whatever is necessary to create a visual picture and to allow you to understand what is being asked.

What Your PSAT Score Means for National Merit Qualification

In 2012, more than 1,550,000 juniors took the PSAT. In the following chart, the column on the left is the score range, and the three columns to the right show what percentage of juniors taking the test scored within that range.

Score range	Reading	Math	Writing
76 - 80	1	1	1
71 - 75	2	2	1
66 - 70	4	4	4
61 - 65	6	9	7
56 - 60	10	12	9
51 - 55	14	15	13
46 - 50	17	16	13
41 - 45	19	17	19
36 - 40	14	12	17
31 - 35	9	7	9
26 - 30	3	3	4
20 - 25	1	2	3

As you're probably aware, the PSAT is no longer scored as three separate sections. Instead, student performances on the Reading and Writing sections are combined to give a single score for both areas: a Reading and Writing score. Also, the range of possible scores has changed from 20-80 on each section to 160-760 on each section. Here is what the previous chart would look like if it were displayed using the new scoring convention.

Score range	Reading and Writing	Math
711 – 760	1	1
661 – 710	2	2
611 – 660	4	4
561 – 610	6	9
511 – 560	10	12
461 – 510	13	15
411 – 460	15	16
361 – 410	19	17
311 – 360	16	12
261 – 310	9	7
211 – 260	3	3
160 – 210	2	2

Most of these changes were made to make it clearer that the PSAT score is supposed to predict or at least correlate with the SAT score. The maximum possible score on the PSAT is now 1520, which is less than the maximum possible score of 1600 on the new SAT, to account for the fact that the SAT is a more difficult test.

Based on this information, your scores should be close to 700 or higher in both categories to guarantee qualification. However, since semi-finalist status is awarded to students in approximately the top 1.5% of composite scores (the sum of your two individual scores), you can have a lower score in one subject as long as your scores in the other is high enough to bring up your composite total. The following chart shows a breakdown of the percentage of juniors receiving given ranges of composite scores.

Composite Range	Percentage Receiving
1446 - 1520	<1
1371 - 1445	1
1296 - 1370	2
1221 - 1295	4
1146 - 1220	6
1071 - 1145	8
996 - 1070	9
921 - 995	10
846 - 920	12
771 - 845	13
696 - 770	12
621 - 695	10
546 - 620	7
471 - 545	4
320 - 470	1

Scoring a 1400 or higher should be enough to ensure that you qualify for semi-finalist status. If you live in a very competitive state (the highest cutoff scores were from California, DC, Massachusetts, New Jersey, and Virginia), you may need another 10 or 20 points to guarantee qualification.

Unless you plan to graduate from high school a year early, only your junior year PSAT scores will be used. You must also be a US citizen or a permanent resident in the process of becoming a US citizen. Although taking the PSAT at one of the October administrations is the easiest way to qualify for the National Merit Program, the NMSC does provide alternatives to students who miss these dates. Contact the NMSC at 1-847-866-5100 for more information.

The initial stages of the Merit Program are judged entirely based on a student's selection index. The selection index is simply the sum of your component scores. In April, 50,000 students with the highest selection indices will be notified and made eligible for NMSC referral service. In September, about 34,000 of these students will be named Commended Students and the remaining 16,000 will be named Semifinalists. Only Semifinalists are eligible to advance further in the competition for Merit Scholarships.

Semifinalists are determined on a state-by-state basis, and the selection index cut-off varies by state and by year. Each state's allotment of semifinalists is determined based on its percentage of the national total of high school graduating seniors.

Semifinalists who meet eligibility standards (students must submit an application, high school record, and SAT I scores among other requirements) will be among the 14,000 National Merit Finalists named in February.

In March and April the NMSC awards 7,600 scholarships to students based upon their abilities, skills, and accomplishments. The three types of scholarships awarded are National Merit Scholarships (2,400), corporate-sponsored scholarships (1,200), and college-sponsored scholarships (4,000).

Some corporations offer a number of scholarships to eligible students (for example, the children of employees) that are not filled entirely by Finalists. These 1,500 scholarships are called Special Scholarships and are chosen from applicants from among the qualified pool that the company has designated.

You can find out more detailed information about the National Merit Program in the PSAT/NMSQT Student Bulletin available in your college counseling office. The College Board maintains information on the PSAT/NMSQT at their website, or you can contact the NMSC directly:

National Merit Scholarship Corporation
1560 Sherman Avenue, Suite 200
Evanston, IL 60201-4897
(847) 866-5100

Practice Test #1

Reading

U.S. Literature

Focus: Students must read and understand a passage from U.S. Literature.

Questions 1-9 refer to the following selection from Little Women by Louisa May Alcott:

"Christmas won't be Christmas without any presents," grumbled Jo, lying on the rug.

"It's so dreadful to be poor!" sighed Meg, looking down at her old dress.

"I don't think it's fair for some girls to have plenty of pretty things, and other girls nothing at all," added little Amy, with an injured sniff.

"We've got Father and Mother, and each other," said Beth contentedly from her corner.

The four young faces on which the firelight shone brightened at the cheerful words, but darkened again as Jo said sadly, "We haven't got Father, and shall not have him for a long time." She didn't say "perhaps never," but each silently added it, thinking of Father far away, where the fighting was.

Nobody spoke for a minute; then Meg said in an altered tone, "You know the reason Mother proposed not having any presents this Christmas was because it is going to be a hard winter for everyone; and she thinks we ought not to spend money for pleasure, when our men are suffering so in the army. We can't do much, but we can make our little sacrifices, and ought to do it gladly. But I am afraid I don't," and Meg shook her head, as she thought regretfully of all the pretty things she wanted.

"But I don't think the little we should spend would do any good. We've each got a dollar, and the army wouldn't be much helped by our giving that. I agree not to expect anything from Mother or you, but I do want to buy Undine and Sintran for myself. I've wanted it so long," said Jo, who was a bookworm.

"I planned to spend mine in new music," said Beth, with a little sigh, which no one heard but the hearth brush and kettle-holder.

"I shall get a nice box of Faber's drawing pencils; I really need them," said Amy decidedly.

"Mother didn't say anything about our money, and she won't wish us to give up everything. Let's each buy what we want, and have a little fun; I'm sure we work hard enough to earn it," cried Jo, examining the heels of her shoes in a gentlemanly manner.

"I know I do—teaching those tiresome children nearly all day, when I'm longing to enjoy myself at home," began Meg, in the complaining tone again.

"You don't have half such a hard time as I do," said Jo. "How would you like to be shut up for hours with a nervous, fussy old lady, who keeps you trotting, is never satisfied, and worries you till you're ready to fly out the window or cry?"

"It's naughty to fret, but I do think washing dishes and keeping things tidy is the worst work in the world. It makes me cross, and my hands get so stiff, I can't practice well at all." And Beth looked at her rough hands with a sigh that anyone could hear that time.

"I don't believe any of you suffer as I do," cried Amy, "for you don't have to go to school with impertinent girls, who plague you if you don't know your lessons, and laugh at your dresses, and label your father if he isn't rich, and insult you when your nose isn't nice."

"If you mean libel, I'd say so, and not talk about labels, as if Papa was a pickle bottle," advised Jo, laughing.

1. Which of the following sentences best describes the theme of this passage?
   a. You should always use the biggest words you know.
   b. The youngest member of a family should do the most work.
   c. Everyone has problems, and it is important to think of others.
   d. You should spend your money on yourself because you deserve it.

2. Which choice gives the best summary of the problems presented in this passage?
   a. Father is away at war, money is scarce, and the sisters are unhappy with their responsibilities.
   b. Mother forbade any presents this Christmas, and the sisters are unhappy with their responsibilities.
   c. The sisters do not have as much money to spend as they would like, and Amy is made fun of at school.
   d. Beth is tired of cleaning and washing dishes, and Father is away at war.

3. What do you know to be true about Father?
   a. He wants the sisters to spend their money on themselves.
   b. He misses his wife and children.
   c. He wants the sisters to give their money to the army.
   d. He is with the army.

4. What do you know to be true about Mother?
   a. She misses her husband.
   b. She is sorry that the family is poor.
   c. She proposed not having presents.
   d. She wants the sisters to spend their money on themselves.

5. Who is the only sister who does NOT specify what she wants to buy with her money?
   a. Amy
   b. Beth
   c. Jo
   d. Meg

6. What does the phrase "no one heard but the hearth brush and kettle holder" tell the reader about where Beth is located in the room?
"I planned to spend mine in new music," said Beth, with a little sigh, which no one heard but the hearth brush and kettle-holder.
   a. Near the stove
   b. By the window
   c. In the kitchen
   d. Closest to the fireplace

7. "'I don't think it's fair for some girls to have plenty of pretty things, and other girls nothing at all,' added little Amy, with an injured sniff." In this sentence, what is the best meaning of "injured"?
   a. Amy sniffs in pain at having injured herself.
   b. Amy sniffs to show her sense of unfairness.
   c. Amy sniffs with hurt feelings at Meg's words.
   d. Amy sniffs because she caught a winter cold.

8. Beth says, "It makes me cross, and my hands get so stiff, I can't practice well at all.'" In the context of this entire passage, Beth refers to what when she says "'practice'"?
   a. Practicing music
   b. Practicing drawing
   c. Practicing teaching
   d. Practicing schoolwork

9. Which evidence shows that this passage takes place during a war?
   a. "...thinking of Father far away, where the fighting was."
   b. "...when our men are suffering so in the army."
   c. "We haven't got Father, and shall not...for a long time."
   d. (a) primarily and also (b) secondarily, but not (c)

History/Social Studies

Passage Set 1
Focus: Students must read and understand a passage on a history topic.

Questions 10-19 refer to the Second Inaugural Address and the Gettysburg Address, both by Abraham Lincoln:

Second Inaugural Address

Fellow-Countrymen:

AT this second appearing to take the oath of the Presidential office there is less occasion for an extended address than there was at the first. Then a statement somewhat in detail of a course to be pursued seemed fitting and proper. Now, at the expiration of four years, during which public declarations have been constantly called forth on every point and phase of the great contest which still absorbs the attention and engrosses the energies of the nation, little that is new could be presented. The progress of our arms, upon which all else chiefly depends, is as well known to the public as to myself, and it is, I trust, reasonably satisfactory and encouraging to all. With high hope for the future, no prediction in regard to it is ventured.

On the occasion corresponding to this four years ago all thoughts were anxiously directed to an impending civil war. All dreaded it, all sought to avert it. While the inaugural address was being delivered from this place, devoted altogether to saving the Union without war, insurgent agents were in the city seeking to destroy it without war—seeking to dissolve the Union and divide effects by negotiation. Both parties deprecated war, but one of them would make war rather than let the nation survive, and the other would accept war rather than let it perish, and the war came.

One-eighth of the whole population were colored slaves, not distributed generally over the Union, but localized in the southern part of it. These slaves constituted a peculiar and powerful interest. All knew that this interest was somehow the cause of the war. To strengthen, perpetuate, and extend this interest was the object for which the insurgents would rend the Union even by war, while the Government claimed no right to do more than to restrict the territorial enlargement of it. Neither party expected for the war the magnitude or the duration which it has already attained. Neither anticipated that the cause of the conflict might cease with or even before the conflict itself should cease. Each looked for an easier triumph, and a result less fundamental and astounding. Both read the same Bible and pray to the same God, and each invokes His aid against the other. It may seem strange that any men should dare to ask a just God's assistance in wringing their bread from the sweat of other men's faces, but let us judge not, that we be not judged. The prayers of both could not be answered. That of neither has been answered fully. The Almighty has His own purposes. "Woe unto the world because of offenses; for it must needs be that offenses come, but woe to that man by whom the offense cometh." If we shall suppose that American slavery is one of those offenses which, in the providence of God, must needs come, but which, having continued through His appointed time, He now wills to remove, and that He gives to both North and South this terrible war as the woe due to those by whom the offense came, shall we discern therein any departure from those divine attributes which the believers in a living God always

- 125 -

ascribe to Him? Fondly do we hope, fervently do we pray, that this mighty scourge of war may speedily pass away. Yet, if God wills that it continue until all the wealth piled by the bondsman's two hundred and fifty years of unrequited toil shall be sunk, and until every drop of blood drawn with the lash shall be paid by another drawn with the sword, as was said three thousand years ago, so still it must be said "the judgments of the Lord are true and righteous altogether."

With malice toward none, with charity for all, with firmness in the right as God gives us to see the right, let us strive on to finish the work we are in, to bind up the nation's wounds, to care for him who shall have borne the battle and for his widow and his orphan, to do all which may achieve and cherish a just and lasting peace among ourselves and with all nations.

Gettysburg Address

Four score and seven years ago our fathers brought forth on this continent, a new nation, conceived in Liberty, and dedicated to the proposition that all men are created equal.

Now we are engaged in a great civil war, testing whether that nation, or any nation so conceived and so dedicated, can long endure. We are met on a great battle-field of that war. We have come to dedicate a portion of that field, as a final resting place for those who here gave their lives that that nation might live. It is altogether fitting and proper that we should do this.

But, in a larger sense, we can not dedicate -- we can not consecrate -- we can not hallow -- this ground. The brave men, living and dead, who struggled here, have consecrated it, far above our poor power to add or detract. The world will little note, nor long remember what we say here, but it can never forget what they did here. It is for us the living, rather, to be dedicated here to the unfinished work which they who fought here have thus far so nobly advanced. It is rather for us to be here dedicated to the great task remaining before us -- that from these honored dead we take increased devotion to that cause for which they gave the last full measure of devotion -- that we here highly resolve that these dead shall not have died in vain -- that this nation, under God, shall have a new birth of freedom -- and that government of the people, by the people, for the people, shall not perish from the earth.

10. In his Second Inaugural Address, Lincoln said, "These slaves constituted a peculiar and powerful interest." In this context, what does "peculiar" most nearly mean?
    a. Odd
    b. Bizarre
    c. Specific
    d. Appropriate

11. In the last sentence of the Gettysburg Address, what did Lincoln most closely mean by "...that this nation, under God, shall have a new birth of freedom"?
    a. Freedom from war
    b. Freedom for all citizens
    c. Freedom for the soldiers
    d. Freedom to own slaves or not

12. In his Second Inaugural Address, Lincoln said, "If we shall suppose that... [God] gives to both North and South this terrible war as the woe due to those by whom the offense came..." Which of the following did he provide as evidence of this supposition?
    a. "Neither party expected for the war the magnitude or the duration which it has already attained."
    b. "Both read the same Bible and pray to the same God, and each invokes His aid against the other."
    c. "Yet, if God wills that it continue...so still it must be said 'the judgments of the Lord are true and righteous altogether.'"
    d. "'Woe unto the world because of offenses; for it must needs be that offenses come, but woe to that man by whom the offense cometh.'"

13. Which of the following comes closest to summarizing the main idea of the Gettysburg Address?
    a. In dedicating this ground, we must moreover save our democracy so soldiers did not die in vain.
    b. In dedicating this ground, we must consecrate and hallow it to honor the soldiers living and dead.
    c. In dedicating this ground, we must ensure the world remembers what we said and they did here.
    d. In dedicating this ground, we must complete soldiers' unfinished work by declaring a cease-fire.

14. In the sentence, "The world will little note, nor long remember what we say here, but it can never forget what they did here", which rhetorical device did Lincoln use?
    a. Epiphora
    b. Anaphora
    c. Repetition
    d. Parallelism

15. Which idea did Lincoln overtly include in both his Second Inaugural Address and Gettysburg Address?
    a. Achieving an enduring peace
    b. The Civil War being God's will
    c. Completing some ongoing tasks
    d. Wishing the war would end soon

16. Why does Lincoln discuss his first inaugural address in this passage?
    a. To prove that the country could have gone in a different direction.
    b. To illustrate how the country had changed since his first inauguration.
    c. To show how much he improved the country during his first term.
    d. To explain that the country was once a place of peace.

17. Which sentence from the address supports the idea that Lincoln believed the North and the South did not have equally justifiable reasons for taking part in the war?
    a. All knew that this interest was somehow the cause of the war.
    b. Neither anticipated that the cause of the conflict might cease with or even before the conflict, itself, should cease.
    c. Both parties deprecated war, but one of them would make war rather than let the nation survive, and the other would accept war rather than let it perish, and the war came.
    d. Each looked for an easier triumph, and a result less fundamental and astounding.

18. How does Lincoln unite the themes of war and religion in his second inaugural address?
    a. He suggests that the war and its end are parts of God's plan.
    b. He says that no man would ask God to help him win a war.
    c. He insists that it is God's responsibility, not his own, to resolve the war.
    d. He quotes from the Bible liberally in order to extend an address he knew was too short.

19. How might reading Lincoln's second inaugural address online differ from hearing it in person?
    a. Lincoln likely was angry while reading his address, and this anger is lost in its translation to online text.
    b. Lincoln's original address was much longer than the version that later appeared online.
    c. Lincoln was an impressive-looking man, and this characteristic could be conveyed online only if the web page includes a photograph of him.
    d. Lincoln would have been able to use his voice to heighten the emotion in his address.

Passage 2
Focus: Students must read and understand a passage from History/Social Studies.

Read the selection from Roosevelt's 1941 State of the Union Address to answer questions 20-29:
    Many subjects connected with our social economy call for immediate improvement.
    As examples:
    We should bring more citizens under the coverage of old-age pensions and unemployment insurance.
    We should widen the opportunities for adequate medical care.
    We should plan a better system by which persons deserving or needing gainful employment may obtain it.
    I have called for personal sacrifice. And I am assured of the willingness of almost all Americans to respond to that call.
    A part of the sacrifice means the payment of more money in taxes. In my Budget Message I will recommend that a greater portion of this great defense program be paid for from taxation than we are paying for today. No person should try, or be allowed, to get rich out of the program; and the principle of tax payments in accordance with ability to pay should be constantly before our eyes to guide our legislation.
    If the Congress maintains these principles, the voters, putting patriotism ahead of pocketbooks, will give you their applause.
    In the future days, which we seek to make secure, we look forward to a world founded upon four essential human freedoms.
    The first is freedom of speech and expression—everywhere in the world.
    The second is freedom of every person to worship God in his own way—everywhere in the world.

The third is freedom from want—which, translated into world terms, means economic understandings which will secure to every nation a healthy peacetime life for its inhabitants—everywhere in the world.

The fourth is freedom from fear—which, translated into world terms, means a world-wide reduction of armaments to such a point and in such a thorough fashion that no nation will be in a position to commit an act of physical aggression against any neighbor—anywhere in the world.

That is no vision of a distant millennium. It is a definite basis for a kind of world attainable in our own time and generation. That kind of world is the very antithesis of the so-called new order of tyranny which the dictators seek to create with the crash of a bomb.

To that new order we oppose the greater conception—the moral order. A good society is able to face schemes of world domination and foreign revolutions alike without fear.

Since the beginning of our American history, we have been engaged in change—in a perpetual peaceful revolution—a revolution which goes on steadily, quietly adjusting itself to changing conditions—without the concentration camp or the quick-lime in the ditch. The world order which we seek is the cooperation of free countries, working together in a friendly, civilized society.

This nation has placed its destiny in the hands and heads and hearts of its millions of free men and women; and its faith in freedom under the guidance of God. Freedom means the supremacy of human rights everywhere. Our support goes to those who struggle to gain those rights and keep them. Our strength is our unity of purpose.

To that high concept there can be no end save victory.

20. Which statement best supports the idea that FDR believed that America is constantly evolving toward a better situation?

a. Since the beginning of our American history, we have been engaged in change—in a perpetual peaceful revolution—a revolution which goes on steadily, quietly adjusting itself to changing conditions—without the concentration camp or the quick-lime in the ditch.

b. This nation has placed its destiny in the hands and heads and hearts of its millions of free men and women; and its faith in freedom under the guidance of God.

c. To that new order we oppose the greater conception—the moral order. A good society is able to face schemes of world domination and foreign revolutions alike without fear.

d. The fourth is freedom from fear—which, translated into world terms, means a world-wide reduction of armaments to such a point and in such a thorough fashion that no nation will be in a position to commit an act of physical aggression against any neighbor—anywhere in the world.

21. Read the following selection from a blog entry on FDR's speech. What aspect of the speech is emphasized?

> ...There is, of course, a lot to love in the speech. It highlights the important social issues of the day, the very same issues our nation is struggling with at the moment. What can we do about our elderly? Do class distinctions matter? The fact of the matter is, no one wants to take care of a sickly aging relative, regardless of class. Then again, most of our elderly don't want to live with their offspring, either—rich or poor. It begs the question...

a. It emphasizes the need for a social safety net for the aging populace.
b. It emphasizes the need for a lack of social class distinctions.
c. It highlights the fact that many of the elderly do not want long-term care.
d. It highlights the idea that people want to live independently.

22. In this text, FDR claims that raising taxes will result in a patriotic populace that will happily support the government. What might be one argument against this idea?
a. Americans are uninterested in pursuing freedom of any kind, and the four freedoms listed here are not considered important.
b. The average citizen already feels overburdened by taxes and feels the money is not being well-spent by the government.
c. Individuals will easily assent to the idea of a greater tax burden since it will naturally lead to a more prosperous state.
d. Patriots of all kinds are part of the natural makeup of America, and some will feel that the support of government is something that should be contemplated and debated.

23. What is a major theme that Roosevelt articulates in his speech?
a. It is important for all people to have access to the benefits of an old-age system that supports citizens when they can no longer work.
b. Patriotic people will feel the need to pay more taxes to the government in order to obtain certain benefits they would not be able to afford.
c. People who want to work should be able to find work without bias and without undue hardship.
d. There are four basic freedoms that are vital to the health of people: speech, worship, freedom from want, and freedom from fear.

24. The last sentence in this passage is, "To that high concept there can be no end save victory." In the context of the preceding text, which of the following is the most precise meaning of the word "end"?
a. Death
b. Purpose
c. Outcome
d. Conclusion

25. FDR spoke of "the so-called new order of tyranny which the dictators seek to create with the crash of a bomb." In the context of this passage, which is the most accurate meaning of the word "order"?
a. A command given by a military leader
b. An authoritative decision or direction
c. An arrangement of items in sequence
d. A system of societal and world politics

26. When FDR spoke of "personal sacrifice", which of these did he explicitly give as an example of it?
     a. Higher taxation
     b. Military service
     c. Arms reduction
     d. Four freedoms

27. FDR described America's constant engagement in change as "a perpetual peaceful revolution...without the concentration camp or the quick-lime in the ditch." In this description, we can infer his implicit reference to which war(s)?
     a. Revolutionary
     b. World War I
     c. World War II
     d. To all of them

28. FDR identified aspects of the social economy needing to be improved immediately. As evidence of this need, which example did he NOT cite in this passage?
     a. Expanding retirement benefits
     b. Expanding healthcare benefits
     c. Expanding draft by the military
     d. Expanding labor opportunities

29. In identifying the four freedoms in this passage, FDR ended his definition of the first three freedoms with "—everywhere in the world" and the fourth with "—anywhere in the world." This is an example of which rhetorical device?
     a. Anastrophe
     b. Antistrophe
     c. Apostrophe
     d. Aposiopesis

Science

Passage 1

Focus: Students must read and understand a passage from a science topic.

Questions 30-38 pertain to the following passage:

<u>Annelids</u>

The phylum Annelida, named for the Latin word *anellus*, meaning "ring", includes earthworms, leeches, and other similar organisms. In their typical form, these animals exhibit bilateral symmetry, a cylindrical cross section, and an elongate body divided externally into segments (*metameres*) by a series of rings (*annuli*). They are segmented internally as well, with most of the internal organs repeated in series in each segment. This organization is termed *metamerism*. Metameric segmentation is the distinguishing feature of this phylum, and provides it with a degree of evolutionary plasticity in that certain segments can be modified and specialized to perform specific functions. For example, in some species certain of the locomotor *parapodia*, or feet, may be modified for grasping, and some portions of the gut may evolve digestive specializations.

The gut is a straight, muscular tube that functions independently of the muscular activity in the body wall. The Annelida resemble the nematodes, another worm phylum, in possessing a fluid-filled internal cavity separating the gut from the body wall. In both phyla, this cavity is involved in locomotion. However, in the annelids this space is formed at a much later time during the development of the embryo, and presumably evolved much later as well. This fluid-filled internal space is called a true *coelom*.

The annelid excretory and circulatory systems are well developed, and some members of the phylum have evolved respiratory organs. The nervous system offers a particular example of metameric specialization. It is concentrated anteriorly into enlarged cerebral ganglia connected to a ventral nerve cord that extends posteriorly and is organized into repeating segmental ganglia.

This phylum includes members bearing adaptations required for aquatic (marine or freshwater) or terrestrial habitats. They may be free-living entities or exist as parasites. Among the best known are the earthworm *Lumbricus*, the water leech *Hirudo*, and the marine worm *Nereis*.

30. What is the purpose of this passage?
   a. To describe the annelid nervous system.
   b. To describe the annelid digestive system.
   c. To introduce distinctive features of annelid anatomy.
   d. To define metamerism.

31. What is meant by the term *metamerism*?
   a. Segmentation of the anatomy
   b. A series of rings
   c. Bilateral symmetry
   d. Evolutionary plasticity

32. What is meant by the term *parapodia*?
   a. Specialization
   b. Grasping appendages
   c. Locomotion
   d. Feet

33. One evolutionary advantage of segmentation is that
   a. Segmented animals have many feet.
   b. Segmented animals have a fluid-filled coelom.
   c. Parts of some segments can become specialized to perform certain functions.
   d. Segments can evolve.

34. Some annelid feet may be specialized in order to
   a. be used for locomotion.
   b. be segmented.
   c. be fluid-filled.
   d. grasp things.

35. The main difference between the Annelida and all other animal phyla is that
   a. the Annelida are worms.
   b. the Annelida include the leeches.
   c. the Annelida are metameric.
   d. the Annelida are aquatic.

36. The purpose of the last paragraph in the passage is to
   a. give familiar examples of members of the annelid phylum.
   b. show that annelids may be parasites.
   c. tell the reader that annelids may be adapted to aquatic environments.
   d. show that there are many annelids in nature and that they are adapted to a wide
   variety of habitats.

37. Which of the following provide(s) evidence to support the statement that metamerism confers
some evolutionary flexibility?
   a. "in some species certain of the...feet may be modified for grasping..."
   b. "...and some portions of the gut may evolve digestive specializations."
   c. "Metameric segmentation is the distinguishing feature of this phylum."
   d. (a) and (b) are both examples of evolutionary flexibility, but (c) is not.

38. The second paragraph discusses annelids and nematodes. Which relationship(s) between these
two phyla does the author establish by describing their respective characteristics?
   a. Comparison
   b. Contrast
   c. Neither
   d. Both

Passage 2
Focus: Students must read and understand a passage from a science topic.

Questions 39-47 are based on the following selection from Albert Einstein's paper on Relativity: The Special and General Theory (1916, revised 1924).

THE PRINCIPLE OF RELATIVITY (IN THE RESTRICTED SENSE)

In order to attain the greatest possible clearness, let us return to our example of the railway carriage supposed to be travelling uniformly. We call its motion a uniform translation ("uniform" because it is of constant velocity and direction, "translation" because although the carriage changes its position relative to the embankment yet it does not rotate in so doing). Let us imagine a raven flying through the air in such a manner that its motion, as observed from the embankment, is uniform and in a straight line. If we were to observe the flying raven from the moving railway carriage, we should find that the motion of the raven would be one of different velocity and direction, but that it would still be uniform and in a straight line. Expressed in an abstract manner we may say : If a mass m is moving uniformly in a straight line with respect to a co-ordinate system K, then it will also be moving uniformly and in a straight line relative to a second co-ordinate system K1 provided that the latter is executing a uniform translatory motion with respect to K. In accordance with the discussion contained in the preceding section, it follows that:

If K is a Galilean co-ordinate system, then every other co-ordinate system K' is a Galilean one, when, in relation to K, it is in a condition of uniform motion of translation. Relative to K1 the mechanical laws of Galilei-Newton hold good exactly as they do with respect to K.

We advance a step farther in our generalization when we express the tenet thus: If, relative to K, K1 is a uniformly moving co-ordinate system devoid of rotation, then natural phenomena run their course with respect to K1 according to exactly the same general laws as with respect to K. This statement is called the principle of relativity (in the restricted sense).

As long as one was convinced that all natural phenomena were capable of representation with the help of classical mechanics, there was no need to doubt the validity of this principle of relativity...

Nevertheless, there are two general facts which at the outset speak very much in favor of the validity of the principle of relativity. Even though classical mechanics does not supply us with a sufficiently broad basis for the theoretical presentation of all physical phenomena, still we must grant it a considerable measure of **"truth,"** since it supplies us with the actual motions of the heavenly bodies with a delicacy of detail little short of wonderful. The principle of relativity must therefore apply with great accuracy in the domain of mechanics. But that a principle of such broad generality should hold with such exactness in one domain of phenomena, and yet should be invalid for another, is a priori not very probable.

We now proceed to the second argument, to which, moreover, we shall return later. If the principle of relativity (in the restricted sense) does not hold, then the Galilean co-ordinate systems K, K1, K2, etc., which are moving uniformly relative to each other, will not be equivalent for the description of natural phenomena. In this case we should be constrained to believe that natural laws are capable of being formulated in a particularly simple manner, and of course only on condition that, from amongst all possible Galilean co-ordinate systems, we should have chosen one (K[0]) of a particular state of motion as our body of reference. We should then be justified (because of its merits for the description of natural phenomena) in calling this system "absolutely at rest," and all other Galilean systems K "in motion." If, for instance, our embankment were the system K[0] then our railway carriage would be a system K, relative to which less simple laws would hold than with respect to K[0]. This diminished simplicity would be due to the fact that the carriage K would be in motion (i.e. "really") with respect to K[0]. In the general laws of nature which have been formulated with reference to K, the magnitude and direction of the velocity of the carriage would necessarily play a part. We should expect, for instance, that the note emitted by an organ pipe placed with its axis parallel to the direction of travel would be different from that emitted if the axis of the pipe were placed perpendicular to this direction.

Now in virtue of its motion in an orbit round the sun, our earth is comparable with a railway carriage travelling with a velocity of about 30 kilometers per second. If the principle of relativity were not valid we should therefore expect that the direction of motion of the earth at any moment would enter into the laws of nature, and also that physical systems in their behavior would be dependent on the orientation in space with respect to the earth. For owing to the alteration in direction of the velocity of revolution of the earth in the course of a year, the earth cannot be at rest relative to the hypothetical system K[0] throughout the whole year. However, the most careful observations have never revealed such anisotropic properties in terrestrial physical space, i.e. a physical non-equivalence of different directions. This is very powerful argument in favor of the principle of relativity.

39. Which of the following choices best supports the claim of Einstein's theory of special relativity as accurate?
    a. the movement of the Earth around the sun
    b. Galilean co-ordinate systems and their application in classical mechanics
    c. the idea of chance in quantum mechanics
    d. the two different parts of relativity

40. What might be one question to ask to begin an argument against Einstein's theory of relativity?
    a. If relativity holds true, what does that say about the classical rules of motion?
    b. If relativity is valid, then why can it not explain all parts of the natural world, including the rules of quantum mechanics?
    c. If the natural laws concerning quantum mechanics are true, then shouldn't the classical rules of motion be suspect?
    d. If the natural laws formulated with reference to K are measurable, then wouldn't the magnitude and direction of the velocity of the carriage be important?

41. Which of the following choices provides the best meaning for the underlined "truth"?
    a. correctness regarding the abstract meaning of classical mechanics
    b. honesty regarding the movement of objects according to the rules of relativity
    c. validity regarding an understanding of the classical rules of motion
    d. exactness regarding the movement of small bodies on a coordinate plane

42. Einstein writes that classical mechanics describes astronomical movements with "a delicacy of detail little short of wonderful." In this context, what is the best synonym for the meaning of "delicacy"?
    a. A fragility
    b. A sensitivity
    c. A rare delight
    d. A soft texture

43. If a reader did not know the meaning of the phrase *a priori*, s/he could ascertain it from the sentence: "But that a principle of such broad generality should hold with such exactness in one domain of phenomena, and yet should be invalid for another, is a priori not very probable." Based on this context, to which of these is its meaning closest?
    a. Existing in the first place
    b. Having the highest priority
    c. Something happening after the fact
    d. General to specific/independently true

44. In the last paragraph, Einstein used the word "anisotropic". What is true about its meaning?
    a. Einstein used and explicitly defined it in the same sentence.
    b. Einstein's meaning is implicit; only physicists would know it.
    c. Einstein coined this term, defining it in an earlier paragraph.
    d. Einstein never defined it, but anyone can tell from context.

45. Within this passage, which of the following conclusions proposed by Einstein is predicated upon the condition that the principle of relativity is valid?
    a. "...then the Galilean co-ordinate systems K, K1, K2, etc., which are moving uniformly relative to each other, will not be equivalent for the description of natural phenomena."
    b. "...natural laws are capable of being formulated in a particularly simple manner, and...only on condition that...we...have chosen one...of a particular state of motion as our body of reference."
    c. "If, relative to K, K1 is a uniformly moving co-ordinate system devoid of rotation...then natural phenomena run their course with respect to K1 according to exactly the same general laws as with respect to K."
    d. "...we should therefore expect that the direction of motion of the earth at any moment would enter into the laws of nature, and also that physical systems in their behavior would be dependent on the orientation in space with respect to the earth."

46. Einstein describes the detail with which classical mechanics describes celestial motions as "little short of wonderful." Rhetorically, this is most an example of which of these?
    a. Understatement
    b. Overstatement
    c. Amplification
    d. Metabasis

- 136 -

47. Which of the following most accurately represents Einstein's use of claims and counterclaims in this passage?

a. From one paragraph to the next, statements of claims and statements of counterclaims are presented alternately; the last two sentences summarize how these contrast.

b. The first three paragraphs present a series of counterclaims; the following four present arguments that logically refute those counterclaims and then support his claims.

c. The first five paragraphs mainly explain his claims; the last two state counterclaims, explaining results to expect if they were true; the last two sentences reassert his claims.

d. Every paragraph begins by presenting a claim, then a counterclaim, then refutation of the counterclaim; and ends with repeating the original claim for emphasis.

Writing and Language

Careers

Focus: Students must make revising and editing decisions in the context of a passage on a careers-related topic.

Software Developer

Software developers are in charge of the entire development process for a software program. They begin by asking how the customer plans to use the software. They design the program and then give instructions to programmers, who write computer code and test it. If the program does not work as expected or people find it too difficult to use, software developers go back to the design process to fix the problems or improve the program. After the program is released to the customer, a developer may perform upgrades and maintenance.

Developers usually work closely with <u>computer programmers</u>. However, in some companies, developers write code themselves instead of giving instructions to computer programmers.

Developers who supervise a software project from the planning stages through implementation sometimes are called information technology (IT) project managers. These workers monitor the project's progress to ensure that it meets deadlines, standards, and cost targets. IT project managers who plan and direct an organization's IT department or IT policies are included in the profile on <u>computer and information systems managers</u>.

The following are types of software developers:
Applications software developers design computer applications, such as word processors and games, for consumers. They may create custom software for a specific customer or commercial software to be sold to the general public. Some applications software developers create complex databases for organizations. They also create programs that people use over the Internet and within a company's intranet.

Systems software developers create the systems that keep computers functioning properly. These could be operating systems that are part of computers the general public buys or systems built specifically for an organization. Often, systems software developers also build the system's interface, which is what allows users to interact with the computer. Systems software developers create the operating systems that control most of the consumer electronics in use today, including those in phones or cars.

1. Which of the following best represents how information is connected in this passage?
   a. Transitions from paragraphs 1-2 and 2-3 begin paragraphs 2 and 3; the transition to both paragraphs 4 and 5 ends paragraph 3.
   b. Transitions from paragraphs 1-2, 2-3, and 3-4 end paragraphs 1, 2, and 3; there is no transition between paragraph 4 and paragraph 5.
   c. Transitions between paragraphs are not present in this passage; each paragraph introduces a new topic with no reference to the last.
   d. Transitions between paragraphs are only evident in the transition from paragraph 3 to paragraph 4, but not in any other place.

2. According to the information in this passage, readers can conclude that Apple's iOS and Google's Android were designed by which of these?
   a. Steve Jobs and Bill Gates respectively
   b. Both (c) and (d) software designers
   c. Applications software designers
   d. Systems software designers

3. Which of the following best describes the organizational structure of this passage from the first paragraph to the others?
   a. Problem to solution
   b. General to specific
   c. Compare-contrast
   d. Cause-and-effect

4. If someone wanted to claim that software developers have nothing more to do with their designs after their programs become available to the public, how would evidence from this passage relate to such a claim?
   a. There is no evidence that relates to such a claim.
   b. There is evidence there that supports this claim.
   c. There is evidence here that will refute this claim.
   d. There is evidence both for and against this claim.

5. Which of the following accurately describes the use of introductions and conclusions in this passage?
   a. An introduction but no conclusion
   b. No introduction but a conclusion
   c. An introduction and a conclusion
   d. No introduction and no conclusion

6. "Software developers are in charge of the entire development process for a software program." Which version has the best noun agreement?
   a. No change
   b. for software programs.
   c. for one software program.
   d. for many software programs.

7. The second paragraph of the passage says that "...in some companies, developers write code themselves" instead of having programmers do it. Which of these is the correct convention in current Standard English?
   a. No change
   b. developers write codes
   c. developers write a code
   d. developers write coding

8. In this passage, the third paragraph states, "Developers who supervise a software project from the planning stages through implementation sometimes are called information technology (IT) project managers." Which version is both least awkward and most correct?
   a. No change
   b. are sometimes called information technology (IT) managers.
   c. are called information technology (IT) managers sometimes.
   d. are called sometimes information technology (IT) managers.

9. A reader unfamiliar with the term "intranet" could determine from the context of the passage that it most precisely means which of these?
   a. A network inside the Internet to which anyone has access
   b. A network the same size as but separate from the Internet
   c. A network smaller than the Internet, specific to a company
   d. A network that is the Internet but as used by one company

10. Based on the context of this passage, which of the following is correct concerning "databases"?
    a. Databases are software operating systems.
    b. Databases are sold to the general public.
    c. Databases are software applications.
    d. Databases are system interfaces.

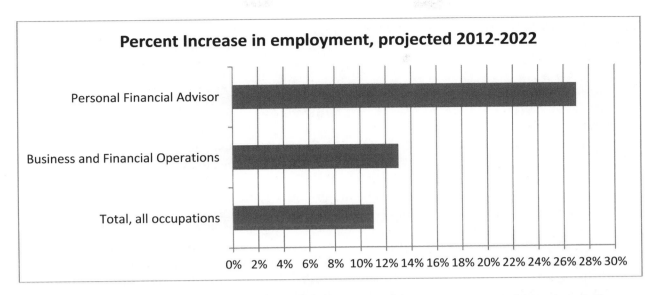

Percent Increase in employment, projected 2012-2022

Adapted from United States Bureau of Labor Statistics, Employment Projections Program. "All occupations" includes all occupations in the United States economy.

11. Based on the information provided in the graph, which of the following is true?
   a. Software developers will be hired more than employees in business and financial or other jobs.
   b. Software developers will be hired at the same rate as business and financial, but not other jobs.
   c. Software developers will be hired more than in all jobs but less than business and financial jobs.
   d. Software developers will not be hired as much as those in business, financial, and all other jobs.

Focus: Students must make revising and editing decisions in the context of a passage on a history/social studies-related topic.

Ernst Lubitsch

The comedy of manners was a style of film popular in the 1930s. These movies expressed the frustrations of the depression-era poor by mocking the swells of the upper classes, and contrasting their gilded lives to the daily grind of the downtrodden masses. One of the greatest directors of this type of film was Ernst Lubitsch, a German filmmaker who eventually came to Hollywood to make some of his greatest films.

Lubitsch's film career began in the silent era. Born in Berlin, in 1892, he worked at first as an actor, subsequently debuting as a director with the film Passion in 1912. He made more than 40 films in Germany, but the advent of sound brought him to Hollywood, where the new technology was most readily available. After the producer Albert Zukor invited him to come to the U.S. in 1923, he pursued his career in the capital of film until the late 1940s. His signature style – a focus on seemingly insignificant details that **(12)** <u>imbued</u> them with symbolism in the context of the film – was just as effective in the "talkies" as it had been in silent films. One of his greatest comedies, Trouble in Paradise, starred Herbert Marshall and Miriam Hopkins and was shot in 1932. A stinging social comedy that skewers the illusions of the upper classes, it would not have been well received in his native Germany of the time.

Trouble in Paradise tells the story of a charming, elegant thief. Marshall plays Gaston Monescu, a man whose charm and elegant manners allow him to work his way into the bosom of high society. In the hotels and clubs of the rich, he manages to gain the trust of wealthy individuals until he swindles them. Monescu courts the rich perfume heiress, Mariette, **(13)** <u>and we can never know of certain of how sincere his affection for her may be.</u> But he is also in love with his accomplice, Lily, a clever thief in her own right. His eventual decision to leave Mariette for her can be seen as an affirmation of the unity of the working class in this very class-conscious film.

The opening scenes of the film provide a classic example of Lubitsch's wry symbolism. The opening shot is of a garbage can, which is duly picked up by a garbage man and dumped onto what seems to be a truck. But, as the camera pans back, we realize that the truck is, in fact, a gondola, and that the scene takes place in Venice. As the gondolier-garbage man breaks into a romantic song, the camera contrasts the elegant city, its palaces and beautiful canals, with the mundane reality of garbage and necessary, low-wage work.

The film continues to contrast the elegant surfaces of society with the corruption that lies beneath. A classic scene is the first meeting between Monescu and Lily, two thieves with polished manners. In an elegant hotel room, the two engage in a genteel banter filled with seductive double-entendres and urbane banalities. But they are not the baron and countess they profess to be, as their behavior soon makes clear. As the supper progresses, they manage to steal one another's wallets, jewelry, and watches. Finally, they reveal the thefts to one another and sort out their belongings, but Monescu has been won over by Lily's cleverness, for he admires her resourcefulness far more than the undeserved wealth of the upper classes.

Lubitsch went on to make many more films during the 1930s, comedies of manners and musical comedies as well. Among his greatest Hollywood films are Design for Living (1933), The Merry Widow (1934), Ninotchka (1939), and Heaven Can Wait (1943). One of the wittiest directors of all time, he made films in English, German and French, always exhibiting the sharpest eye for detail. His films challenged the intellect of his viewers, and they never disappointed. The juxtaposition of seemingly contradictory elements was always central to his style, as he exposed the falsehoods he found in his world.

12.
    a. No Change
    b. engulfed
    c. enchanted
    d. emboldened

13.
    a. No Change
    b. and we are not to certain of how sincere his affection for her may be.
    c. and we will never know certain of how sincere his affection for her may be.
    d. and we are never certain of how sincere his affection for her may be.

14. Which of the following terms would *not* be a good description of Lubitsch's film style, as it is described in the text?
    a. Sophisticated
    b. Erudite
    c. Chic
    d. Boisterous

15. One of the tools that Lubitsch used to mock the upper classes, as shown in the text, was
    a. Lighting.
    b. Talking pictures.
    c. Juxtaposition of contradictory elements.
    d. Urbane banalities.

16. Lubitsch's signature style can be described as
    a. Double-entendres and urbane banalities.
    b. Using apparently insignificant details as symbols.
    c. Charm and elegant manners.
    d. Corruption underlying high society.

17. Lubitsch first came to the U.S in 1923 because
    a. His films were not well received in Germany.
    b. He was fleeing the Nazi regime.
    c. He was invited by a producer.
    d. He could not make films with sound in Germany.

18. The text tells us that Lubitsch's first film, *Passion* was
    a. An early "talkie."
    b. A comedy of manners.
    c. A film starring Miriam Hopkins.
    d. None of the above.

19. Without considering gender, which two characters have the most in common?
    a. Monescu and Lily
    b. Monescu and Mariette
    c. Lily and Mariette
    d. Monescu and Lubitsch

20. The scene with the garbage gondola at the opening of the film shows that
    a. The rich need supporting services.
    b. Venice is kept clean by gondoliers.
    c. Elegance may be only a veneer.
    d. Gondoliers sing romantic ballads.

21. Monescu most admires
    a. Lily's wealth.
    b. Lily's cleverness.
    c. Mariette's money.
    d. Venetian gondolas.

22. In the film, Lily pretends to be
    a. A perfume heiress.
    b. A countess.
    c. A wealthy dowager.
    d. Monescu's partner.

Humanities

Focus: Students must make revising and editing decisions in the context of a passage on a humanities-related topic.

Buddhism, Western Society, and the Self

In Western society, the individual self is generally prioritized over the collective self. This is evidenced in such things as the privatization of medicine and conceptions of ownership. In recent decades, however, there has been an increased tension in Western societies between institutions and ideologies that prioritize the individual and those groups that prioritize the collective. This is evidenced in the struggles that Western Buddhists face.

Central to Buddhist belief is the idea of "egolessness." While this term may seem to imply the absence of the individual ego or selfhood, this is not the case; rather, "egolessness" is a prioritization of the relationships between and among people over selfish concerns. "Egolessness" may also be thought of as an antonym of "ego-toxicity," that condition where an individual places his or her concerns before any other person or group's concerns. In Western societies, ego-toxicity is the reigning condition. Buddhists who live in such societies often find themselves caught between their ideology of egolessness and environmental ego-toxicity.

While a Western perspective might find it difficult to **(23)** <u>understand how a Buddhist can keep egolessness;</u> in Western society, Buddhists are able to maintain such a perspective as a natural consequent of their beliefs. The Western perspective expects moral actions to be quid pro quo; to put it another way, a Westerner assumes that if he or she does something considered "good," then he or she should and will be rewarded. Buddhists, on the other hand, believe that good should be done out of compassion for all beings, and to do good is to do good for all beings, including the self. Approaching society and social action in an egoless manner has begun to become more prevalent in secular institutions and movements, such as the transition to a more socialized form of medical treatment in some Western countries. The struggle between the ego and the collective continues, however.

Buddhist practitioners show through their actions that it is possible to do good in the world without giving up one's personhood. **(24)** <u>When ego-toxicity is abandoned, is it possible to care for one's self and the rest of the world through compassionate, egoless behavior.</u>

23.
    a. No Change
    b. understand how a Buddhist could maintain egolessness,
    c. understand how a Buddhist could stay egolessness
    d. believe what a Buddhist could maintain egolessness

24.
   a. No Change
   b. When ego-toxicity can be abandoned it is possible for one's self to care for the rest of the world through compassionate, egoless behavior.
   c. When ego-toxicity is abandoned it could be possible to care for one's self and the rest of the world through compassionate, egoless behavior.
   d. When ego-toxicity is abandoned, it is possible to care for one's self and the rest of the world through compassionate, egoless behavior.

25. What is the purpose of the first paragraph?
   a. To criticize Buddhist notions of the self.
   b. To criticize contemporary Western notions of the self.
   c. To introduce the tension between individuality and collectivity in Western society.
   d. To introduce the idea of "egolessness."

26. According to the passage, what is "egolessness?"
   a. The complete denial of the self.
   b. The rejection of psychoanalytic notions of ego, superego, and id.
   c. The prioritization of self over others.
   d. The prioritization of relationships between and among people.

27. Which of the following best describes the purpose of the second paragraph?
   a. It introduces the distinction between "egolessness" and "ego-toxicity."
   b. It makes light of the conflicts that Buddhists in Western societies experience.
   c. It praises egolessness as the only moral way of living.
   d. It harshly denounces ego-toxicity.

28. Based on the passage, "*quid pro quo*" most likely means:
   a. "something for nothing."
   b. "good merits money."
   c. "to each his own."
   d. "something for something."

29. According to the passage, why do Buddhists do good deeds?
   a. Doing good brings direct, personal benefits to the person doing the action.
   b. They do good so that they may go to heaven when they die.
   c. If they do not do good, they will be reincarnated again.
   d. Doing good for one person is doing good for all beings.

30. In this passage, which sentence in the first paragraph states a main idea that is developed in subsequent paragraphs?
   a. The second sentence
   b. The fourth sentence
   c. The third sentence
   d. The first sentence

31. This sentence appears in the second paragraph: "In Western societies, ego-toxicity is the reigning condition." Which of the following would be the most logical organization?
    a. No change
    b. Move it to the end of the paragraph
    c. Move it to the paragraph's beginning
    d. Move it out of the paragraph entirely

32. Which of these accurately describes a pattern in the first and/or last sentences of all the paragraphs in this passage?
    a. The last sentence of each paragraph identifies half a main conflict; the final sentence completes it.
    b. The first sentence of each paragraph identifies a main conflict, with the final sentence reiterating.
    c. The first sentence of each paragraph identifies a main conflict, with the final sentence resolving it.
    d. The last sentence of each paragraph identifies a main conflict, with the final sentence resolving it.

33. The style, mode, or type of text in this passage is best characterized as which of these?
    a. Description
    b. Persuasion
    c. Exposition
    d. Narration

Science

Focus: Students must make revising and editing decisions in the context of a passage on a science-related topic.

How are Hypotheses Confirmed?

Most scientists agree that while the scientific method is an invaluable methodological tool, it is not a failsafe method for arriving at objective truth. It is debatable, for example, whether a hypothesis can actually be confirmed by evidence.

When the hypothesis is of a form, "All x are y," which is commonly believed that a piece of evidence that is both x and y confirms the hypothesis. For example, for the hypothesis "All monkeys are hairy," a particular monkey that is hairy is thought to be a confirming piece of evidence for the hypothesis. A problem arises when one encounters evidence that disproves a hypothesis: while no scientist would argue that one piece of evidence proves a hypothesis, it is possible for one piece of evidence to disprove a hypothesis. To return to the monkey example, one hairless monkey out of one billion hairy monkeys disproves the hypothesis "All monkeys are hairy." Single pieces of evidence, then, seem to affect a given hypothesis in radically different ways. For this reason, the confirmation of hypotheses is better described as probabilistic.

Hypotheses that can only be proven or disproven based on evidence need to be based on probability because sample sets for such hypotheses are too large. In the monkey example, every single monkey in the history of monkeys would need to be examined before the hypothesis could be proven. By making confirmation a function of probability, one may make provisional or working conclusions that allow for the possibility of a given hypothesis being **(34)** <u>dissipated</u> in the future. In the monkey case, then, encountering a hairy monkey would slightly raise the probability that "all monkeys are hairy," while encountering a hairless monkey would slightly decrease the probability that "all monkeys are hairy." This method of confirming hypotheses is both counterintuitive and controversial, **(35)** <u>but it allowed for evidence to equitably effect hypotheses</u> and it does not require infinite sample sets for confirmation or disconfirmation.

34.
   a. No Change
   b. distilled
   c. disconfirmed
   d. destroyed

35.
   a. No Change
   b. but it allows for evidence to equitably effect hypotheses
   c. but it allowed for evidence to equitably affect hypotheses
   d. but it allows for evidence to equitably affect hypotheses

36. Which of the following best states the main idea of the second paragraph?
    a. One hairy monkey proves the hypothesis "All monkeys are hairy."
    b. The same piece of evidence can both confirm and disconfirm a hypothesis.
    c. Confirming and disconfirming evidence affect hypotheses differently.
    d. The scientific method is not a failsafe method for arriving at objective truth.

37. Which of the following is true of hypotheses of the form "All x are y"?
    a. Something that is neither x nor y disproves the hypothesis.
    b. Something that is both x and y disproves the hypothesis.
    c. Something that is x but not y disproves the hypothesis.
    d. Something that is y but not x disproves the hypothesis.

38. In the third paragraph, why does the author discuss the "sample set" of monkeys?
    a. To show that there are significant differences between monkey species.
    b. To show that all monkeys are hairy.
    c. To show that just a few monkeys can prove the hypothesis "all monkeys are hairy."
    d. To show that practical concerns make confirmation or disconfirmation a function of probability.

39. Using the same reasoning as that in the passage, an automobile with eighteen wheels does what to the following hypothesis: "All automobiles have only four wheels"?
    a. It proves the hypothesis.
    b. It raises the hypothesis's probability.
    c. It disproves the hypothesis.
    d. It decreases the hypothesis's probability.

40. Which of the following best describes this passage?
    a. The main idea of this entire passage is in the first sentence.
    b. The main idea of the first paragraph is in the first sentence.
    c. The main passage idea is both the first paragraph sentences.
    d. This passage's main idea is not in first paragraph sentences.

41. According to the passage, which of the following is true?
    a. It is possible to prove a hypothesis by simply giving only one piece of evidence.
    b. It is possible to prove but not disprove a hypothesis with one piece of evidence.
    c. It is possible to disprove but not prove a hypothesis with one piece of evidence.
    d. It is not possible to prove or disprove a hypothesis using one piece of evidence.

42. The last sentence of the second paragraph reads, "For this reason, the confirmation of hypotheses is better described as probabilistic." Which of the following is most accurate about this sentence?
    a. This sentence is not relevant to the passage topic and should be deleted.
    b. This sentence is not relevant to this paragraph and should be relocated.
    c. This sentence draws an inference related to the topic but not to purpose.
    d. This sentence draws a logical conclusion, based on preceding sentences.

43. This passage ends with, "...<u>it does not require infinite sample sets for confirmation or disconfirmation.</u>" This statement refers to information found where in the passage?
  a. Most specifically in the initial sentence in this same paragraph
  b. Most specifically in the second sentence of the same paragraph
  c. Most specifically the fourth sentence of the previous paragraph
  d. Most specifically the information is not found in any paragraph

44. Which of these is correct regarding the sentence boundaries in this passage?
  a. This passage contains a sentence fragment.
  b. This passage contains one run-on sentence.
  c. This passage contains neither type of error.
  d. This passage contains both types of errors.

Math - Calculator

Questions 1-4 pertain to the following information:

Elli wants to plant a flower garden that contains only roses and tulips. However, she has a limited amount of space for the garden, and she can only afford to buy a specific number of each plant. Elli has enough space to plant a total of 20 flowers, and she wants to spend a total of $100 to purchase the flowers. Roses cost $14 per plant and tulips cost $4 per plant. Let R represent the number of roses and let T represent the number of tulips Elli will plant in her garden.

1. Which system of linear equations can be used to solve for the number of roses and tulips Elli will plant in her garden?

a. $\begin{cases} 4R + 14T = 20 \\ R + T = 100 \end{cases}$

b. $\begin{cases} R + T = 20 \\ 14R + 4T = 100 \end{cases}$

c. $\begin{cases} R + T = 20 \\ 4R + 14T = 100 \end{cases}$

d. $\begin{cases} 14R + 4T = 20 \\ 14R + 4T = 100 \end{cases}$

2. How many roses will Elli plant in her flower garden?
   a. 4
   b. 16
   c. 18
   d. 2

3. How many tulips will Elli plant in her flower garden?
   a. 4
   b. 16
   c. 18
   d. 2

4. Based on the information provided, why might Elli plant more tulips than roses in her garden?
   a. Because tulips require less space than roses
   b. Because tulips are less expensive than roses
   c. Because tulips are prettier than roses
   d. Because tulips require less fertilizer than roses

5. Which of the following represents the solution of the following system of linear equations?
$$5x + 9y = -7$$
$$2x - 4y = 20$$

    a. $x = 3, y = 2$
    b. $x = 4, y = 3$
    c. $x = 4, y = -3$
    d. $x = 3, y = -2$

Use the information below to answer question 6:

    José is participating in a school fundraiser by selling packages of cookie dough and soft pretzels. His order form is shown below.

Customer name	Packages of cookie dough	Packages of pretzels	Total cost
Cedric	1	4	$42
Madhavi	3	2	$51
James	2	?	$24
Mei Ling	2	1	?

6. The cost per package of cookie dough is $_____. James ordered ___ packages of pretzels. The total cost of Mei Ling's order is $_____.

7. If $\frac{1}{2x} + \frac{1}{x} = \frac{1}{6}$, then $x =$
    a. 2
    b. 4
    c. 9
    d. 12

8. Which of the following data sets could be represented by the histogram shown below?

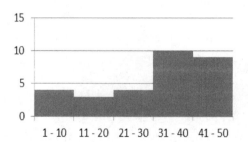

    a. 6, 7, 7, 8, 12, 13, 18, 22, 26, 27, 28, 31, 36, 36, 36, 36, 37, 38, 38, 38, 39, 41, 41, 41, 42, 42, 43, 43, 48, 49
    b. 2, 3, 4, 4, 8, 9, 10, 10, 11, 15, 19, 21, 21, 21, 21, 22, 24, 24, 25, 29, 31, 33, 40, 43, 45, 46, 48, 48, 49, 50
    c. 1, 2, 8, 8, 9, 9, 12, 13, 15, 15, 16, 17, 18, 19, 19, 21, 29, 31, 31, 35, 36, 38, 41, 42, 42, 45, 46, 47, 47, 49
    d. 1, 4, 4, 5, 10, 10, 10, 12, 12, 16, 20, 22, 23, 23, 25, 27, 31, 31, 37, 39, 40, 41, 41, 43, 45, 46, 48, 49, 49, 50

9. A taxi service charges $5.50 for the first 1/5 of a mile, $1.50 for each additional 1/5 of a mile, and 20¢ per minute of waiting time. Joan took a cab from her home to a flower shop 8 miles away, where she bought a bouquet, and then another 3.6 miles to her mother's house. The driver had to wait 9 minutes while she bought the bouquet. What was the fare?
 a. $101.80
 b. $120.20
 c. $92.80
 d. $91.20

10. Prizes are to be awarded to the best pupils in each class of an elementary school. The number of students in each grade is shown in the table, and the school principal wants the number of prizes awarded in each grade to be proportional to the number of students. If there are twenty prizes, how many should go to fifth-grade students?

Grade	1	2	3	4	5
Students	35	38	38	33	36

 a. 5
 b. 4
 c. 6
 d. 3

11. The probability that Bryan goes to the store is 0.18. The probability that he goes to the movies is 0.34. The probability that he goes to the store, given that he goes to the movies, is 0.46. What is the probability he goes to the store or to the movies?
 a. 32.38%
 b. 36.36%
 c. 40.28%
 d. 44.46%

12. Suppose Ashley will receive a $6,000 scholarship if she chooses University A, a $4,500 scholarship if she chooses University B, and a $5,500 scholarship if she chooses University C. The probabilities that she will attend each university are equal. Which of the following best represents the expected value for the scholarship amount she will receive?
 a. $4,833
 b. $5,155
 c. $5,333
 d. $5,525

13. Calculate the fifth term of the sequence defined as $f(0) = 2$, $f(n + 1) = 2f(n) - 1$ for $n \geq 1$.
 a. 9
 b. 17
 c. 32
 d. 33

14. The table below displays the value of $h(x)$ for nine different values of x.

x	−4	−3	−2	−1	0	1	2	3	4
$h(x)$	−16	−8	−4	−2	−1	−0.5	0	2	6

What is the value of $h^{-1}(-2)$?
    a. $h^{-1}(-2) = -4$
    b. $h^{-1}(-2) = -1$
    c. $h^{-1}(-2) = 1$
    d. $h^{-1}(-2) = 3$

15. Which frequency table is represented by the histogram shown below?

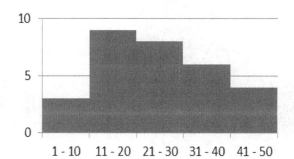

a.

Interval	Frequency
1 – 10	3
11 – 20	9
21 – 30	8
31 – 40	6
41 – 50	4

c.

Interval	Frequency
1 – 10	3
11 – 20	9
21 – 30	8
31 – 40	5
41 – 50	4

b.

Interval	Frequency
1 – 10	3
11 – 20	8
21 – 30	8
31 – 40	6
41 – 50	3

d.

Interval	Frequency
1 – 10	2
11 – 20	9
21 – 30	8
31 – 40	6
41 – 50	4

16. In an election in Kimball County, Candidate A obtained 36,800 votes. His opponent, Candidate B, obtained 32,100 votes. 2,100 votes went to write-in candidates. What percentage of the vote went to Candidate A?
    a. 51.8%
    b. 53.4%
    c. 52.6%
    d. 46.8%

17. Given the ordered pairs below, in the form, $(x, f(x))$, which represent values and their corresponding probabilities, what is the expected value?
$(0, 18), (1, 12), (2, 20), (3, 24), (4, 10), (5, 36), (6, 4)$
   a. 354
   b. 362
   c. 368
   d. 374

18. You draw two cards from a deck with cards labeled $1 - 6$ and then graph the probabilities of the expected value of picking a 3 after choosing 2 cards. Which of the following represents the probabilities that correspond to x-values of 0, 1, and 2 cards?
   a. $\frac{2}{3}, \frac{1}{3}, 0$
   b. $\frac{1}{3}, \frac{1}{6}, 0$
   c. $\frac{2}{3}, \frac{1}{3}, \frac{1}{5}$
   d. $\frac{1}{3}, \frac{1}{6}, \frac{1}{9}$

For questions 19-20, consider the set of data below:
   38 49 22 36 45 27 38 47 20 21 19 38 17 28 15 18 42 17 25 33 31

19. Organize the data using a stem-and-leaf plot.

   1 |
   2 |
   3 |
   4 |

20. State the mean, median, and mode(s). If necessary, round to the nearest tenth.
   Mean: _____
   Median: _____
   Mode: _____

21. Given the equation, $\frac{2}{x+4} = \frac{3}{x}$, what is the value of x?
   a. 10
   b. 12
   c. −12
   d. −14

22. Which of the following represents the points of intersection of the line, $x + y = -6$ and a circle, given by the equation, $(x - 2)^2 + (y + 4)^2 = 16$?
   a. $(2, -6)$ and $(-2, 4)$
   b. $(-2, -4)$ and $(2, -8)$
   c. $(2, 4)$ and $(-2, 8)$
   d. $(-2, -6)$ and $(2, -12)$

23. What is the solution to the equation, $\frac{x}{x+4} - \frac{3}{4} = \frac{4}{x+4}$?
    a. $x = 22$
    b. $x = 24$
    c. $x = 26$
    d. $x = 28$

24. Which of the following represents the solutions of the system of equations, $\begin{array}{l} y = x + 2 \\ y = x^2 + 2 \end{array}$?
    a. $(1, 3)$ and $(2, 0)$
    b. $(3, 1)$ and $(0, 2)$
    c. $(1, 3)$ and $(0, 2)$
    d. $(3, 1)$ and $(2, 0)$

25. The path of ball thrown into the air is modeled by the first quadrant graph of the equation $h = -16t^2 + 47t + 3$, where h is the height of the ball in feet and t is time in seconds after the ball is thrown. The maximum height of the ball occurs at $t = $ _____ seconds, and the ball hits the ground at $t = $ _____ seconds. If necessary, round answers to the nearest tenth.

26. What is the range of the function $g(x) = 2x^2 + 8x + 5$?
    a. $g(x) \geq -3$
    b. $g(x) > -2$
    c. $g(x) \leq -2$
    d. All real numbers

27. The area of a rectangular bedroom is 120 ft², and the perimeter of the room is 44 ft. On a house plan drawn to a $\frac{1}{24}$ scale, what is the length in inches of the longer side of the rectangle representing the room? _____

28. In the figure, C is the center of the circle and $m\angle ACD = 110°$.

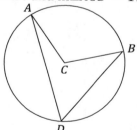

Calculate $m\angle ADB$.

$m\angle ACD = $ _____

29. A typical soda can is approximately 4.8 in tall with a diameter of about 2.2 in. Assuming that the can is a perfect cylinder, what is its volume? If necessary, round your answer to the nearest tenth.

Its volume is approximately _____ in³.

30. In isosceles triangle ABC, the length of each leg is 13 and the length of the base is 10. Calculate the area of $\triangle ABC$. Write an exact answer in simplest form.

    a. 60

    b. 65

    c. 130

    d. $\frac{25\sqrt{3}}{2}$

31. In the figure, C is the center of the circle with radius 4. The length of minor arc AB is 3π. Calculate the area of sector ACB. Write your answer in terms of π.

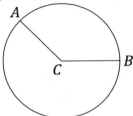

    a. $A = 3\pi$

    b. $A = 4\pi$

    c. $A = 6\pi$

    d. $A = 8\pi$

Math - No-Calculator

1. Given the system of equations, $\begin{array}{l} 3x + 6y = 36 \\ 2x + 9y = 34 \end{array}$, which of the following equations may be added to produce the correct y-value solution?

    a. $\begin{array}{l} 6x + 15y = 72 \\ -6x - 36y = -102 \end{array}$

    b. $\begin{array}{l} 6x + 12y = 72 \\ -6x - 27y = -102 \end{array}$

    c. $\begin{array}{l} 6x + 12y = 108 \\ -6x - 27y = -102 \end{array}$

    d. $\begin{array}{l} 6x + 15y = 108 \\ -6x - 36y = -72 \end{array}$

2. Jonathan pays a \$65 monthly flat rate for his cell phone. He is charged \$0.12 per minute for each minute used, in a roaming area. Which of the following expressions represents his monthly cell phone bill for x roaming minutes?

    a. $65 + 0.12x$
    b. $65x + 0.12$
    c. $65.12x$
    d. $65.12 + 0.12x$

3. Which of the following equations is represented by the graph shown below?

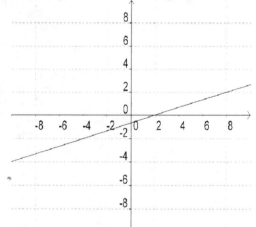

    a. $14x - 21y = 7$
    b. $12x - 6y = 16$
    c. $7x - 21y = 14$
    d. $16x - 18y = 12$

4. A taxi ride costs \$4.25 for the first mile and \$0.70 for each mile after the first. Which of the following functions $c(d)$ gives the total cost (in dollars) of traveling d miles (assuming that $d \geq 1$)?

    a. $c(d) = 3.55 + 0.70(d + 1)$
    b. $c(d) = 3.55 + 0.70(d - 1)$
    c. $c(d) = 4.25 + 0.70d$
    d. $c(d) = 4.25 + 0.70(d - 1)$

5. A pump fills a cylindrical tank with water at a constant rate. The function $L(g) = 0.3g$ represents the water level of the tank (in feet) after g gallons are pumped into the tank. The function $w(t) = 1.2t$ represents the number of gallons that can be pumped into the tank in t minutes. Write a function $L(t)$ for the water level of the tank after t minutes.

    a. $L(t) = 0.25t$
    b. $L(t) = 0.36t$
    c. $L(t) = 0.9t$
    d. $L(t) = 3.6t$

6. Adam has \$10 more than Betty. If Adam were to give \$15 to Betty, then she would have twice as much money as Adam. Write this situation as a system of equations.

    a. $A = B + 10$
       $B + 15 = 2A$

    b. $B = A + 10$
       $B + 15 = 2A$

    c. $A = B + 10$
       $B + 15 = 2(A - 15)$

    d. $B = A + 10$
       $B + 15 = 2(A - 15)$

7. Linear functions grow by equal differences over equal intervals. By what amount does the linear function $f(x) = 4x - 8$ grow by over every interval whose length is 5?

    a. -40
    b. 12
    c. 20
    d. 40

8. The linear function $g(x)$ is graphed below.

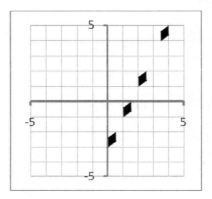

Write an explicit formula for $g(x)$.
    a. $g(x) = -2x - 3$
    b. $g(x) = -5x + 2$
    c. $g(x) = 2x - 3$
    d. $g(x) = 5x + 2$

9. What is the solution to the inequality, $3x + 18 > 6$?
    a. $x > -4$
    b. $x < -4$
    c. $x > -8$
    d. $x < -8$

10. What is the range of the function $g(x) = x - 2$?
    a. $g(x) \geq -8$
    b. $g(x) \geq 8$
    c. $g(x) > 0$
    d. All real numbers

11. Which of the following represents the difference of $(3x^3 - 9x^2 + 6x) - (8x^3 + 4x^2 - 3x)$?
    a. $-5x^3 - 13x^2 + 9x$
    b. $11x^3 - 13x^2 + 3x$
    c. $-5x^3 - 5x^2 + 3x$
    d. $5x^3 + 13x^2 + 9x$

12. Which of the following represents the sum of $(12x^3 - 8x + 6x^2 - 3)$ and $(8x^2 - 20x^3 + 6 - 2x)$?
    a. $-8x^3 + 14x^2 - 10x + 3$
    b. $20x^3 - 28x^2 + 12x - 5$
    c. $-8x^3 + 2x^2 + 6x + 3$
    d. $32x^2 + 14x^2 - 10x - 5$

13. The graph of $y = (x + 3)(x^2 - x - 2)$ has x-intercepts _____ and y-intercept _____.

14. Which of the following is the graph of $y = -2(x - 2)^2 + 1$.

a.

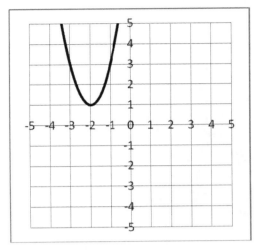

b.

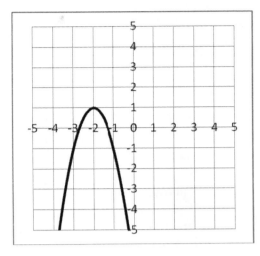

c.

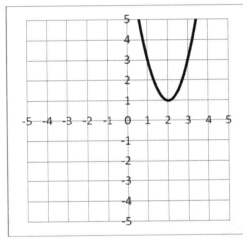

d.

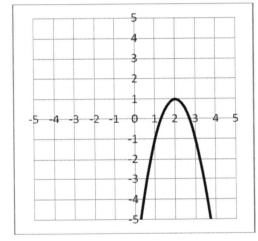

15. What is the domain of the function $f(x) = 2x^2 + 5x - 12$?
   a. $x \geq \dfrac{3}{2}$
   b. $x \leq -4$
   c. $-4 \leq x \leq \dfrac{3}{2}$
   d. All real numbers

16. What is the domain of the function $f(x) = \sqrt{x + 5}$?
   a. $x \geq -5$
   b. $x \geq 5$
   c. $x > 0$
   d. All real numbers

17. In the figure, *ABCD* is a rectangle. Lines *m* and *n* are parallel to $\overline{AB}$ and $\overline{BC}$, respectively, and intersect at point *P*. In addition, they each bisect rectangle. Which transformation of *ABCD* will NOT result in an image that coincides with the original rectangle?

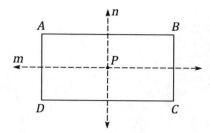

a. A reflection across *m*
b. A reflection across *n*
c. A 90° rotation about *P*
d. A 180° rotation about *P*

Answers and Explanations #1

Reading

U.S. Literature

1. C: The selection does not portray the themes offered in choices A, B, and D.

2. A: Choice B is incorrect because Mother did not forbid any presents. Choices C and D give some of the problems presented in the selection, but do not offer a complete summary.

3. D: The passage states: "'We haven't got Father, and shall not have him for a long time.' She didn't say 'perhaps never,' but each silently added it, thinking of Father far away, where the fighting was." The other choices may be true of Father, but they are not specified in this selection.

4. C: Although choices A and B may be true, they are not specified in this selection. Jo believes choice D to be true, but whether or not she is right is not stated: "'Mother didn't say anything about our money, and she won't wish us to give up everything. Let's each buy what we want, and have a little fun; I'm sure we work hard enough to earn it,' cried Jo."

5. D: The other sisters all specify what they want to buy. Choice A: "'I shall get a nice box of Faber's drawing pencils; I really need them,' said Amy decidedly." Choice B: "'I planned to spend mine in new music,' said Beth." Choice C: "'I do want to buy Undine and Sintran for myself. I've wanted it so long,' said Jo."

6. D: The presence of a hearth brush and kettle-holder indicate a fireplace, and the fact that the fireplace "hears" Beth's sigh when no one else does indicates that Beth is closest to it.

7. B: "Injured" in the context of this sentence means Amy feels that her sense of fairness, vanity, and pride have been injured—not that she has a physical injury (a) or hurt feelings at Meg's words (c), which were "'It's so dreadful to be poor!'"—basically more in agreement with Amy's subsequent sentiment than containing anything to hurt Amy's feelings. There is nothing in this passage indicating Amy has a cold (d); she sniffs to emphasize her sense of unfairness at being deprived of the pretty things some girls have.

8. A: Five paragraphs before this quotation, Beth says she planned to spend her dollar "in new music," so in the context of this entire passage alone we can assume she means practicing music. (We would know from reading the entire novel that Beth plays piano.) Drawing (b) is what Amy does: she says she will buy Faber's drawing pencils with her dollar. Teaching (c) is what Meg does; she complains about it in this passage. Schoolwork (d) is what Amy complains about following Beth's complaint about washing dishes and housecleaning.

9. D: (a) most explicitly shows there is a war going on by describing their father being "where the fighting was." (b) also alludes to war by mentioning "our" army men suffering. (c) only indicates that their father is not with his family and they may be separated for a long time, but it does not say where he is or why.

History/Social Studies

Passage 1

10. C: "Peculiar" can mean odd (a) or bizarre (b), but these make no sense in this context. "Peculiar" can also mean specific (c), unique, particular, distinctive, or characteristic, which is the meaning in this case, because Lincoln was referring to the specific and unique situation that, "One-eighth of the whole population were colored slaves, not distributed generally over the Union, but localized in the southern part of it," and the specific interest these slaves constituted. Appropriate (d) is another synonym offered by a thesaurus for the second (correct) meaning, but its denotation of suitable or fitting does not make sense in this context as specific, unique, particular, distinctive, etc. does.

11. B: The closest meaning is freedom for all citizens, which would include slaves. Lincoln issued the Emancipation Proclamation over nine months before the Gettysburg Address, but the Civil War was still being fought over the issue of slavery. He called for "us the living" to finish the "unfinished work" of soldier and "highly resolve that these dead shall not have died in vain" by giving the nation a "new birth of freedom". Without reaffirming the nation's bases of freedom and equality, the nation would "perish from the earth" and the soldiers would have died in vain. The entire paragraph leads up to this meaning. This does not indicate freedom from war (a): the speech does not say ending the war would bring freedom; but by restoring the nation's original foundations of freedom and equality for which soldiers fought, the dead would not die in vain—not that soldiers should be freed from fighting the war (c). Slavery violated the foundations of US democracy; hence (d) makes no sense in this context.

12. D: Lincoln's Biblical quotation established the subsequent supposition that the war is an example of the woe for causing offenses described in the quotation (just as previously in the same sentence he supposed American slavery was one of the offenses that must needs come). (a) does not support the supposition that God gave the war as woe; if anything, it supports his contention that despite their basic differences regarding slavery, "Both parties deprecated war" (second paragraph, last sentence). (b) reinforces the parallelism and comparison/contrast established in the second paragraph ("saving the Union without war/destroy it without war"; "make war rather than let the nation survive/accept war rather than let it perish") and continued in the third ("Neither...expected....Neither anticipated....Each looked for....") rather than supporting that war was God's giving both sides woe for offenses. (c) supports that even though everyone wanted the war to end soon ("Fondly...away", penultimate sentence), if it lasted longer it would be God's will.

13. A: Lincoln was reminding his audience that the nation was formed with the ideas of liberty and equality as foundations—seen symmetrically in the opening and closing sentences—and reasoning that upholding those ideals was the best way to honor the soldiers who fought for that nation. (b) is not the main idea as he explicitly stated in the third paragraph, first sentence, "we can not consecrate – we cannot hallow – this ground" because the soldiers had done so "far beyond our poor power to add or detract." He continues to say their deeds will never be forgotten even though his and others' words would—making (c) incorrect. Completing soldiers' unfinished work refers not to declaring a cease-fire (d) in particular, but to ensuring the nation's democratic government and its founding principles would not "perish from the earth."

14. D: By using the same syntactic structure in "what we say here" and "what they did here", Lincoln employed parallel structure to reinforce his message contrasting words vs. deeds. Epiphora (a), epistrophe, is repeating the same words/phrases at the *ends* of sentences/clauses. An example in Lincoln's Gettysburg Address is: "that government of the people, by the people, for the people..." in its final sentence. Anaphora (b) is repeating the same words/phrases at the *beginnings* of

- 164 -

clauses/sentences, as Dickens did in the opening of *A Tale of Two Cities*: "It was the best of times, it was the worst of times, it was the age of wisdom, it was the age of foolishness..." etc. (he used "it was" 10 times in one sentence). Repetition (c) involves simply repeating the same word/phrase/clause multiple times. Parallelism/parallel structure does not require exact word repetition, but symmetrical sentence/clause structure arranging the same parts of speech in the same word order.

15. C: In the Second Inaugural Address, Lincoln said in the final paragraph, "...let us strive on to finish the work we are in..." and in the Gettysburg Address, third paragraph, "...to be dedicated here to the unfinished work which they who fought here have thus far so nobly advanced." He spoke of (a), (b), and (d) in the former speech, but not overtly in the latter.

16. B: In the opening paragraph of his second inaugural address, Lincoln discusses his first address, describing how the first actions in the coming Civil War were just beginning to take place. The country had suffered much since then as the war got underway and continued throughout his first term as president. This change in the nation inspired the plea for an end to the hostilities that dominates his second inaugural address.

17. C: Lincoln believed that the South was wrong for making war by trying to secede from the union, and the North was right for trying to maintain the union by refusing to accept the hostile action. This quote shows he believed the actions of the North were more justifiable than those of the South.

18. A: Lincoln states that "if God wills that it [the war] continue ... until every drop of blood drawn with the lash shall be paid by another drawn with the sword, as was said three thousand years ago, so still it must be said 'the judgments of the Lord are true and righteous altogether.'" This statement indicates Lincoln's believe that the war was a product of God's will.

19. D: Lincoln delivered his Second Inaugural Address after a time of great hardship for the United States: the Civil War. His plea for the country's resolution of its severe problems must have been an emotional experience for the president, and his voice must have conveyed this emotionality as he read the speech. As a result, reading the document online could not have quite the same emotional impact as hearing it in person.

Passage 2
20. A: Since the beginning of our American history, we have been engaged in change—in a perpetual peaceful revolution—a revolution which goes on steadily, quietly adjusting itself to changing conditions—without the concentration camp or the quick-lime in the ditch.
This is the only statement listed here that directly supports the idea that FDR thought that America is constantly moving toward a better way of life.

21. A: It emphasizes the need for a social safety net for the aging populace. While the other ideas in Choices B and C are clearly mentioned in the blog, they are not derived from the speech. Choice A is the only one that discusses an idea that shows up in the speech.

22. B: The average citizen already feels overburdened by taxes and feels the money is not being well-spent by the government. The argument that needs to be evaluated is that people will be happy to give more money in taxes to the government. It would be safe to raise the counterargument that the general population may already believe they are paying enough in taxes and don't think the government is spending that money wisely. Not everyone will be happy to give

more to the government to spend. Choices A and D do not address the question. Choice C actually agrees with FDR's premise.

23. D: There are four basic freedoms that are vital to the health of people: speech, worship, freedom from want, and freedom from fear. This speech is typically referred to as the "Four Freedoms" speech. In it, FDR articulates the basic freedoms he believes in. These freedoms are the central focus of the speech, since it supports the other ideas that he is focusing on (ie, social issues). Choice A is a detail in the speech, Choice B is not articulated, and Choice C is not in the speech.

24. C: FDR spoke of freedom, defining it in the previous paragraph as "the supremacy of human rights everywhere." This is the "high concept" he refers to in the following paragraph/sentence. In this context, the "end" of victory does not mean death (a). It does not precisely mean purpose (b), as in the common phrase "a means to an end" (a way of achieving a purpose): he was not saying victory was the only purpose of the concept, but rather that this concept could have no other outcome (c) or result than victory. "End" can also mean conclusion (d), i.e., the termination or finishing of something, which does not fit the meaning in this context quite as precisely as (c) because it does not imply cause and effect as "outcome" does.

25. D: After describing the four freedoms he identified, FDR said the vision of a world founded on those freedoms was "no vision of a distant millennium" but "a definite basis for a kind of world attainable in our own time and generation. That kind of world is the very antithesis of the so-called new order of tyranny..." referring to the "order" that dictators wanted to impose, to which "we oppose the greater conception—the moral order. He further described the "cooperation of free countries, working together in a friendly, civilized society" as the "world order which we seek". This context establishes that "order" more nearly means a system of societal and world politics (d) rather than a military leader's command (a); an authoritative decision or direction (b), e.g., a court order or a doctor's order; or an arrangement in sequence (c), e.g., alphabetical, numerical, or chronological order.

26. A: Following the paragraph beginning, "I have called for personal sacrifice", FDR said, "A part of the sacrifice means the payment of more money in taxes" for "a greater portion of this great defense program". While he called for taxpayers to support the military, in this passage he did not equate personal sacrifice with serving in the military (b). While he described worldwide arms reduction (c), he did not equate this with personal sacrifice, but with the fourth freedom: freedom from fear. The four freedoms (d) he identified were "essential human freedoms", i.e., things all human beings had rights to, not examples of personal sacrifice.

27. D: FDR implicitly referred to the American Revolutionary War (a) by contrasting it with the process of continual change which he characterized as America's ongoing *perpetual peaceful revolution*". He continued a pattern of implicit contrast by further characterizing this peaceful revolution as adjusting to change "without the concentration camp or the quick-lime in the ditch." Concentration camps were established by the Nazis during World War II as part of the Holocaust; quicklime was used in trenches during World War I (b), when trench warfare was widely practiced. In World War II (c), soldiers dug more individual foxholes than trenches (though there were some); but quicklime was also used by Nazis in mass graves of people they murdered and on the floors of train cattle cars transporting people to concentration camps, labor camps, and death camps.

28. C: In this passage there is no mention of expanding the draft of citizens into military service. As examples of aspects of the social economy needing "immediate improvement", FDR cited, "We should bring more citizens under the coverage of old-age pensions...." (a); "We should widen the

- 166 -

opportunities for adequate medical care" (b); and "We should plan a better system by which persons deserving or needing gainful employment may obtain it" (d).

29. B: Antistrophe is repeating a word/phrase at the end of each sentence/clause as FDR did in the successive sentences (which are also paragraphs) defining the four freedoms. Anastrophe (a) is inverting word order for emphasis, e.g., Longfellow's "the forest primeval" (*Evangeline*) or JFK's "**Ask not** what your country can do for you...." Apostrophe (c) is interrupting dialogue or narration to address the reader, audience, or a personification thereof directly ("Dear reader, what would you do in my place?" or an actor in a play speaking to the audience instead of other actors). Aposiopesis (d) is abruptly leaving a statement unfinished, e.g., "You do that once more and I'll—".

Science

Passage 1
30. C: The passage describes several distinctive features of annelid anatomy and tells how some of them differ from other worms.

31. A: The term is defined in the text as an organization of the anatomy into segments.

32. D: The term is defined in the text between commas.

33. C: The text gives the example of feet specializing into grasping organs to illustrate this evolutionary advantage of segmental plasticity.

34. D: The text gives the example of parapodia modified for grasping to illustrate evolutionary plasticity among metameres.

35. C: The text defines metemeres as segments, and discusses segmentation as the distinguishing feature of the phylum.

36. D: The paragraph tells us that annelids can live in salt or fresh water and on land, and then gives examples.

37. D: Stating that metameric segmentation is the distinguishing feature of the Annelid phylum (c) is stating a fact; though it is true, simply identifying this characteristic does not automatically inform the reader of the evolutionary flexibility it confers. The author establishes this flexibility by writing, "...certain segments can be modified and specialized to perform specific functions." To illustrate such modification and specialization, the author continues with (a) and (b), which are both actual examples of such modification and specialization.

38. D: The author compares (a) annelids and nematodes as both having a fluid-filled internal *coelum* or cavity separating the body wall and gut, and both having this cavity involved in their locomotion. The author also contrasts (b) the two phyla in that annelids develop this cavity much later during both embryonic growth and ("presumably") evolutionary progress. Hence both (d) relationships are established, meaning (c) [Neither] is incorrect.

Passage 2
39. A: the movement of the Earth around the sun. Only this choice provides support for the idea of special relativity. Choice B. is used in the explanation, but does not provide support on its own.

Choice C. is actually part of a counterargument to relativity. Choice D. only indicates that there are two sections, and does not provide any support.

40. B: If relativity is valid, then why can it not explain all parts of the natural world, including the rules of quantum mechanics? Only this choice deals closely with an argument against relativity. The classical laws of motion are in agreement with relativity. Choice C. does not pose an argument against relativity and Choice D. focuses on asking a detailed question about the thought experiment, not the entire theory.

41. C: validity regarding an understanding of the classical rules of motion. The word "truth" was quoted because Einstein was referring to the understanding of the laws of motion we had before relativity, which did indeed seem to provide the correct answers for a great deal of physics questions. However, according to the other sentences around this word, we can conclude that it does not refer to an absolute truth because relativity turns classical ideas on their heads.

42. B: Corresponding to the noun "delicacy", one meaning of the adjective "delicate" is fragile (a) or easily damaged. This meaning is not supported by the context. As it modifies "detail", delicacy here refers to how sensitively and specifically classical mechanics describes the movements of stars, planets, etc. Another meaning of a delicacy is an expensive and/or rare delight (c), especially regarding food; e.g., caviar is considered a delicacy. This meaning makes no sense in this context. Delicacy can also refer to soft texture (d), e.g., the delicacy of a lace fabric. This meaning does not relate to the subject matter.

43. D: *A priori* is Latin, meaning literally "from the one before". In the context of Einstein's discussion, he means that because the principle of relativity can be generalized so broadly across domains, its applying so precisely in one domain predicts it would apply with comparable accuracy in another domain; and therefore, that its being valid for one domain but not another is not very likely. It is *a priori* not very likely when considering this application of a general principle to a specific domain, and this unlikeliness is logically true/valid independent of observation or experience.

44. A: Einstein used and defined this term in the same sentence: "However, the most careful observations have never revealed such anisotropic properties in terrestrial physical space, i.e., a physical non-equivalence of different directions." The latter boldfaced portion is the definition. Hence the meaning is explicit, not implicit; and physicists are not the only ones who would know the meaning (b) without the definition: it is also used in biology, botany, medicine, optics, and zoology, for example. Einstein did not coin this term (c); its origin is c. 1875-1880, and Einstein was born in 1879. He also had not defined it in an earlier paragraph (c) of this passage, but within the same sentence where he used it. Thus it is not true that he never defined it (d). Neither is it true that anyone can tell its meaning from context (d) here. If it were, he would not have defined it for his audience/readers.

45. C: As Einstein indicated in the sentence following this one, "This statement is called the principle of relativity (in the restricted sense)." The statements in (a), (b), and (d) are all conclusions predicated upon the condition that this principle were NOT true: (a) begins with "If the principle of relativity (in the restricted sense) does not hold," continuing with the "then" clause quoted. (b) continues from (a), saying, "In this case we should be constrained to believe that..." finishing with the clause quoted. (d) is prefaced by, "If the principle of relativity were not valid" and continues with the clause quoted.

46. A: The quoted phrase is most an example of understatement. To emphasize through reversal how exquisite he found the detail provided by classical mechanics, Einstein downplayed it by describing it as less than wonderful, but only a little less. He further qualified this by not writing "*nothing* short of wonderful", but "*little* short of wonderful", making it comparative rather than absolute. An example of overstatement (b) or hyperbole in this case would be something like "the most wonderful ever seen", "too wonderful to be believed", etc. Amplification (c) is repeating a word/phrase but with added details or expanded description for emphasis; e.g., "...it supplies us with the actual motions of the heavenly bodies with a delicacy of detail—a delicacy of detail so fine that it can only be perceived as wonderful." Metabasis (d) is a transitional summary that recapitulates what was said previously and predicts what will be said next, to clarify and organize discourse.

47. C: Of the first five paragraphs, the first four are completely positive in Einstein's assertions and explanations of his claims; the fifth is also mainly positive, with only a hint of counterclaim in its last sentence refuted to emphasize the claim's validity ("But that [this] principle...should hold...in one domain...and yet...be invalid for another, is a priori not very probable."). The last two paragraphs present counterclaims, introduced by "If the principle of relativity does not hold..." and similar clauses, followed by "then..." conclusions illustrating the logically necessary yet improbable results of such counterclaims.

Writing and Language

Careers

1. A: Paragraph 2 begins with a transition from paragraph 1 by referring to the same topic—what software developers do—as it further specifies this. Paragraph 3 begins with a transition from paragraph 2 by referring to information in both paragraphs 1 and 2 as it gives additional details about developers sometimes called IT project managers. The last sentence in paragraph 3 creates a transition by introducing the subtopics of paragraphs 4 and 5. This is the *only* place where the transition is explicitly at the end of the preceding paragraph (b) rather than introducing the next one. Since there are between-paragraph transitions in this passage, (c) is incorrect. Since there are multiple transitions, (d) is also incorrect.

2. D: The passage identifies systems software designers as those who design operating systems; Apple's iOS and Google's Android are operating systems. The late Steve Jobs (a) did not design any original Apple operating systems (OSs); he was not an engineer and did not write code. He did make changes and additions to others' designs. (Except for the Apple II "monitor" program which included Allen Baum's assistance, Steve Wozniak designed all of the Apple I and Apple II OSs by himself.) Bill Gates (a) co-founded the Microsoft Corporation with Paul Allen; he did not design Google's Android OS. Besides, this passage does not mention either name. Applications software designers (c) design games, programs, and other software applications rather than OSs; the passage makes this distinction. Hence (b) is incorrect.

3. B: The first paragraph of this passage gives a general description of what software developers do. The succeeding paragraphs all give more specific details about this topic. This passage does not introduce a problem and then provide a solution for it (a). Although it does describe the different types of software (applications and operating systems) designed by different types of software developers (applications software developers and systems software developers) respectively, it simply identifies what they each design without discussing their similarities and differences; and does not point out similarities and differences (c) otherwise or overall between aspects of software development. It does not explain how certain factors caused certain effects (d) regarding the topic.

4. C: The first paragraph of this passage states that software developers return to their design processes to improve their programs or solve problems if customers find the programs too hard to use or the programs do not work as expected; and that developers may conduct maintenance and upgrades for their programs after they become available to the public. This information is evidence that refutes the claim described in the question. Therefore (a) is incorrect. There is no evidence in the passage to support this claim (b); therefore, (d) is also incorrect.

5. A: This passage has an introduction(s): The first sentence introduces both the first paragraph and the entire passage topic; and the entire first paragraph can also be considered an introduction to the rest of the passage as it gives a more general summary of the topic, while the other paragraphs provide more specific details. There is no conclusion, which can be expected in a passage which could be excerpted from a longer work. Since there is an introduction but no conclusion, (b) is incorrect. Since there is no conclusion, (c) is incorrect. Since there is an introduction, (d) is incorrect.

6. B: To agree with the plural noun "(software) developers", "for software programs" should also be plural. The sentence as is (a) combines plural and singular nouns. Version (c) further specifies the singular by adding "one", but the singular object still disagrees with the plural subject; also, "one"

changes the meaning. While (d) uses a plural object to agree with the plural subject, it also further specifies "programs" by adding "many", which changes the meaning.

7. A: This clause is correct as it is. Current convention dictates that "code", i.e., computer programming code, is a mass (collective or non-count) noun; and "writing code" is the conventional expression. Because the sense of "code" in this context is NOT as a count noun, both using the plural "codes" (b) and specifying a singular count noun by using the article "a" (c) are incorrect. Although the word "coding" has become convention as a synonym for "*writing* code", this "-ing" progressive participle is only used that way—as a verb, but NOT as a noun or synonym for "code" (d).

8. B: Although in some cases it is preferable to keep the auxiliary verb ("are") and verb participle ("called") together, this depends on the individual instance. If placing a modifier outside the two reads or sounds awkward, placing it between them as in this case is better. "...are sometimes called" is not only smoother and less awkward than "sometimes are called"; the latter also is less clear: in that position, "sometimes" could modify either "supervise" before it or "called" after it. Placing the adverb at the end of the sentence (c) also reads awkwardly, plus detracts from the emphasis on the descriptor "information technology (IT) project managers" by following it with another word; and moreover interrupts the transition to the next sentence, "These workers...." Placing "sometimes" after "called" (d) is not only awkward but incorrect. To be correct and make sense, "sometimes" would need commas to signal its intervention between predicate and object to modify the verb (i.e., "are called, sometimes, information...."); but this would still be more awkward than (b).

9. C: By identifying both "the Internet" and "within a company's intranet" in the same sentence, the reader can infer that an intranet belongs to a single company, unlike the Internet. Company intranets have access restricted to the company's employees, owners, and other authorized users (a). Intranets are neither as large as the Internet, nor separate from it (b) because they use protocols and software developed for the Internet. An intranet does not refer to the Internet as used by one specific company (d), which does not make sense since any company with Internet access can use the Internet.

10. C: The context of the passage establishes that databases are software applications in the fourth paragraph by identifying applications software developers as designing computer applications and then stating, "Some applications software developers create complex <u>databases</u> for organizations." From the context, (a) is incorrect because the passage differentiates applications from operating systems, including databases in paragraph 4 about applications developers but not in paragraph 5 about systems developers. Paragraph 4 also specifies "databases for organizations"; it only identifies "commercial software to be sold to the general public", not databases (b). Paragraph 5 defines system interfaces (d) as enabling users to interact with operating systems and the computers running them. The passage never equates databases with interfaces and moreover differentiates them by identifying databases as applications developed by applications developers but interfaces as developed by systems developers.

11. D: The graph shows that all occupations are projected to increase in employment by 11% from 2012-2022; occupations in business and financial operations are projected to increase by 13% during the same period; and occupations as personal financial advisors are projected to increase by 27% during that time. Even without comparing these numbers, one can easily see by looking at the bars in the graph that the third category is projected to increase by far more than the first two. Therefore, if software developers are included in the total of all occupations, which is projected to increase by less the other two, (d) is true. The other choices are not true because the bar including software developers would have to be longer than the other two for software developer

employment to be projected to increase by the same amount as (b), or more than either (c) or both of (a) the others.

History/Social Studies

12. A: *Imbued* in this context means *permeated* or *saturated*, which is the sense that this sentence is trying to convey.

13. D: The wording in this revision option is the only one that makes grammatical sense.

14. D: Choices A, B, and C all have similar meanings and match the text's description of Lubitsch's film style as elegant or sophisticated.

15. C: This phrase is used in the last sentence to describe the Lubitsch style.

16. B: Lubitsch's focus on seemingly irrelevant details as symbols is described in the text as his signature style. (Paragraph 2)

17. C: Lubitsch was invited in 1923 by Albert Zukor.

18. D: Made in 1912, the film could not have been a talkie, as it was not until 1923 that Lubitsch went to Hollywood to use sound technology. And the text tells us nothing of the film's content or cast.

19. A: Monescu and Lily were both thieves who posed as members of high society. Mariette was a real heiress, and Lubitsch, of course, was a director, not a character in the film.

20. C: This, indeed, is the underlying theme of the entire movie, as shown by the characters of Monescu and Lily, who appear to be elegant but are, in fact, thieves.

21. B: Lily has no wealth of her own, but Monescu finally chooses her over Mariette and her fortune. (Paragraph 5)

22. B: Lily passes herself off as a countess and Montescu poses as a baron (Paragraph 5).

Humanities

23. B: This is the only revision of the phrase that uses proper grammar and punctuation.

24. D Since the sentence ends with a period, it may not be phrased as a question, this is the correct revision.

25. C: In general, the first paragraph in an essay (of any length) introduces the discussion at hand or frames a particular debate. Most introductory paragraphs do not introduce extensive content. In this paragraph, there is no clear stance taken on either Buddhist or Western notions of the self, and so choices A and B are inappropriate. Choice C is a good answer because it stresses that the purpose of the first paragraph is to introduce a tension and not to make judgments one way or another. Choice D is inappropriate because "egolessness" is not discussed until the second paragraph. The best choice, then, is C.

26. D: Insofar as this is a definition question, the reader should look back to the passage for the exact wording of the definition. Doing so reveals that choice A is inappropriate because

it is explicitly rejected as a valid definition within the passage. Choice B is inappropriate because superego and id are not mentioned within the passage. Choice C is inappropriate because it is the definition for "ego-toxicity." Choice D is a good choice because it is the definition of "egolessness" given in the passage.

27. A: This question is easy to over think. In the second paragraph "egolessness" and "ego-toxicity" are defined and contrasted. The purpose of this paragraph, then, should mention this in some form. Choice A is good because it captures the fact that these terms are distinguished in the paragraph. Choice B is inappropriate because the paragraph only mentions the conflict that Buddhists feel—there is no judgment made on the conflict. Choices C and D are inappropriate because the paragraph does not praise one perspective over another.

28. D: Looking to the passage, it seems as if "*quid pro quo*" means something like "if I do something, then I will be rewarded with something good." Choice A is not a good choice because it says "if I don't do anything, I will get something good." Choice B is inappropriate because money is not mentioned. While choice C might seem like a good choice, the passage does not really talk about what people deserve as much as it talks about what people should do or how they should behave. Choice D is a good choice because "something for something" implies the sort of exchange described in the passage.

29. D: This question asks for a detail from the passage, not for a larger, general idea. Choice A is inappropriate because this position describes ego-toxicity, not Buddhist egolessness. Choice B is inappropriate not only because Buddhists do not act out of expectation of reward, but also because the passage does not mention heaven. Choice C is inappropriate because the passage does not address the idea of reincarnation. Choice D is the best choice because in addition to doing good out of compassion, Buddhists do good because it is good for all beings.

30. C: In the first paragraph, the third sentence identifies increased tension in recent decades between individualism and collectivism in the West. This is developed in subsequent paragraphs by the discussion of ego-toxicity vs. egolessness reflecting individualism vs. collectivism. The second sentence (a) provides evidence supporting the first sentence, not a main idea. The fourth sentence (b) provides evidence supporting the third sentence. The first sentence (d) focuses only on Western emphasis of individualism over collectivism, not on the tension between the two that is a main idea on which the following paragraphs elaborate.

31. A: The sentence is in the best position for the most logical organization. Moving it to the end of the paragraph (a) would be illogical because as it is now, it precedes the sentence "Buddhists who live in <u>such societies</u>....", which refers back to <u>"In Western societies..."</u> so reversing their order would make no sense. Moving it to the beginning of the paragraph (c) would interrupt the transition between the previous paragraph's last sentence, "...the struggles that Western Buddhists face" and the second paragraph's first sentence, "Central to Buddhist belief is the idea of 'egolessness.'" The latter sentence logically follows the former one. Not only would moving the quoted sentence interrupt this logical progression; it would moreover mention ego-toxicity prematurely—before it is introduced in the second paragraph's third sentence. The quoted sentence should not be removed entirely from the paragraph (d) as it further specifies ego-toxicity, introduced and defined in the previous sentence, as prevalent in Western societies; hence it provides essential information.

32. D: The last sentence in each paragraph of this passage identifies "struggles", "caught between", "The struggle...continues"—all referring to a main conflict between individualism and collectivism—and the final sentence resolves it by stating that abandoning ego-toxicity enables compassionate caring for self and others. Hence none of these sentences identifies only half of this conflict, and the final sentence is not the only one to complete it (a). The first sentence of each paragraph does not identify this main conflict (b), (c); only the first sentence of the third paragraph does. In the first paragraph, the first sentence identifies Western emphasis of one over the other, not the conflict between them. In the second paragraph, the first sentence identifies the idea of "egolessness" central to Buddhist belief, not its conflict with ego-toxicity identified later in the paragraph. The final sentence does not simply reiterate the conflict (b) but resolves it.

33. B: This passage is best characterized as persuasive because the author is making a point, arguing in its favor, and providing evidence to support it. Descriptive (a) text paints a vivid picture of a person, place, thing, scene, or situation by providing many specific sensory details to help readers imagine they are really experiencing it. Expository (c) prose provides factual information objectively without adding the author's opinions or seeking to convince readers of anything. Narrative (d) text tells readers a story.

Science
34. C: In terms of determining their validity, hypotheses are confirmed or disconfirmed. None of the other options are meaningful.

35. D: Since the sentence begins in the present tense, it should continue in the present tense as well. The proper verb to be used in this clause is *affect*, meaning to have an impact, not *effect*, meaning to bring about.

36. C: With a complex passage like this one, main idea questions may require a re-reading of the relevant portion of the passage because some answer choices may not apply to the question. Answer choice D, for example, is the main idea of the first paragraph, not the second. Answer choices A and B on the other hand, are details that are directly contradicted by the passage. C is the only answer choice that is not contradicted by the passage and applies to the specified paragraph.

37. C: Even though this question seems like it requires logical operations, it actually asks for a detail from the passage. Choice A is inappropriate because something that is neither x nor y is irrelevant to the passage. Choice B is inappropriate because something that is both x and y proves the hypothesis. Choice C is a good choice because, using the monkey example, a monkey (x) that has no hair (y) disproves the hypothesis "all monkeys are hairy." Choice D is inappropriate because it is irrelevant to the passage. An example of something that is y but not x could be a hairy llama.

38. D: This is also a detail question. It asks why the author discusses "sample sets." A good answer to this question will say something about probability and/or the size of sample sets. Choice A is inappropriate because the passage does not discuss different monkey species. Choice B is inappropriate because the sample set example shows that it is practically impossible to prove that all monkeys are hairy. Choice C is inappropriate because the passage shows that neither large nor small sample sets can prove hypotheses. Choice D is the best choice because the passage shows that to prove a hypothesis about monkeys, the sample set needed would be functionally too large— every monkey past, present, and future, would have to be examined.

39. D: This question asks the reader to apply information learned in the passage to a new instance. In this case, an eighteen-wheel automobile will lower the probability of the hypothesis "all

automobiles have only four wheels." Choices A and C are inappropriate because they refer to proving and disproving and not lowering probability. Choice B is inappropriate because it refers to raising and not lowering probability. Choice D is the best answer because an eighteen wheel automobile decreases the probability that all automobiles have only four wheels.

40. A: The main idea of the entire passage is found in the first sentence of the first paragraph. This is not the main idea of only the first paragraph (b) since the entire first paragraph itself is comprised of only two sentences. The second sentence of the first paragraph gives an example of the main idea stated in the first paragraph rather than being included with the first sentence as the main idea (c). Since (a) is correct, (d) is incorrect.

41. C: According to the second paragraph, third sentence, it is NOT possible to prove a hypothesis using only one single piece of evidence (a). However, it IS possible to disprove a hypothesis with just one piece of evidence (b), (c). Therefore, (d) is incorrect.

42. D: This paragraph uses examples to establish the idea that "Single pieces of evidence...seem to affect a given hypothesis in radically different ways." Based on the preceding sentences in this paragraph, which show how it can be impossible to prove a hypothesis using evidence if even one piece of evidence can disprove, the conclusion in the paragraph's last sentence that it is better to describe confirming hypotheses as probabilistic (i.e., rather than absolute) is a logical one. Since it is, this sentence is not irrelevant to the passage topic and should not be deleted (a). It is not irrelevant to this particular paragraph and should not be moved to another paragraph (b). This sentence can be said to infer and is related to the topic, but it is not unrelated to the purpose (c), which apparently is to discuss hypothesis confirmation and propose one method, identifying its disadvantages and advantages.

43. B: The second sentence of the same last passage paragraph states, "In the monkey example, every single monkey in the history of monkeys would need to be examined before the hypothesis could be proven or disproven." In the last passage sentence, "...infinite sample sets for confirmation or disconfirmation" refers directly to that second sentence (quoted above here). The initial sentence of this paragraph (a) states that evidence-based hypotheses must use probability because sample sets are too large, which agrees with the sentence following it, but does not specifically identify infinite sample sets as that second sentence following it does. The fourth sentence of the previous paragraph (c) shows how even one piece of evidence out of a very large—but NOT infinite—sample size of one billion can disprove a hypothesis rather than showing how infinite sample sizes are required. Since (b) is correct, (d) is incorrect.

44. C: This passage does not contain any sentence fragments (a) as all sentences are complete, each having a subject and predicate and all necessary function words, etc. There are no run-on sentences in this passage (b) as all sentences are separated appropriately with capitalized first letters and periods at the ends and use correct internal punctuation. Since (c) is correct, (d) is incorrect.

Math - Calculator

1. B: Since Elli will plant a total of 20 flowers, the number of roses plus the number of tulips is 20 or $R + T = 20$. Each rose costs \$14; so multiply the number of roses by 14. Each tulip costs \$4; so multiply the number of tulips by 4. Elli has a total of \$100 to spend on roses and tulips. So $14R + 4T = 100$.

2. D: Use a linear system of equations to find the number of roses. See the explanation for question 36. In this case, the system of equations is $R + T = 20$ and $14R + 4T = 100$. Begin with $R + T = 20$ and solve for T.

$$R + T = 20$$
$$T = 20 - R$$

Now substitute the equation for T into the equation $14R + 4T = 100$.

$$14R + 4T = 100$$
$$14R + 4(20 - R) = 100$$
$$14R + 80 - 4R = 100$$
$$10R = 20$$
$$R = 2$$

Therefore, Elli will plant 2 roses in her garden.

3. C: The number of roses, R is 2 and $R + T = 20$. Therefore, $T = 20 - 2 = 18$. Hence, Elli will plant 18 tulips in her garden.

4. B: Based on the given information, roses cost \$14 while tulips cost only \$4. Therefore, tulips are less expensive than roses. No information is given about the amount of space or fertilizer tulips require or about which flower Elli thinks is prettier.

5. C: Using the method of elimination to solve the system of linear equations, each term in the top equation may be multiplied by −2, while each term in the bottom equation may be multiplied by 5. Doing so produces two new equations with x-terms that will add to 0. The sum of $-10x - 18y = 14$ and $10x - 20y = 100$ may be written as $-38y = 114$, where $y = -3$. Substituting the y-value of −3 into the top, original equation gives $5x + 9(-3) = -7$. Solving for x gives $x = 4$. Thus, the solution is $= 4$, $y = -3$.

6. \$12.00, 0, \$31.50:
Writing and solving a system of equations is one way to determine the cost of a package of cookie dough. Let c represent the cost of each package of cookie dough and p the cost of each package of pretzels. An individual's order cost is equal the number of packages of cookie dough ordered times the cost per package of dough plus the number of packages of pretzels ordered times the cost per package of pretzels. Using the information from the order form for Cedric's and Madhavi's orders,

$$3c + 2p = 51$$
$$1c + 4p = 42$$

A system of linear equations can be solved using a variety of methods, including the elimination (or linear combination) method shown here. Since the question asks for the cost of cookie dough, eliminate the variable p by multiplying the top equation by -2

$$-2(3c + 2p = 51) \rightarrow -6c - 4p = -102$$

and combining the result with the other equation. Then, solve the resulting equation for c.

$$-6c - 4p = -102$$
$$\underline{+\ 1c + 4p = \quad 42}$$
$$-5c \qquad = -60$$
$$c = 12$$

James bought two packages of cookie dough for $12.00 each; since his order total was $24.00, he must not have purchased any packages of pretzels.

To determine Mei Ling's total order cost, first find the cost per package of pretzels. Madhavi bought one package of cookie dough for $12.00, and her order total was $42.00; it follows that she spent $42.00 − $12.00 = $30.00 on four packages of pretzels. Each package of pretzels therefore costs $\frac{\$30}{4}$=$7.50.

Mei Ling ordered two packages of cookies at $12.00 per package and one package of pretzels at $7.50 per package, so her order total was 2($12.00) + ($7.50) = $31.50.

7. C: Probably the simplest way to solve this equation is to first get rid of the fractions by multiplying each term by their lowest common denominator, which is $6x$: then we have $\frac{6x}{2x} + \frac{6x}{x} = \frac{6x}{6}$, which reduces to 3 + 6 = x. So, x = 3 + 6 = 9.

8. A: The data set, shown in Choice A, correctly represents a frequency of 4 for the interval 1 – 10, a frequency of 3 for 11 – 20, a frequency of 4 for 21 – 30, a frequency of 10 for 31 – 40, and a frequency of 9 for 41 – 50.

9. C: The total distance traveled was 8 + 3.6 = 11.6 miles. The first 1/5 of a mile is charged at the higher rate. Since 1/5 = 0.2, the remainder of the trip is 11.4 miles. Thus, the fare for the distance traveled is computed as $5.50 + 5(11.4)($1.50) = $91.00. To this, the charge for waiting time must be added, which is simply 9($0.20) = $1.80. Finally, add the two charges, $91 + $1.80 = $92.80.

10. B: First, determine the proportion of students in the fifth grade. Since the total number of students is 180, this proportion is $\frac{36}{180}$ = 0.2, or 20%. Next, determine the same proportion of the total prizes, which is 20% of 20, or 0.2(20) = 4.

11. B: The probability of events, A or B, may be written as $P(A \text{ or } B) = P(A) + P(B) - P(A \text{ and } B)$. The probabilities of A and B are given, as is the probability of A, given B, so first use the formula $P(A \text{ and } B) = P(B) \cdot P(A|B)$. Thus, $P(A \text{ and } B) = 0.34 \cdot 0.46 = 0.1564$. Substituting all probabilities gives 0.18 + 0.34 − 0.1564, which equals 0.3636. Thus, the probability that he goes to the store or to the movies is 36.36%.

12. C: The expected value is equal to the sum of the products of the scholarship amounts and probability she will attend each college, or $\frac{1}{3}$. Thus, the expected value is $\left(6000 \cdot \frac{1}{3}\right) + \left(4500 \cdot \frac{1}{3}\right) + \left(5500 \cdot \frac{1}{3}\right)$, which equals 5,333. So, she can expect to receive $5,333.

13. A: The data set, shown in Choice A, correctly represents a frequency of 4 for the interval 1 – 10, a frequency of 3 for 11 – 20, a frequency of 4 for 21 – 30, a frequency of 10 for 31 – 40, and a frequency of 9 for 41 – 50.

14. C: The probability of independent events, A and B, may be found using the formula, $P(A \text{ and } B) = P(A) \cdot P(B)$. Thus, the probability she draws a jack, replaces it, and then draws an ace card may be represented as $P(A \text{ and } B) = \frac{4}{52} \cdot \frac{4}{52}$, which simplifies to $P(A \text{ and } B) = \frac{1}{169}$.

15. A: The frequency table for Choice A correctly shows the frequencies represented by the histogram. The frequencies of values, falling between 1 and 10 is 3, between 11 and 20 is 9, between 21 and 30 is 8, between 31 and 40 is 6, and between 41 and 50 is 4.

16. A: Candidate A's vote percentage is determined by the number of votes that he obtained, divided by the total number of votes cast, and then multiplied by 100 to convert the decimal into a percentage. Therefore,
Candidate A's vote percentage $= \frac{36,800}{36,800+32,100+2,100} = \frac{36,800}{71,000} = 51.8\%$.

17. C: The expected value is equal to the sum of the products of the probabilities and their x-values. Thus, the expected value is $(0 \cdot 18) + (1 \cdot 12) + (2 \cdot 20) + (3 \cdot 24) + (4 \cdot 10) + (5 \cdot 36) + (6 \cdot 4)$. The expected value equals 368.

18. A: The table below represents the probabilities:

x	f(x)
0	$\frac{\binom{1}{0}\binom{5}{2}}{\binom{6}{2}} = \frac{2}{3}$
1	$\frac{\binom{1}{1}\binom{5}{1}}{\binom{6}{2}} = \frac{1}{3}$
2	$\frac{\binom{1}{2}\binom{5}{0}}{\binom{6}{2}} = 0$

19. 1 | 5 = 15:

1	5, 7, 7, 8, 9
2	0, 1, 2, 5, 7, 8
3	1, 3, 6, 8, 8, 8
4	2, 5, 7, 9

20. Mean: 29.8; Median: 28; Mode: 38: The mean, or average, is equal to the sum of the data divided by the number of values in the data set.
Mean $= \frac{15+17+17+18+19+20+21+22+25+27+28+31+33+36+38+38+38+42+45+47+49}{21} = \frac{626}{21} = 29.8$
The median is the middle number or the average of the two middle numbers in the set of data organized from least to greatest. Since there are 21 numbers in the data set, the median is the eleventh number, below and above which there are ten numbers. The eleventh number is 28.

The mode is the value that occurs with the greatest frequency in the set. If all values occur with equal frequency, there is no mode; if more than one value appears with the highest frequency, there is more than one mode. In this set, there is one mode, namely 38, which appears three times in the set of data.

21. C: The least common denominator of $x(x + 4)$ may be multiplied by both rational expressions. Doing so gives $2x = 3(x + 4)$ or $2x = 3x + 12$. Solving for x gives $x = -12$.

22. B: Graphing the linear equation and a circle, with a center at $(2, -4)$ and radius of 4, shows points of intersection of $(-2, -4)$ and $(2, -8)$.

23. D: The equation may be solved by multiplying each term on each of the equation by the least common denominator, or $4(x + 4)$. Doing so gives $4(x + 4) \cdot \frac{x}{x+4} - 4(x + 4) \cdot \frac{3}{4} = 4(x + 4) \cdot \frac{4}{x+4}$, which simplifies to $4x - 3x - 12 = 16$, where $x = 28$.

24. C: When graphing the equations, the points of intersection represent the solutions of the system of equations. The line and parabola intersect at the points, $(1, 3)$ and $(0, 2)$. Thus, the solutions of the system include the points, $(1, 3)$ and $(0, 2)$. Substitution of the x- and y-values into each equation produces true statements.

25. 1.5, 3: The ball follows a parabolic path, and the ball's maximum height occurs at the vertex of the parabola. Since the equation of the parabola is given in the form $h = at^2 + bt + c$, the t-value of the vertex can be found using $\frac{-b}{2a} = \frac{-47}{2(-16)} \approx 1.5$. The ball reaches a maximum height about 1.5 seconds after having been thrown into the air.

When the ball hits the ground, its height is zero. Substitute 0 for h into the equation and solve for t.
$$h = -16t^2 + 47t + 3$$
$$0 = -16t^2 + 47t + 3$$
Factor and use the zero-product property.
$$0 = (-16t - 1)(t - 3)$$
$$0 = -16t - 1 \quad 0 = t - 3$$
$$1 = -16t \quad 3 = t$$
$$-\frac{1}{16} = t$$
Since t cannot be negative, $t = 3$. The ball hits the ground three seconds after having been thrown into the air.

26. A: The range of a function is the set of all possible output values for the function. In this case, the output for $g(x)$ is the function itself, $g(x)$. To find the range, first graph the given function.

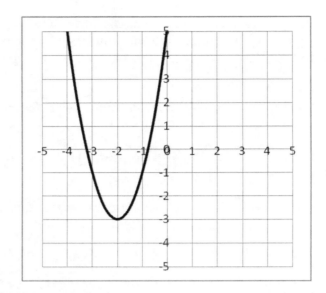

Notice that the graph is a U-shaped parabola, which means that its vertex is a minimum (rather than a maximum). Because of this, the range is the set of y-values above (and including) the minimum. In this case, the minimum is the point (-2,-3). Therefore, the range of $g(x)$ is $g(x) \geq -3$.

27. 6 inches: The area of a rectangle is equal to its length times its width, while the perimeter is the sum of the four sides, or the sum of twice the length and twice the width. So, to find the dimensions of the rectangle, set up and solve a system of equations. Here, the substitution method of solving is shown.

$$lw = 120 \;\rightarrow l = \frac{120}{w}$$
$$2l + 2w = 44$$
$$2\left(\frac{120}{w}\right) + 2w = 44$$
$$\frac{240}{w} + 2w = 44$$
$$w\left(\frac{240}{w} + 2w\right) = w(44)$$
$$240 + 2w^2 = 44w$$
$$2w^2 - 44w + 240 = 0$$
$$2(w^2 - 22w + 120) = 0$$
$$w^2 - 22w + 120 = 0$$
$$(w - 10)(w - 12) = 0$$
$$w = 10 \;\text{ or } w = 12$$

If the width is 10 ft, the length is 12 ft, or if the width is 12 ft, the length is 10 ft.

On the house plan, the scale is $\frac{1}{24}$, which means that a 1 ft length is represented as 1/24th of a foot on the plan. 1/24th of a foot is $\left(\frac{1}{24}\right)(12") = \frac{12"}{24} = \frac{1"}{2}$. So, the 12' side of the room is represented as a 6" side of a rectangle on the house plan.

28. 55: Since $m\angle ACD = 110°$, the measure of $\overset{\frown}{AB}$ is 110°. In a circle, the measure of an inscribed angle is equal to one half of the measure of the intercepted arc. Since $\angle ADB$ is an inscribed angle, its measure is half of m$\overset{\frown}{AB}$, or $110° \div 2 = 55°$.

29. 18.2: The formula for the volume of a cylinder is $V = \pi r^2 h$, where r is the radius of the cylinder and h is its height. The diameter of the soda can is 2.2 in, so its radius is $2.2 \div 2 = 1.1$ in. Thus, the volume of the can is

$$V = \pi(1.1)^2(4.8)$$
$$\approx 18.2 \text{ in}^3$$

30. A: An isosceles triangle is a triangle with two congruent sides called its *legs*. The other side is called the *base* of the triangle. First draw isosceles triangle ABC.

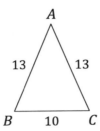

To calculate its area, we must find the height h of the triangle, so draw an altitude from A.

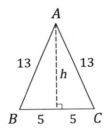

Use the Pythagorean Theorem to calculate h.

$$a^2 + b^2 = c^2$$
$$h^2 + 5^2 = 13^2$$
$$h^2 + 25 = 169$$
$$h^2 = 144$$
$$h = 12$$

The formula for the area of a triangle is $A = \frac{1}{2}Bh$, where B is the length of the base and h is the height. The base of ΔABC is 10 and its height is 12. Use these values to calculate the triangle's area.

$$A = \frac{1}{2}(10)(12)$$
$$= 60$$

31. C: The circumference of a circle is given by the formula $C = 2\pi r$, where r is the length of the radius. One section of a circle is called an *arc*, and it is proportional to the central angle that defines the arc. Thus, the length of an arc with central angle θ (in degrees) is given by the formula

$$L = 2\pi r \cdot \frac{\theta}{360}$$

Calculate the measure of the central angle.

$$3\pi = 2\pi(4) \cdot \frac{\theta}{360}$$
$$3\pi = 8\pi \cdot \frac{\theta}{360}$$
$$\frac{3}{8} = \frac{\theta}{360}$$
$$135 = \theta$$

Thus, m∠ACB = 135°. A sector is a slice of a circle bounded by two radii. The area of a sector with angle θ (in degrees) is given by the formula

$$A = \pi r^2 \cdot \frac{\theta}{360}$$

Substitute the value of the radius and angle into this formula and simplify the result.

$$A = \pi(4)^2 \cdot \frac{135}{360}$$
$$= 16\pi \cdot \frac{135}{360}$$
$$= 6\pi$$

Math - No-Calculator

1. B: Using the method of elimination to solve the system of equations, each term in the top equation may be multiplied by 2, while each term in the bottom equation may be multiplied by –3. Doing so produces two new equations with x-terms that will add to 0; $2(3x + 6y) = 2(36)$ can be written as $6x + 12y = 72$; $-3(2x + 9y) = -3(34)$ can be written as $-6x - 27y = -102$. Thus, the equations, $\begin{aligned} 6x + 12y &= 72 \\ -6x - 27y &= -102 \end{aligned}$, may be added to find the correct y-value solution.

2. A: The flat rate of $65 represents the y-intercept, and the charge of $0.12 per roaming minute used represents the slope. Therefore, the expression representing his monthly phone bill is $65 + 0.12x$.

3. C: The slope of the line may be determined by calculating the ratio of the change in y-values per change in corresponding x-values. Using the points, $(2, 0)$ and $(8, 2)$, the slope may be written as $\frac{2-0}{8-2}$, which equals $\frac{1}{3}$. Substituting the slope into the slope-intercept form of an equation gives $y = \frac{1}{3}x + b$. Substituting a pair of corresponding x- and y-values into the equation will reveal the y-intercept. Substituting the x- and y-values from the point, $(2, 0)$, gives: $0 = \frac{1}{3}(2) + b$, where $b = -\frac{2}{3}$. Thus, the equation of the line is $y = \frac{1}{3}x - \frac{2}{3}$. The equation, $7x - 21y = 14$, may be written as the same equation, when solved for y.

4. D: The cost of the taxi ride is the sum of two functions, a constant function for the first mile and a linear function for the rest of the ride. The constant function is $c_1(d) = 4.25$ since the cost of the first mile is $4.25. For the linear part, subtract 1 from d to exclude the first mile, and then multiply the result by 0.70 since it costs $0.70 per mile. The result is $c_2(d) = 0.70(d - 1)$. Finally, write the function for the total cost of the taxi ride by adding the two functions.
$$c(d) = c_1(d) + c_2(d)$$
$$= 4.25 + 0.70(d-1)$$

5. B: The first function $L(g)$ gives the water level after g gallons are pumped into the tank. The second function $w(t)$ gives the number of gallons pumped into the tank after t minutes, which the first function calls g. Consequently, we can have L act on w: the composition of the functions $L(w(t))$ is the water level of the tank after t minutes. Calculate $L(w(t))$.

$$L(w(t)) = 0.3 \cdot w(t)$$
$$= 0.3 \cdot 1.2t$$
$$= 0.36t$$

Thus, the function $L(t) = 0.36t$ represents the water level of the tank after t minutes.

6. C: T the first sentence, "Adam has $10 more than Betty," can be written as $A = B + 10$, where A represents the amount of money Adam has and B represents the amount of money Betty has.

Next translate the second sentence "If Adam were to give $15 to Betty, then she would have twice as much money as Adam." This means that if Adam had $15 less (represented by the expression $A - 15$) and Betty had $15 more ($B + 15$), then Betty would have two times what Adam would have. So, the correct equation is $B + 15 = 2(A - 15)$.

7. C: The length of an interval is the difference between its endpoints. For example, the length of the interval [2, 4] is 2. To determine how the given function grows over an interval of length 5, determine the value of f at each endpoint of that interval. Since linear functions grow by equal differences over equal intervals, you can use any interval of length 5, and your answer will apply to all such intervals. For example, you can use the interval [0, 5]:

$$f(0) = 4(0) - 8$$
$$= 0 - 8$$
$$= -8$$

$$f(5) = 4(5) - 8$$
$$= 20 - 8$$
$$= 12$$

Since $f(0) = -8$ and $f(3) = 12$, the function increases by $12 - (-8) = 20$ over this interval, and over any interval of length 5.

8. C: Linear functions can be written in the form $g(x) = ax + b$. To determine the value of a, notice that $g(x)$ increases by 2 every time x increases by 1. For instance, when x goes from 0 to 1, the value of y goes from -3 to -1; and when x goes from 1 to 2, the value of y increases from -1 to 1. Since $g(x)$ increases by 2, the value of a is 2, so the function is $g(x) = 2x + b$. Next calculate the value of b. From the graph, you can tell that $g(0) = -3$. Use this to calculate b:

$$g(0) = -3$$
$$2(0) + b = -3$$
$$0 + b = -3$$
$$b = -3$$

Thus, the function is $g(x) = 2x - 3$.

Alternatively, writing an explicit formula in the form $g(x) = ax + b$ means solving for two variables, a and b. Use the information given in the graph to write two equations relating these two variables in terms of x and $g(x)$:

$$-3 = a(0) + b$$
$$1 = a(2) + b$$

The first readily solves to $b = -3$, which you can substitute into the second to solve for a:

$$1 = a(2) - 3$$
$$4 = a(2) = 2a$$
$$a = 2$$

Thus, the function is $g(x) = 2x - 3$.

9. A: The inequality may be solved by first subtracting 18 from both sides. Doing so gives $3x > -12$. Dividing both sides of the inequality by 3 gives $x > -4$.

10. D: The range of a function is the set of all possible output values for the function. In this case, the output for $g(x)$ is the function itself, $g(x)$. Examine the given function. Let's say you choose some particular real number for $g(x)$. For any choice you make, you can find an x-value that will result in that choice by simply adding 2 to it. For example, say you choose $g(x) = -3$. Then you can use

$x = -3 + 2 = -1$ to get your original value because $g(-1) = -1 - 2 = -3$. Since this will work for any real value for $g(x)$, the range of $g(x)$ is all real numbers.

You can see this visually by graphing the function. In the graph below, notice that the function can go up and down without end.

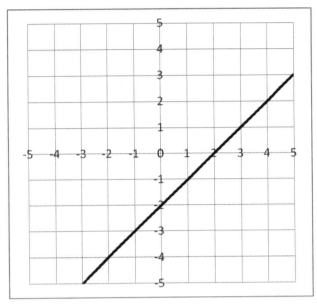

11. A: After distributing the minus sign across the second trinomial, the expression can be rewritten as $3x^3 - 9x^2 + 6x - 8x^3 - 4x^2 + 3x$. Combining like terms gives $-5x^3 - 13x^2 + 9x$.

12. A: The sum can be written as $12x^3 - 8x + 6x^2 - 3 + 8x^2 - 20x^3 + 6 - 2x$. Combining like terms and writing the expression in standard form gives: $-8x^3 + 14x^2 - 10x + 3$.

13. $x = -3, \ 2, \ -1; y = -6$: $y = (x + 3)(x^2 - x - 2)$ is a cubic equation written as a product of a linear and quadratic factor, $x - 3$ and $x^2 - x - 2$, respectively. The quadratic expression can be further factored to $(x - 2)(x + 1)$, so $y = (x + 3)(x^2 - x - 2) = (x + 3)(x - 2)(x + 1)$. The x-intercepts of the graph of y occur when $y = 0$, so to find the x-intercepts, solve $0 = (x + 3)(x - 2)(x + 1)$ using the zero-product property.

$$x + 3 = 0 \qquad x - 2 = 0 \qquad x + 1 = 0$$
$$x = -3 \qquad x = 2 \qquad x = -1$$

The y-intercept of the graph of the equation occurs when $x = 0$, so solve $y = (0 + 3)(0^2 - 0 - 2) = (3)(-2) = -6$.

14. D: Since the equation is in the form $y = a(x - h)^2 + k$, the graph is a parabola. For an equation in this form, the vertex is (h,k), and the parabola either opens up (is U-shaped) or opens down (is an upside-down U) depending on the value of A: If a is positive, the parabola opens up, and if a is negative, it opens down. Moreover, if $|a|$ is greater than one, the graph is wider than the parent function $y = x^2$, and if $|a|$ is smaller than one, the graph is skinnier than the parent function.

15. D: The domain of a function is the set of all possible input values for the function. In this case, the input for $f(x)$ is x. The easiest way to find the domain of $f(x)$ is to determine for which values of x the function is undefined. Then you can exclude those values from the domain.

Examine the given function. Notice that it does not contain a square root sign, a logarithm, or a fraction with x in the denominator. Therefore, the function will be defined for all real numbers. You can see this visually by graphing the function. In the graph below, notice that the function can go to the left and right without end.

16. A: The domain of a function is the set of all possible input values for the function. In this case, the input for $f(x)$ is x. The easiest way to find the domain of $f(x)$ is to determine for which x-values the function is undefined. Then, you can exclude those values from the domain.

Examine the given function. Notice that $f(x)$ has a square-root sign. Since negative numbers do not have real square roots, we need to exclude all the x-values that will make the expression under the square root negative. The expression $x + 5$ is negative only when x is strictly less than -5. Therefore, the domain is all values greater than or equal to -5, or $x \geq -5$.

17. C: Since $ABCD$ is a rectangle, opposite sides are equal and all the angles are right angles. Moreover, m and n are parallel to the sides of the rectangle and bisect the rectangle, so they are both perpendicular to the sides of the rectangle. Consider the four given choices:
- If you reflect $ABCD$ across m, then $\overline{AB}$ and $\overline{BC}$ will switch places, so the image $A'B'C'D'$ will look like the original rectangle.
- Similarly, if you reflect $ABCD$ across n, then $\overline{BC}$ and $\overline{AD}$ will switch places, so the image will look like the original as well.
- However, if you rotate the rectangle $90°$ about point P, the image will be a "tall" rectangle, rather than a "long" (or "wide") rectangle, so the image will not look like the original.
- Finally, if you rotate the rectangle $180°$ about point P, then both pairs of opposite sides of the rectangle will switch places.

Practice Test #2

Reading

World Literature

Focus: Students must read and understand a passage from World Literature.

Questions 1-9 refer to the following selection from Pride and Prejudice by Jane Austen:

It is a truth universally acknowledged, that a single man in possession of a good fortune, must be in want of a wife.

However little known the feelings or views of such a man may be on his first entering a neighbourhood, this truth is so well fixed in the minds of the surrounding families, that he is considered the rightful property of some one or other of their daughters.

"My dear Mr. Bennet," said his lady to him one day, "have you heard that Netherfield Park is let at last?"

Mr. Bennet replied that he had not.

"But it is," returned she; "for Mrs. Long has just been here, and she told me all about it."

Mr. Bennet made no answer.

"Do you not want to know who has taken it?" cried his wife impatiently.

"You want to tell me, and I have no objection to hearing it."

This was invitation enough.

"Why, my dear, you must know, Mrs. Long says that Netherfield is taken by a young man of large fortune from the north of England; that he came down on Monday in a chaise and four to see the place, and was so much delighted with it, that he agreed with Mr. Morris immediately; that he is to take possession before Michaelmas, and some of his servants are to be in the house by the end of next week."

"What is his name?"

"Bingley."

"Is he married or single?"

"Oh! Single, my dear, to be sure! A single man of large fortune; four or five thousand a year. What a fine thing for our girls!"

"How so? How can it affect them?"

"My dear Mr. Bennet," replied his wife, "how can you be so tiresome!" You must know that I am thinking of his marrying one of them."

"Is that his design in settling here?"

"Design! Nonsense, how can you talk so! But it is very likely that he may fall in love with one of them, and therefore you must visit him as soon as he comes."

"I see no occasion for that. You and the girls may go, or you may send them by themselves, which perhaps will be still better, for as you are as handsome as any of them, Mr. Bingley may like you the best of the party."

1. What is the central idea of this selection?
    a. A new neighbor is due to arrive who may become good friends with Mr. and Mrs. Bennet.
    b. A new neighbor is due to arrive who may be a prospective husband for one of the Bennet daughters.
    c. A new neighbor is due to arrive who may be a good business connection for Mr. Bennet.
    d. A new neighbor is due to arrive who has expressed an interest in marrying one of the Bennet daughters.

2. How does Mrs. Bennet feel about the arrival of Mr. Bingley?
    a. Mrs. Bennet is excited about the arrival of Mr. Bingley.
    b. Mrs. Bennet is nervous about the arrival of Mr. Bingley.
    c. Mrs. Bennet is afraid the arrival of Mr. Bingley will upset Mr. Bennet.
    d. Mrs. Bennet is indifferent to the arrival of Mr. Bingley.

3. What does Mrs. Bennet expect from Mr. Bennet?
    a. Mrs. Bennet expects Mr. Bennet to invite Mr. Bingley to a dinner party.
    b. Mrs. Bennet expects Mr. Bennet to offer one of his daughters in marriage to Mr. Bingley.
    c. Mrs. Bennet expects Mr. Bennet to pay a visit to Mr. Bingley.
    d. Mrs. Bennet expects Mr. Bennet to invite Mr. Bingley to a ball in his honor.

4. What does Mrs. Bennet expect from Mr. Bingley?
    a. Mrs. Bennet expects Mr. Bingley to be interested in marrying one of her daughters.
    b. Mrs. Bennet expects Mr. Bingley to be interested in receiving a visit from Mr. Bennet.
    c. Mrs. Bennet expects Mr. Bingley to love living at Netherfield Park.
    d. Mrs. Bennet expects Mr. Bingley to ask for her help in choosing a wife for himself.

5. Which of the following statements best describes Mrs. Bennet's feelings about her husband as indicated by this selection?
    a. Mrs. Bennet is tired of her husband.
    b. Mrs. Bennet is exasperated by her husband.
    c. Mrs. Bennet is afraid of her husband.
    d. Mrs. Bennet is indifferent toward her husband.

6. This selection is set in England at the beginning of the 19th century. Drawing on information from this selection, what could you conclude was a primary goal for young women in England during this time period?
    a. To marry
    b. To marry a man with money
    c. To entertain the neighbors
    d. To be courted by as many men as possible

7. "It is a truth universally acknowledged, that a single man in possession of a good fortune, must be in want of a wife."
Which of the following most nearly matches the meaning of the underlined phrase?
    a. Everyone knows
    b. The universe has decided
    c. It is a documented fact
    d. It is best to tell the truth

8. "It is a truth universally acknowledged, <u>that a single man in possession of a good fortune, must be in want of a wife.</u>"
Which of the following most nearly matches the meaning of the underlined phrase?
    a. An unmarried man always wants to get married.
    b. An unmarried man must want to give his money away.
    c. An unmarried man with money always wants to get married.
    d. An unmarried man can increase his fortune by getting married.

9. "Is that his design in settling here?"
What does the word design mean in the context of this selection?
    a. Intention
    b. Drawing
    c. Creation
    d. Improvisation

History/Social Studies

Passage 1
Focus: Students must read and understand a passage from History/Social Studies.

Read the following selection from <u>Ten American Girls from History</u> *by Kate Dickinson Sweetser to answer questions 10-18:*

[Clara has begun her work of ministering to soldiers on the front lines of the civil war. Her tireless efforts and care have taken her to some of the most horrific battles of the war]

Clara Barton!—Only the men who lay wounded or dying on the battle-field knew the thrill and the comfort that the name carried. Again and again her life was in danger—once at Antietam, when stooping to give a drink of water to an injured boy, a bullet whizzed between them. It ended the life of **<u>the poor lad</u>**, but only tore a hole in Clara Barton's sleeve. And so, again and again, it seemed as if a special Providence protected her from death or injury. At Fredericksburg, when the dead, starving and wounded lay frozen on the ground, and there was no effective organization for proper relief, with swift, silent efficiency Clara Barton moved among them, having the snow cleared away and under the banks finding famished, frozen figures which were once men. She rushed to have an old chimney torn down and built fire-blocks, over which she soon had kettles full of coffee and gruel steaming.

As she was bending over a wounded rebel, he whispered to her: "Lady, you have been kind to me … every street of the city is covered by our cannon. When your entire army has reached the other side of the Rappahannock, they will find Fredericksburg only a slaughter-pen. Not a regiment will escape. Do not go over, for you will go to certain death."

She thanked him for the kindly warning and later told of the call that came to her to go across the river, and what happened. She says:

"At ten o'clock of the battle day when the rebel fire was hottest, the shells rolling down every street, and the bridge under the heavy cannonade, a courier dashed over, and, rushing up the steps of the house where I was, placed in my hand a crumpled, bloody piece of paper, a request from the lion-hearted old surgeon on the opposite shore, establishing his hospitals in the very jaws of death:

"'Come to me,' he wrote. 'Your place is here.'

<u>"The faces of the rough men working at my side, which eight weeks before had flushed with indignation at the thought of being controlled by a woman, grew ashy white as they guessed the nature of the summons, … and they begged me to send them, but save myself.</u> I could only allow them to go with me if they chose, and in twenty minutes we were rocking across the swaying bridge, the water hissing with shot on either side.

"Over into that city of death, its roofs riddled by shell, its every church a crowded hospital, every street a battle-line, every hill a rampart, every rock a fortress, and every stone wall a blazing line of forts.

- 190 -

"Oh, what a day's work was that! How those long lines of blue, rank on rank, charged over the open acres, up to the very mouths of those blazing guns, and how like grain before the sickle they fell and melted away.

"An officer stepped to my side to assist me over the débris at the end of the bridge. While our hands were raised in the act of stepping down, a piece of an exploding shell hissed through between us, just below our arms, carrying away a portion of both the skirts of his coat and my dress, rolling along the ground a few rods from us like a harmless pebble in the water. The next instant a solid shot thundered over our heads, a noble steed bounded in the air and with his gallant rider rolled in the dirt not thirty feet in the rear. Leaving the kind-hearted officer, I passed on alone to the hospital. In less than a half-hour he was brought to me—dead."

She was passing along a street in the heart of the city when she had to step aside to let a regiment of infantry march by. At that moment General Patrick saw her, and, thinking she was a frightened resident of the city who had been left behind in the general exodus, leaned from his saddle and said, reassuringly:

"You are alone and in great danger, madam. Do you want protection?"

With a rare smile, Miss Barton said, as she looked at the ranks of soldiers, "Thank you, but I think I am the best-protected woman in the United States."

10. What can be inferred from the fact that the men's faces turned "white" in the underlined sentence?
    a. The men were afraid that Clara would be seriously hurt or killed by going to help.
    b. The men had not wanted Clara to tend to them or order them around when she first arrived.
    c. The men were terrified of the coming war and wanted Clara to escape with them.
    d. The men did not want to be moved to the hospital on the other side of the bridge.

11. Which of the following might be a good title for the above selection?
    a. Clara Barton: "The Angel of the Battlefields"
    b. "The Angel of the Civil War"
    c. Civil War Nurses and the Work of Clara Barton
    d. "When the Fighting Was Over: Clara Barton, Civil War Hero"

12. Why does the author mention the instances when Clara's life had been in danger on the battlefield?
    a. To show that Clara was an unwilling participant in the initial war effort.
    b. To help the reader picture how Clara seemed to not really be a part of the battle.
    c. To compare how many battles she lived through with how many armed men had not.
    d. To illustrate how battles were turned through the care she provided.

13. Which of the following best explains why the author referred to one of the soldiers as "the poor lad"?
    a. She wanted to show that the man had little or no material belongings.
    b. She wanted to build sympathy for the young man who died.
    c. She wanted to show that the soldier had only been a young boy, not a man.
    d. She wanted to create an image in the mind of the reader about the soldier.

14. Clara Barton is quoted describing the old surgeon across the river as "establishing his hospitals in the very jaws of death". In the context of this passage, what does this phrase mean?
    a. He was treating in hospitals which were all destroyed.
    b. He was treating wounded though he was near death.
    c. He was treating wounded soldiers, who all then died.
    d. He was treating wounded soldiers on the battlefields.

15. This passage's first paragraph describes a close call when a bullet whizzed between Clara and a boy. What happened?
    a. The bullet killed the boy, but it only wounded Clara.
    b. The bullet wounded both the boy and Clara.
    c. The bullet wounded the boy, but it missed Clara.
    d. The bullet killed the boy, but it missed Clara.

16. The last sentence begins, "With a rare smile, Miss Barton said..." In this context, what is the meaning of "rare" describing her smile?
    a. Miss Barton had an unusually great smile.
    b. Miss Barton's smile was fine/precious.
    c. Miss Barton did not smile very often.
    d. Miss Barton had an admirable smile.

17. Which of the following excerpts provides evidence of Barton's positive feelings for the Union army?
    a. "'...a noble steed...and with his gallant rider...'"
    b. "...a wounded rebel...whispered... 'Lady, you have been kind to me...'"
    c. "How those long lines of blue, rank on rank, charged over the open acres..."
    d. "...the kind-hearted officer...In less than a half-hour he was brought to me—dead.'"

18. "Over into that city of death, its roofs riddled by shell, its every church a crowded hospital, every street a battle-line, every hill a rampart, every rock a fortress, and every stone wall a blazing line of forts." This sentence makes use of which literary device?
    a. Alliteration
    b. Parallelism
    c. Paradoxes
    d. Periphrasis

Passage 2
Focus: Students must read and understand a passage from a history/social studies topic.

Questions 19-27 are based on the following passages:

Black History Month began as Negro History Week, established by black historian Carter G. Woodson in 1926. Fifty years later, in 1976, the week was expanded to encompass the month of February. Opinions differ on whether its continued observance is the best way to ensure a shared knowledge, interest, and respect for all that is encompassed in African American history.

Passage 1:

Black History Month is unnecessary. In a place and time in which we overwhelmingly elected an African American president, we can and should move to a post-racial approach to education. As *Detroit Free Press* columnist Rochelle Riley wrote in a February 1 column calling for an end to Black History Month, "I propose that, for the first time in American history, this country has reached a point where we can stop celebrating separately, stop learning separately, stop being American separately."

In addition to being unnecessary, the idea that African American history should be focused on in a given month suggests that it belongs in that month alone. It is important to instead incorporate African American history into what is taught every day as American history. It needs to be recreated as part of mainstream thought and not as an optional, often irrelevant, side note. We should focus efforts on pushing schools to diversify and broaden their curricula.

There are a number of other reasons to abolish it: first, it has become a shallow commercial ritual that does not even succeed in its (limited and misguided) goal of focusing for one month on a sophisticated, intelligent appraisal of the contributions and experiences of African Americans throughout history. Second, there is a paternalistic flavor to the mandated bestowing of a month in which to study African American history that is overcome if we instead assert the need for a comprehensive curriculum. Third, the idea of Black History Month suggests that the knowledge imparted in that month is for African Americans only, rather than for all people.

Passage 2:

Black History Month is still an important observance. Despite the important achievement of the election of our first African American president, the need for knowledge and education about African American history is still unmet to a substantial degree. Black History Month is a powerful tool in working towards meeting that need. There is no reason to give up that tool now, and it can easily coexist with an effort to develop a more comprehensive and inclusive yearly curriculum.

Having a month set aside for the study of African American history doesn't limit its study and celebration to that month; it merely focuses complete attention on it for that month. There is absolutely no contradiction between having a set-aside month and having it be present in the curriculum the rest of the year.

Equally important is that the debate *itself* about the usefulness of Black History Month can, and should, remind parents that they can't necessarily count on schools to teach African American history as thoroughly as many parents would want.

Although Black History Month has, to an extent, become a shallow ritual, it doesn't have to be. Good teachers and good materials could make the February curriculum deeply informative, thought-provoking, and inspiring. The range of material that can be covered is rich, varied, and full of limitless possibilities.

Finally, it is worthwhile to remind ourselves and our children of the key events that happened during the month of February. In 1926, Woodson organized the first Black History Week to honor the birthdays of essential civil rights activists Abraham Lincoln and Frederick Douglass. W. E. B. DuBois was born on February 23, 1868.

The 15th Amendment, which granted African Americans the right to vote, was passed on February 3, 1870. The first black U.S. senator, Hiram R. Revels, took his oath of office on February 25, 1870. The National Association for the Advancement of Colored People (NAACP) was founded on February 12, 1909. Malcolm X was shot on February 21, 1965.

19. The author's primary purpose in Passage 1 is to:
    a. argue that Black History Month should not be so commercial.
    b. argue that Black History Month should be abolished.
    c. argue that Black History Month should be maintained.
    d. suggest that African American history should be taught in two months rather than just one.

20. It can be inferred that the term "post-racial" in the second sentence of Passage 1 refers to an approach that:
    a. treats race as the most important factor in determining an individual's experience.
    b. treats race as one factor, but not the most important, in determining an individual's experience.
    c. considers race after considering all other elements of a person's identity.
    d. is not based on or organized around concepts of race.

21. Which of the following statements is true?
    a. The author of Passage 1 thinks that it is important for students to learn about the achievements and experience of African Americans, while the author of Passage 2 does not think this is important.
    b. The author of Passage 2 thinks that it is important for students to learn about the achievements and experience of African Americans, while the author of Passage 1 does not think this is important.
    c. Neither author thinks that it is important for students to learn about the achievements and experience of African Americans.
    d. Both authors think that it is important for students to learn about the achievements and experience of African Americans.

22. The author of Passage 1 argues that celebrating Black History Month suggests that the study of African American history can and should be limited to one month of the year. What is the author of Passage 2's response?
    a. Black History Month is still an important observance.
    b. Black History Month is a powerful tool in meeting the need for education about African American history.
    c. Having a month set aside for the study of African American history does not limit its study and celebration to that month.
    d. Black History Month does not have to be a shallow ritual.

23. Why does the author of Passage 2 believe that the debate itself about Black History Month can be useful?
    a. The people on opposing sides can come to an intelligent resolution about whether to keep it.
    b. African American history is discussed in the media when the debate is ongoing.
    c. The debate is a reminder to parents that they can't count on schools to teach their children about African American history.
    d. Black History Month doesn't have to be a shallow ritual.

24. Which of the following does the author of Passage 1 not give as a reason for abolishing Black History Month?
    a. It has become a shallow ritual.
    b. There is a paternalistic feel to being granted one month of focus.
    c. It suggests that the month's education is only for African Americans.
    d. No one learns anything during the month.

25. Which of the following does neither author claim occurred in February?
    a. W.E.B. DuBois's birthday
    b. Abraham Lincoln's birthday
    c. The signing of the Emancipation Proclamation
    d. The founding of the NAACP

26. What does the author of Passage 2 say about the range of material that can be taught during Black History Month?
    a. It is rich and varied.
    b. It is important.
    c. It is an unmet need.
    d. It is comprehensive.

27. Which event happened first?
    a. The passing of the 15th Amendment
    b. The birth of W.E.B. DuBois
    c. The establishment of Black History Month
    d. The founding of the NAACP

Science

Passage 1

Focus: Students must read and understand a passage from a science topic.

Questions 28-37 pertain to the following passage:

<u>Comets</u>

Comets are bodies that orbit the sun. They are distinguishable from asteroids by the presence of coma or tails. In the outer solar system, comets remain frozen and are so small that they are difficult to detect from Earth. As a comet approaches the inner solar system, solar radiation causes the materials within the comet to vaporize and trail off the nuclei. The released dust and gas forms a fuzzy atmosphere called the coma, and the force exerted on the coma causes a tail to form, pointing away from the sun.

Comet nuclei are made of ice, dust, rock and frozen gases and vary widely in size: from 100 meters or so to tens of kilometers across. The comas may be even larger than the Sun. Because of their low mass, they do not become spherical and have irregular shapes.

There are over 3,500 known comets, and the number is steadily increasing. This represents only a small portion of the total comets existing, however. Most comets are too faint to be visible without the aid of a telescope; the number of comets visible to the naked eye is around one a year.

Comets leave a trail of solid debris behind them. If a comet's path crosses the Earth's path, there will likely be meteor showers as Earth passes through the trail of debris.

Many comets and asteroids have collided into Earth. Some scientists believe that comets hitting Earth about 4 billion years ago brought a significant proportion of the water in Earth's oceans. There are still many near-Earth comets.

Most comets have oval shaped orbits that take them close to the Sun for part of their orbit and then out further into the Solar System for the remainder of the orbit. Comets are often classified according to the length of their orbital period: short period comets have orbital periods of less than 200 years, long period comets have orbital periods of more than 200 years, single apparition comets have trajectories which cause them to permanently leave the solar system after passing the Sun once.

28. What does the passage *not* list as a component of comet nuclei?
    a. solar radiation
    b. dust
    c. frozen gases
    d. rock

29. What does the passage claim distinguishes comets from asteroids?
   a. The make-up of their nuclei
   b. The presence of coma or tails
   c. Their orbital periods
   d. Their irregular shapes

30. What would a comet with an orbital period of 1,000 years be called?
   a. a short period comet
   b. a long period comet
   c. a single apparition comet
   d. an elliptical comet

31. According to the passage, which of the following is true?
   a. There are 350 known comets and the number is steadily increasing.
   b. There are 3,500 known comets and the number is staying the same.
   c. There are 3,500 known comets and many more comets that aren't known.
   d. Most comets are visible to the naked eye.

32. According to the passage, why do comets have irregular shapes?
   a. because they are not spherical
   b. because they have orbital periods
   c. because of their low mass
   d. because of their tails

33. What does the passage claim about the size of comets?
   a. Some are tens of kilometers across and the coma can be larger than the Sun
   b. Some are tens of kilometers across and the coma is never larger than the Sun
   c. Some are 100 meters across and the coma is never larger than the Sun
   d. The smallest comet is at least a kilometer and the coma can be larger than the Sun

34. According to the passage, what shape is the orbit of most comets?
   a. circular
   b. square
   c. linear
   d. oval

35. According to the first passage, what does the name "single apparition comets" mean?
   a. They only appear during the part of their orbit that is nearer to the Sun.
   b. They stay in the solar system even though they are only apparent once.
   c. Their orbital periods are so long they only appear once across millennia.
   d. They only remain in the solar system long enough to pass the Sun once.

36. Which of the following does the first passage author give as evidence of comets' low mass?
   a. Their irregular shapes
   b. Their nuclei's content
   c. The size of the comas
   d. Their variability in size

37. According to the first passage, what can cause meteor showers?
    a. Multiple comets and asteroids collide into the Earth.
    b. Large groups of meteors enter Earth's atmosphere.
    c. A comet explodes causing meteors to shower down.
    d. The Earth passes through a comet's solid debris trail.

Passage 2
Focus: Students must read and understand a passage from a science topic.

Questions 38-47 pertain to the following passage:

Periodic Table

The periodic table groups elements with similar chemical properties together. The grouping of elements is based on atomic structure. It shows periodic trends of physical and chemical properties and identifies families of elements with similar properties. It is a common model for organizing and understanding elements. In the periodic table, each element has its own cell that includes varying amounts of information presented in symbol form about the properties of the element. Cells in the table are arranged in rows (periods) and columns (groups or families). At minimum, a cell includes the symbol for the element and its atomic number. The cell for hydrogen, for example, which appears first in the upper left corner, includes an "H" and a "1" above the letter. Elements are ordered by atomic number, left to right, top to bottom.

In the periodic table, the groups are the columns numbered 1 through 18 that group elements with similar outer electron shell configurations. Since the configuration of the outer electron shell is one of the primary factors affecting an element's chemical properties, elements within the same group have similar chemical properties. Previous naming conventions for groups have included the use of Roman numerals and upper-case letters. Currently, the periodic table groups are: Group 1, alkali metals; Group 2, alkaline earth metals; Groups 3-12, transition metals; Group 13, boron family; Group 14; carbon family; Group 15, pnictogens; Group 16, chalcogens; Group 17, halogens; Group 18, noble gases.

In the periodic table, there are seven periods (rows), and within each period there are blocks that group elements with the same outer electron subshell (more on this in the next section). The number of electrons in that outer shell determines which group an element belongs to within a given block. Each row's number (1, 2, 3, etc.) corresponds to the highest number electron shell that is in use. For example, row 2 uses only electron shells 1 and 2, while row 7 uses all shells from 1-7.

For example, hydrogen is in the s-block as its highest-energy electron is in the s-orbital. The f-block is organized separately from the rest of the periodic table and includes atoms or ions that have valence electrons in f-orbitals.

Atomic radii will decrease from left to right across a period (row) on the periodic table. In a group (column), there is an increase in the atomic radii of elements from top to bottom. Ionic radii will be smaller than the atomic radii for metals, but the opposite is true for non-metals. From left to right, electronegativity, or an atom's likeliness of taking another atom's electrons, increases. In a group, electronegativity decreases from top to bottom. Ionization energy or the amount of energy needed to get rid of an atom's outermost electron, increases across a period and decreases down a group. Electron affinity will become more negative across a period but will not change much within a group. The melting point decreases

38. This passage states, "Previous naming conventions for groups have included the use of Roman numerals and upper-case letters." From the context of the paragraph containing this sentence, what is the current naming convention for groups in the periodic table?
a. Element name words
b. Lower-case letters
c. Roman numerals
d. Arabic numerals

39. In the first paragraph the author writes, "The cell for hydrogen...includes an 'H' and a '1' above the letter." From the context of this paragraph, what does the "H" represent?
a. The cell's alphabetical order
b. The symbol for the element
c. The element name's initial letter
d. The atomic number of the element

40. Among the following, what is evidence that the groups in the periodic table contain chemically similar elements?
a. "Since the configuration of the outer electron shell is one of the primary factors affecting an element's chemical properties, elements within the same group have similar chemical properties."
b. "In the periodic table, the groups are the columns numbered 1 through 18 that group elements with similar outer electron shell configurations."
c. "In the periodic table, each element has its own cell that includes varying amounts of information presented in symbol form about the properties of the element."
d. "Ionization energy or the amount of energy needed to get rid of an atom's outermost electron increases across a period and decreases down a group."

41. The author provides evidence of periodic trends, i.e., that various chemical/electronic properties are arranged in either ascending or descending order by periods/rows and groups/columns in which paragraph(s) of this passage?
a. In the first paragraph
b. The fourth paragraph
c. The second and third
d. In all the paragraphs

42. Which of these is correct regarding information in the passage about how cells are arranged in the periodic table?
a. Periods are vertical; groups are horizontal.
b. Periods are horizontal; groups are vertical.
c. Cells are called periods, rows called groups.
d. Cells have no vertical/horizontal ordering.

43. The periodic trends described in the last paragraph of the passage mainly depict what kind of relationship?
    a. Sequence
    b. Cause-effect
    c. Parts to whole
    d. Comparison-contrast

44. From the description of periodic trends in the fourth paragraph, the reader might infer that what kind of relationship between periods and groups is not necessarily or always the case, but occurs often?
    a. Inverse
    b. Converse
    c. A direct one
    d. None of these

45. According to the passage, what determines which group an element belongs to within a block?
    a. The element's atomic number determines this
    b. The number given each period determines this
    c. The highest-number electron shell in use does
    d. The number assigned to that element's group

46. Which of these describes the structural movement of this passage from beginning to end?
    a. It gives general facts throughout.
    b. It moves from general to specific.
    c. It gives specific facts throughout.
    d. It moves from specific to general.

47. What best identifies the purpose of this passage?
    a. To explain the relationship of electron shell configuration to chemical properties
    b. To explain the differences between periods and groups within the periodic table
    c. To explain why the periodic table exists and is used in chemistry in the first place
    d. To explain functions, organization, conventions, and trends of the periodic table

Writing and Language

Careers

Focus: Students must make revising and editing decisions in the context of a passage on a careers-related topic.

Dieticians and Nutritionists

Dietitians and nutritionists evaluate the health of their clients. Based on their findings, dietitians and nutritionists advise clients on which foods to eat—and those foods to avoid—to improve their health.

Some dietitians and nutritionists provide customized information for specific individuals. For example, a dietitian or nutritionist might teach a client with high blood pressure how to use less salt when preparing meals. Others work with groups of people who have similar needs. For example, a dietitian or nutritionist might plan a diet with limited fat and sugar to help patients lose weight. They may work with other healthcare professionals to coordinate patient care.

Dietitians and nutritionists who are self-employed may meet with patients, or they may work as consultants for a variety of organizations. They may need to spend time on marketing and other business-related tasks, such as scheduling appointments and preparing informational materials for clients.

Although many dietitians and nutritionists do similar tasks, there are several specialties within the occupations. The following are examples of types of dietitians and nutritionists:

Clinical dietitians and nutritionists provide medical nutrition therapy. They work in hospitals, long-term care facilities, clinics, private practice, and other institutions. They create nutritional programs based on the health needs of patients or residents and counsel patients on how to lead a healthier lifestyle. Clinical dietitians and nutritionists may further specialize, such as working only with patients with kidney diseases or those with diabetes.

Community dietitians and nutritionists develop programs and counsel the public on topics related to food and nutrition. They often work with specific groups of people, such as adolescents or the elderly. They work in public health clinics, government and nonprofit agencies, health maintenance organizations (HMOs), and other settings.

Management dietitians plan meal programs. They work in food service settings such as cafeterias, hospitals, prisons, and schools. They may be responsible for buying food and for carrying out other business-related tasks such as budgeting. Management dietitians may oversee kitchen staff or other dietitians.

1. Where in this passage is the material in a paragraph introduced by the last sentence in the preceding paragraph to create a transition?
    a. To introduce the information in the last paragraph
    b. This technique is used between all the paragraphs
    c. Material is introduced only in beginning sentences
    d. Information in any paragraph is never introduced

2. Which of these lists the topics of each passage paragraph in the same sequence as they appear?
    a. Clients; functions; specialties; self-employed
    b. Specialties; self-employed; functions; clients
    c. Self-employed; specialties; clients; functions
    d. Functions; clients; self-employed; specialties

3. According to the passage, which can be included for self-employed dietitians and nutritionists?
    a. Administrative activities
    b. All these can be included
    c. Assembling information
    d. Promoting their services

4. The first paragraph of this passage states that dietitians and nutritionists give advice about how clients can eat "to improve their health." Where in the passage is evidence included that supports this point?
    a. There is no supporting evidence
    b. The second and last paragraphs
    c. All paragraphs include evidence
    d. Only the last paragraph has this

5. According to the evidence in this passage, which types of dietitians and nutritionists are *most* likely to perform job duties including overseeing staff, budgeting, and purchasing foods?
    a. Clinical dietitians and nutritionists
    b. Community dietitians and nutritionists
    c. Management dietitians are the most likely
    d. All of these are equally likely to perform these

6. In the first paragraph, this passage states that "dietitians and nutritionists advise clients on which foods to eat—and those foods to avoid—to improve their health." Which of the following accurately describes the use of dashes in the underlined portion?
    a. The dashes are incorrect and no punctuation is required.
    b. The dashes should be replaced with a pair of parentheses.
    c. The dashes should be removed and commas used instead.
    d. The dashes are correct and appropriate for this sentence.

7. "For example, a dietitian or nutritionist might teach a client with high blood pressure how to use less salt when preparing meals." What type of sentence is this?
    a. A simple sentence
    b. A complex sentence
    c. A compound sentence
    d. A compound-complex sentence

8. "...a dietitian or nutritionist might plan <u>a diet with limited fat and sugar to help patients lose weight.</u>" Which of the following would have noun agreement?
    a. a diet with limited fat and sugar to help a patient lose weight.
    b. diets with limited fat and sugar to help patients lose weight.
    c. Both (a) and (b)
    d. No change

9. The passage says community dietitians and nutritionists frequently work with <u>"specific groups of people"</u>. Based on the sentence context, what kinds of "specific groups" are these?
    a. People with specific diseases
    b. People in specific age groups
    c. People in the general public
    d. People specifically in HMOs

10. "<u>Dietitians and nutritionists who are self-employed may meet with patients, or they may work as consultants for a variety of organizations.</u>" From this sentence as it is written, what must the reader infer?
    a. Dietitians and nutritionists consulting for organizations are always self-employed.
    b. Dietitians and nutritionists only meet with patients when they work as consultants.
    c. Dietitians and nutritionists meet with patients whether or not they are consultants.
    d. Dietitians and nutritionists do not meet with patients when working as consultants.

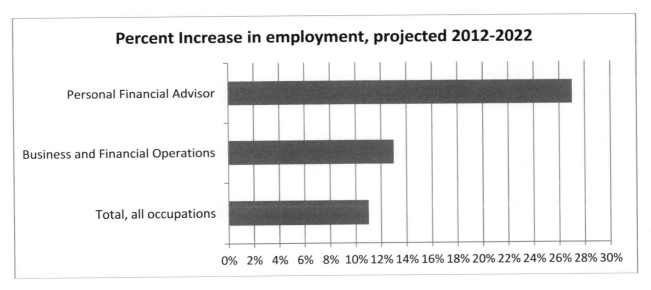

Adapted from United States Bureau of Labor Statistics, Employment Projections Program. "All occupations" includes all occupations in the United States economy.

11. According to the graph provided, what can readers *most accurately* conclude about the occupations of dietitians and nutritionists in general?

    a. Dietitian and nutritionist occupations are expected to increase by more than other occupations.

    b. Dietitian and nutritionist occupations are expected to increase by less than another occupation.

    c. Dietitian and nutritionist occupations are expected to increase by less than the other positions.

    d. Dietitian and nutritionist occupations are expected to increase by a percent equal to the others.

History/Social Studies

Focus: Students must make revising and editing decisions in the context of a passage on a history/social studies-related topic.

This passage is adapted from "Sailing Around the World" by Capt. Joshua Slocum.

I had not been in Buenos Aires for a number of years. The place where I had once landed from packets in a cart was now built up with magnificent docks. Vast fortunes had been spent in remodeling the harbor; London bankers could tell you that. The port captain after assigning the *Spray* a safe berth with his compliments
5   sent me word to call on him for anything I might want while in port and I felt quite sure that his friendship was sincere. **(12)** <u>The sloop has been well cared for at Buenos Aires; her dockage and tonnage dues are all free, and the</u> yachting fraternity of the city welcomed her with a good will. In town, I found things not so greatly changed as about the docks and I soon felt myself more at home.

10   From Montevideo I had forwarded a letter from Sir Edward Hairby to the owner of the "Standard", Mr. Mulhall, and in reply to it was assured of a warm welcome to the warmest heart, I think, outside of Ireland. Mr. Mulhall, with a prancing team, came down to the docks as soon as the *Spray* was berthed, **(13)** <u>and would have me go to his house at once, where a room was waiting</u>. And it was New Year's day, 1896. The
15   course of the *Spray* had been followed in the columns of the "Standard."

Mr. Mulhall kindly drove me to see many improvements about the city, and we went in search of some of the old landmarks. The man who sold lemonade on the plaza when first I visited this wonderful city I found selling lemonade still at two cents a glass; he had made a fortune by it. His stock in trade was a wash tub and a
20   neighboring hydrant, a moderate supply of brown sugar, and about six lemons that floated on the sweetened water. The water from time to time was renewed from the friendly pump, but the lemon went on forever, and all at two cents a glass.

But we looked in vain for the man who once sold whisky and coffins in Buenos Aires; the march of civilization had crushed him -- memory only clung to his name.
25   Enterprising man that he was, I fain would have looked him up. I remember the tiers of whisky barrels, ranged on end, on one side of the store, while on the other side, and divided by a thin partition, were the coffins in the same order, of all sizes and in great numbers. The unique arrangement seemed in order, for as a cask was emptied a coffin might be filled. Besides cheap whisky and many other liquors, he sold
30   "cider" which he manufactured from damaged Malaga raisins. Within the scope of his enterprise was also the sale of mineral waters, not entirely blameless of the germs of disease. This man surely catered to all the tastes, wants, and conditions of his customers.

Farther along in the city, however, survived the good man who wrote on the side of
35   his store, where thoughtful men might read and learn: "This wicked world will be destroyed by a comet! The owner of this store is therefore bound to sell out at any price and avoid the catastrophe." My friend Mr. Mulhall drove me round to view the fearful comet with streaming tail pictured large on the merchant's walls.

12.

    a. No Change

    b. The sloop is well cared for at Buenos Aires; her dockage and tonnage dues were all free, and the

    c. The sloop was well cared for at Buenos Aires; her dockage and tonnage dues were all free, and the

    d. The sloop will stay well cared for at Buenos Aires; while her dockage and tonnage dues were all free, and the

13.

    a. No Change

    b. and would have asked me go to his house at once, where a room was waiting

    c. and would like me to go to his house at once, where a room was waiting

    d. and would be pleased if I would go to his house at once, where a room was waiting

14. The passage suggests that the *Spray* was

    a. A packet.

    b. A sailboat.

    c. A bus.

    d. A jet of water.

15. The author found that, since his previous visit, the greatest changes in Buenos Aires had taken place:

    a. Downtown.

    b. At the harbor.

    c. At a lemonade stand.

    d. At the bank.

16. The author was shown around Buenos Aires by Mr. Mulhall. How did he come to know Mr. Mulhall?

    a. They had previously met in Ireland.

    b. They had met on the author's first visit to the city.

    c. They met through a letter of introduction.

    d. They met on the docks.

17. The passage suggests that the "Standard" (Line 11) was

    a. A steam packet.

    b. A sailboat.

    c. A newspaper.

    d. An ocean chart.

18. The author uses the term "landmarks" (Line 17) to refer to

    a. Monuments.

    b. Merchants.

    c. Banks.

    d. Buildings.

19. The passage suggests that the lemonade vendor used fresh lemons
    a. Whenever the flavor got weak.
    b. Every morning.
    c. Almost never.
    d. When he could get them.

20. The meaning of the word "fain" (Line 25) is closest to
    a. Anxiously.
    b. Willingly.
    c. Desperately.
    d. Indifferently.

21. The description of the mineral waters sold by the whiskey merchant (line 31) suggests that these waters
    a. Could cure disease.
    b. Were held in casks.
    c. Were not very clean.
    d. Were mixed with the cider.

22. The passage suggests that the merchant with the picture of the comet on his walls had
    a. Malaga raisins.
    b. Been in Buenos Aires when the author first visited.
    c. Painted the sign himself.
    d. Lived for a very long time.

Humanities

Focus: Students must make revising and editing decisions in the context of a passage on a humanities-related topic.

New Zealand Inhabitants

The islands of New Zealand are among the most remote of all the Pacific islands. New Zealand is an archipelago, with two large islands and a number of smaller ones. Its climate is far cooler than the rest of Polynesia. Nevertheless, according to Maori legends, it was colonized in the early fifteenth century by a wave of Polynesian voyagers who traveled southward in their canoes and settled on North Island. At this time, **(23)** New Zealand will already be known to the Polynesians, who had probably first landed there some 400 years earlier.

The Polynesian southward migration was limited by the availability of food. Traditional Polynesian tropical crops such as taro and yams will grow on North Island, but the climate of South Island is too cold for them. Coconuts will not grow on either island. The first settlers were forced to rely on hunting and gathering, and, of course, fishing. Especially on South Island, most settlements remained close to the sea. At the time of the Polynesian **(24)** incursion, enormous flocks of moa birds had their rookeries on the island shores. These flightless birds were easy prey for the settlers, and within a few centuries had been hunted to extinction. Fish, shellfish and the roots of the fern were other important sources of food, but even these began to diminish in quantity as the human population increased. The Maori had few other sources of meat: dogs, smaller birds, and rats. Archaeological evidence shows that human flesh was also eaten, and that tribal warfare increased markedly after the moa disappeared.

By far the most important farmed crop in prehistoric New Zealand was the sweet potato. This tuber is hearty enough to grow throughout the islands, and could be stored to provide food during the winter months, when other food-gathering activities were difficult. The availability of the sweet potato made possible a significant increase in the human population. Maori tribes often lived in encampments called *pa*, which were fortified with earthen embankments and usually located near the best sweet potato farmlands.

23.
   a. No Change
   b. New Zealand is already known by the Polynesians
   c. New Zealand has already been known to the Polynesians
   d. New Zealand was already known to the Polynesians

24.
   a. No Change
   b. import
   c. influx
   d. gathering

25. A definition for the word *archipelago* is
    a. A country
    b. A place in the southern hemisphere
    c. A group of islands
    d. A roosting place for birds

26. This article is primarily about what?
    a. The geology of New Zealand
    b. New Zealand's early history
    c. New Zealand's prehistory
    d. Food sources used by New Zealand's first colonists.

27. According to the passage, when was New Zealand first settled?
    a. In the fifteenth century
    b. Around the eleventh century
    c. Thousands of years ago
    d. On South Island

28. Why did early settlements remain close to the sea?
    a. The people liked to swim.
    b. The people didn't want to get far from the boats they had come in.
    c. Taro and yams grow only close to the beaches.
    d. They were dependent upon sea creatures for their food.

29. Why do you suppose tribal warfare increased after the moa disappeared?
    a. Increased competition for food led the people to fight.
    b. Some groups blamed others for the moa's extinction.
    c. They had more time on their hands since they couldn't hunt the moa, so they fought.
    d. One group was trying to consolidate political control over the entire country.

30. How did the colder weather of New Zealand make it difficult for the Polynesians to live there?
    a. The Polynesians weren't used to making warm clothes.
    b. Cold water fish are harder to catch.
    c. Some of them froze.
    d. Some of their traditional crops would not grow there.

31. What was a significant difference between the sweet potato and other crops known to the Polynesians?
    a. The sweet potato provided more protein.
    b. The sweet potato would grow on North Island.
    c. The sweet potato could be stored during the winter.
    d. The sweet potato could be cultured near their encampments.

32. Why was it important that sweet potatoes could be stored?
    a. They could be eaten in winter, when other foods were scarce.
    b. They could be traded for fish and other goods.
    c. They could be taken along by groups of warriors going to war.
    d. They tasted better after a few weeks of storage.

33. Why do you suppose the *pa* were usually located near sweet potato farmlands?
    a. So they could defend the best farmlands from their fortified camps.
    b. So they could have ready access to their most important source of food.
    c. So they could transport the potatoes easily into camp for storage.
    d. All of the above are probably true.

Science

Focus: Students must make revising and editing decisions in the context of a passage on a science-related topic.

Cilia and Flagella

Cilia and flagella are tubular structures found on the surfaces of many animal cells. They are examples of organelles, sub-cellular structures that perform a particular function. By beating against the surrounding medium in a swimming motion, they may endow cells with motility or induce the medium to circulate, as in the case of gills. Ciliated cells typically each contain large numbers of cilia 2 -10 μm (micrometer) long. In contrast, flagellated cells usually have one or two flagella, and the structures can be as long as 200 μm. For both types of structure, the diameters are less than 0.5 μm.

Although they share similar structures, the motion of the two organelles is somewhat different. Flagella beat in a circular, undulating motion that is continuous. The effective stroke of a cilium's beat, which generates the power, is followed by a more languid recovery to the original position. During the recovery stroke, they are brought in close to the membrane of the cell. Cilia usually beat in coordinated waves, so that at any given moment some are in the midst of their power stroke while others are recovering. This provides for a steady flow of fluid past gill surfaces or the epithelia lining the lungs or digestive tract.

The construction of both organelles is very similar. A portion of the cell membrane appears to be stretched over a framework made of tubulin polymers. A polymer is a long, chain-like molecule made of smaller units that are strung together. In this case, the subunits are molecules of the protein tubulin. The framework, or skeleton, of a cilium or flagellum consists of 9 pairs of tubulin polymers spaced around the periphery, and two more single polymers of tubulin that run along the center of the shaft. This is called a 9+2 pattern.

The motion of the organelles results from chemical reactions that cause the outer polymers to slide past one another. **(34)** <u>By doing so, they force the overall structure</u> to bend. This is similar to the mechanism of contraction of skeletal muscle. In cilia and flagella, the nine outer polymer pairs of the skeleton have along their lengths molecules of a rod-shaped protein called dynein. The dynein rods can grasp, or bind to, the neighboring tubulin polymer. Energy is then used to drive a chemical reaction that causes the dynein arms to bend, causing one tubulin polymer to move along the length of the other. Through a coordinated series of thousands of such reactions, the cilium or flagellum will beat.

Cilia have also provided some of the best evidence for the inheritance of traits by a mechanism that does not involve DNA. A *Paramecium* is a single-celled ciliated protist that lives in ponds. In one variety, the stroke cycle of the cilia is clockwise (right-handed). In another variety, it is counter-clockwise (left-handed). When the cells divide, left-handed cells give rise to more left-handed cells, and *vice versa*. T.M. Sonneborn of Indiana University managed to cut tiny pieces of cell membrane from a left-handed *Paramecium* and graft them onto a right-handed one. **(35)** <u>The cell</u>

survived, and the direction of the stroke did not change, despite the fact that the cilia were now in a cell with a right-handed nucleus and surrounded by right-handed cilia, they continued to rotate to the left. A *paramecium* reproduces by dividing, and Sonneborn followed the transplanted patch for several generations, but it did not change direction. This suggested that the direction of rotation is a property of the cilium itself, and is not influenced by the DNA in the nucleus. In another experiment, Sonneborn transplanted the nucleus of a right-handed cell into a left-handed cell from which the original nucleus had been removed. The cell's cilia kept their counter-clockwise direction of rotation. Further, when this cell divided, all subsequent generations maintained it as well. This proved that the direction of rotation could be inherited in a manner completely independent of the chromosomal DNA.

One theory to explain this is the concept of *nucleation*. According to this idea, the tubulin proteins in left- and right-handed *Paramecia* are the same, so that the genes that give rise to them are also identical. However, once they begin to chain together in a left- or right-handed manner, they continue to do so. Therefore the direction of rotation does not depend upon the genes, but rather on some basal structure that is passed on to the cell's offspring when it divides.

34.
  a. No Change
  b. By doing it so they force the overall structure
  c. By doing so, it force the overall structure
  d. By doing that, it can forces the overall structure

35.
  a. No Change
  b. The cell survived, and the direction of the stroke did not change, but despite the fact
  c. The cell survived, and the direction of the stroke did not change. Despite the fact
  d. The cell survived, and the direction of the stroke did not change, even though despite the fact

36. Cilia and flagella are both
  a. Proteins.
  b. Sub-cellular structures that perform a particular function.
  c. Organelles that beat in a continuous undulating motion.
  d. Single-celled protists

37. According to the passage, where would you expect to find cilia?
  a. Stomach lining
  b. Back of the hand
  c. Lining of the heart
  d. Circulatory system

38. According to the passage, how many tubulin polymers make up the entire 9+2 pattern seen in cilia and flagella?
  a. 11
  b. 9
  c. 20
  d. 2

39. Two proteins mentioned in this passage are
    a. Tubulin and Paramecium.
    b. Tubulin and dynein.
    c. Tubulin and flagellin.
    d. Tubulin and Sonneborn.

40. Which of the following explains how the beating motion of flagella is caused?
    a. The two central polymers slide past one another.
    b. Dynein causes the outer polymer pairs to slide past one another.
    c. Dynein causes each of the outer polymers to bend.
    d. The organelle increases in diameter.

41. Polymers are always
    a. Made of protein.
    b. Made of tubulin.
    c. Made of subunits.
    d. Arranged in a 9+2 array.

42. The passage implies that T.M. Sonneborn was
    a. A zookeeper.
    b. A scientist at Indiana University.
    c. A chemist.
    d. A medical practitioner.

43. It was shown that, if cilia with a counterclockwise rotation are grafted onto a cell whose native cilia beat clockwise, the transplants will
    a. Beat clockwise.
    b. Stop beating.
    c. Beat randomly.
    d. Beat counterclockwise.

44. The passage describes cilia and flagella and tells us that
    a. Cilia may be 200 µm long.
    b. Flagella are less than 0.5 µm long.
    c. Cells can have more than two flagella.
    d. Flagella are less than 0.5 µm in diameter.

Math – Calculator

1. Solve the following system of equations.

$$y = 3x + 2$$
$$2x + y = 7$$

    a. $x = -1, y = 5$
    b. $x = -1, = 9$
    c. $x = 1, y = 5$
    d. $x = 1, y = 9$

2. The table below lists values for x and $f(x)$.

x	$f(x)$
1	2
2	5
3	10
4	17
5	26

Which of the following equations describes the relationship between x and $f(x)$?
    a. $f(x) = x + 1$
    b. $f(x) = x^2$
    c. $f(x) = (-x)^2$
    d. $f(x) = x^2 + 1$

3. Which of the following equations represents the relationship between x and y, shown in the table below?

x	y
−3	−21
−1	−3
0	6
2	24
5	51

    a. $y = 9x + 6$
    b. $y = 7x$
    c. $y = 3x + 18$
    d. $y = 12x + 6$

4. Kim is given $21 to buy gallons of milk and cartons of eggs. Each gallon of milk costs $3.50, and each carton of eggs costs $1.75. Which of the following graphs represents the possible combinations of gallons of milk and cartons of eggs she may purchase?

a.

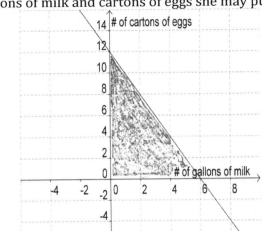

c.

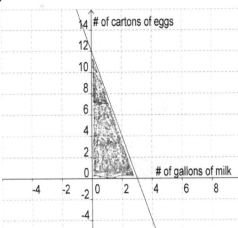

b.

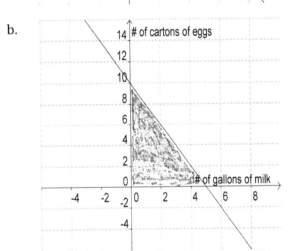

d.

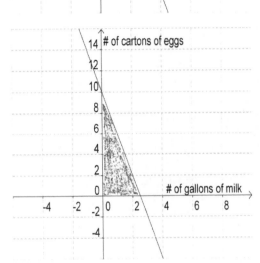

5. If the two lines $2x + y = 0$ and $y = 3$ are plotted on a typical xy coordinate grid, at which point will they intersect?

    a. -1.5, 3
    b. 1.5, 3
    c. -1.5, 0
    d. 4, 1

6. What is the value of $\frac{x^3+2x}{x+3}$ when $x = -1$?

    a. $-\frac{3}{2}$
    b. $-\frac{2}{3}$
    c. $\frac{1}{2}$
    d $\frac{3}{4}$

7. What is the value of $\frac{2x-2}{x-3}$ when $x = -1$?

    a. 0
    b. 1
    c. 2
    d. −2

8. A seller purchases wholesale merchandise and sells it in his store with a mark-up of 25%. Store inventory that does not readily sell is placed on clearance and marked down by 20%. What percentage profit does the seller make on clearance sales? _____

9. An MP3 player is set to play songs at random from the fifteen songs it contains in its memory. Any song can be played at any time, even if it is repeated. There are 5 songs by Band A, 3 songs by Band B, 2 by Band C, and 5 by Band D. If the player has just played two songs in a row by Band D, what is the probability that the next song will also be by Band D?

    a. 1 in 5
    b. 1 in 3
    c. 1 in 9
    d. 1 in 27

10. 9.5% of the people in a town voted for a certain proposition in a municipal election. If the town's population is 51,623, about how many people in the town voted for the proposition?

    a. 3,000
    b. 5,000
    c. 7,000
    d. 10,000

11. A reporter for a school newspaper surveys the students at the school to ask if they prefer chocolate, vanilla, or strawberry ice cream. Of the students who answer her question, 35% prefer vanilla, and 40% prefer chocolate. What percent of the students she surveyed prefer strawberry?

    a. 15%
    b. 25%
    c. 45%
    d. There is not enough information to say.

12. Six people sit around a circular table at a party. If two of these people are the party's hosts and must sit next to each other, how many different possibilities are there for the order of the six people around the table? (Rotations are not counted as different orders.)

    a. 24
    b. 48
    c. 120
    d. 240

13. Mrs. Patterson's classroom has sixteen empty chairs. All of the chairs are occupied when every student is present. If 2/5 of the students are absent, how many students make up her entire class?

    a 16 students
    b. 32 students
    c. 24 students
    d. 40 students

14. The probability that Alisha chooses a philosophy class is 0.30. The probability that she chooses a qualitative methods class, given that she chooses a philosophy class, is 0.40. Finally, the probability she chooses a philosophy class or a qualitative methods class is 0.62. What is the probability she chooses a qualitative methods class?
   a. 0.32
   b. 0.38
   c. 0.44
   d. 0.52

Question 15 is based on the following figure (not drawn to scale):

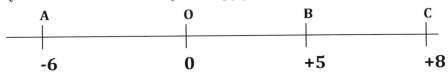

A	O	B	C
-6	0	+5	+8

15. In the figure, A, B, and C are points on the number line, where O is the origin. What is the ratio of the distance BC to distance AB?
   a. 3:5
   b. 8:5
   c. 8:11
   d. 3:11

16. Given the probability distribution table shown below, what is the expected value?

x	$f(x)$
0	0.23
1	0.21
2	0.17
3	0.14
4	0.12
5	0.09
6	0.04

   a. 1.82
   b. 1.96
   c. 2.02
   d. 2.14

17. The numbers of volunteers in different states are shown in the table below. Which of the following statements is true?

Texas	8	17	18	19	20	21	21	21	22	28	29	31	41	45	48
New Mexico	7	11	15	29	30	30	31	33	34	36	37	42	44	44	45

   a. The numbers of volunteers in Texas have a greater median and mean.
   b. The numbers of volunteers in Texas have a greater median and a smaller mean.
   c. The numbers of volunteers in Texas have a smaller median and mean.
   d. The numbers of volunteers in Texas have a smaller median and a greater mean.

18. Given the table shown below, what is the probability that a student is a Democrat or prefers math?

	History	Science	Math	Total
Democrat	13	30	37	23
Republican	20	38	12	35
Total	33	68	49	58

a. $\frac{23}{51}$

b. $\frac{35}{58}$

c. $\frac{33}{58}$

d. $\frac{7}{17}$

Questions 19 and 20 are based on the following table:

Kyle bats third in the batting order for the Badgers baseball team. The table below shows the number of hits that Kyle had in each of 7 consecutive games played during one week in July.

Day of Week	Number of Hits
Monday	1
Tuesday	2
Wednesday	3
Thursday	1
Friday	1
Saturday	4
Sunday	2

19. What is the mode of the numbers in the distribution shown in the table?
    a. 1
    b. 2
    c. 3
    d. 4

20. What is the mean of the numbers in the distribution shown in the table?
    a. 1
    b. 2
    c. 3
    d. 4

21. Todd will win $10 if he rolls a 3 or 4, $8 if he rolls a 2, and $12 if he rolls any other number. Which of the following best represents the amount of money he can expect to win?
    a. $9.37
    b. $9.67
    c. $10.67
    d. $11.37

22. Solve the inequality $2x^2 + 5x - 12 \geq 0$ for x.
    a. $-2 \leq x \leq 3$
    b. $x \leq -2$ or $x \geq 3$
    c. $-4 \leq x \leq \frac{3}{2}$
    d. $x \leq -4$ or $x \geq \frac{3}{2}$

23. Solve the equation $\sqrt{4x - 3} + 2 = x$ for x.
    a. $x = 1$
    b. $x = 7$
    c. $x = -1$ and $x = 7$
    d. $x = 1$ and $x = 7$

24. If $f(x)$ is a quadratic function with roots at $x = -4$ and $x = 6$, what is $f(x)$?
    a. $f(x) = x^2 - 24$
    b. $f(x) = x^2 - 10x + 24$
    c. $f(x) = x^2 - 2x - 24$
    d. $f(x) = x^2 + 2x - 24$

25. Which of the following represents the sum of $\frac{3}{x+2} + \frac{x}{x^2+10x+16}$?
    a. $\frac{3}{x+2}$
    b. $\frac{x+6}{x+8}$
    c. $\frac{2(x+6)}{(x+2)(x+8)}$
    d. $\frac{4(x+6)}{(x+8)(x+2)}$

26. Which of the following represents the product of $(4x^3 - 2x + 4)(x - 8)$?
    a. $4x^4 - 32x^3 + 18x - 32$
    b. $4x^4 - 32x^3 - 18x^2 - 2x - 12$
    c. $4x^4 - 32x^3 - 2x^2 + 20x - 32$
    d. $4x^4 - 28x^3 - 2x^2 + 16x - 4$

27. In the figure, $ABCD$ is a parallelogram. The angles are $m\angle B = (3x)°$ and $m\angle C = (4x + 5)°$. Find $m\angle A$.
    a. $m\angle A = 95°$
    b. $m\angle A = 100°$
    c. $m\angle A = 105°$
    d. $m\angle A = 110°$

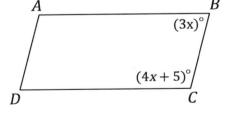

28. In the figure, the radius of circle C is 8. Find the area of the shaded sector. If necessary, round your answer to the nearest tenth.
The area is approximately _____.

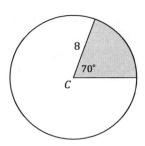

29. The figure shows the shape of a large swimming pool in a Las Vegas resort. The pool is a rectangle with semicircles on either end. If the pool is 8 ft deep throughout, what is the volume of the pool? Round your answer to the nearest cubic foot if necessary.

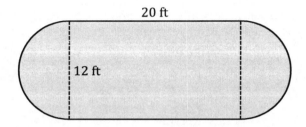

The volume of the pool is approximately _____ ft³.

30. In the figure, $\triangle ABC$ is an equilateral triangle with sides of length 10 in. Circle O is inscribed in this triangle, so that it is tangent to $\triangle ABC$ at three points. Calculate the radius of circle O. Write an exact answer in simplest form.
The radius is _____ in.

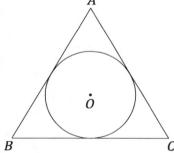

31. Simplify: $4(-3 + 5i) + 6(1 - 3i)$.
    a. $18 + 38i$
    b. $13 + 18i$
    c. $-6 + 2i$
    d. $-6 - 2i$

Math - No-Calculator

1. A librarian makes 50% more per hour for each hour that he works in excess of 40 hours each week. The linear function $s(h) = 27h + 720$ represents his weekly salary (in dollars) if he works h hours more than 40 hours that week. For example, his weekly salary is $s(10) = 990$ dollars if he works 50 hours in one week (because 10 + 40 = 50). What is his hourly wage after he has already worked the initial 40 hours in one week?

    a. $7.20 per hour
    b. $18.00 per hour
    c. $27.00 per hour
    d. $72.00 per hour

2. Which of these expresses the equation $y = 4x - 2$ as x in terms of y?

    a. $x = 4y - 2$
    b. $x = -4y + 2$
    c. $x = \frac{1}{4}y + 2$
    d. $x = \frac{1}{4}y + \frac{1}{2}$

3. Graph on the number line the solution to the inequality $2|x + 3| - 9 \geq -1$.

4. The solution to which of the following systems of inequalities is graphed below?

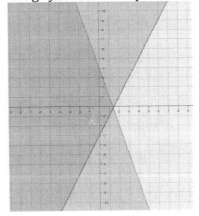

    a. $y < -3x + 4$
        $4x - 2y \leq 6$

    b. $y \geq 2x - 3$
        $y < 3x + 4$

    c. $x < -3y + 4$
        $y + 3 \leq 2x$

    d. $y > 4 - 3x$
        $y \leq 2x - 3$

5. Which of the following is the correct graph of the system of inequalities below?

$$x - y > 1$$
$$2x + y > 2$$

a.
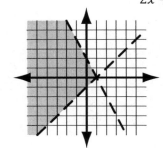

c.
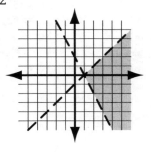

b.
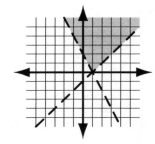

d.
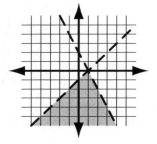

6. Which of the following is equivalent to $-2x < 5$?
   a. $x < 1$
   b. $x > 1$
   c. $x < -1$
   d. $x > -1$

7. A certain exam has 30 questions. A student gets 1 point for each question he gets right and loses half a point for a question he answers incorrectly; he neither gains nor loses any points for a question left blank. If C is the number of questions a student gets right and B is the number of questions he leaves blank, which of the following represents his score on the exam?
   a. $C - \frac{1}{2}B$
   b. $C - \frac{1}{2}(30 - B)$
   c. $C - \frac{1}{2}(30 - B - C)$
   d. $(30 - C) - \frac{1}{2}(30 - B)$

8. A building has a number of floors of equal height, as well as a thirty-foot spire above them all. If the height of each floor in feet is h, and there are n floors in the building, which of the following represents the building's total height in feet?
   a. $n + h + 30$
   b. $nh + 30$
   c. $30n + h$
   d. $30h + n$

9. If $x + y > 0$ when $x > y$, which of the following cannot be true?
   a. $x = 6$ and $y = -1$
   b. $x = -3$ and $y = 0$
   c. $x = -4$ and $y = -3$
   d. $x = 3$ and $y = -3$

10. Simplify the expression $\frac{x^2+2x-24}{5x-20}$.
    a. $\frac{x-4}{5}$
    b. $\frac{x+6}{5}$
    c. $\frac{(x-4)(x+6)}{5(x-4)}$
    d. $\frac{(x+4)(x+6)}{5(x-4)}$

11. Simplify the expression $x^6 \cdot (3x)^2$.
    a. $3x^8$
    b. $3x^{12}$
    c. $9x^8$
    d. $9x^{12}$

12. A theater manager estimates that he will sell 600 tickets to a play if he prices tickets at $10 each. He also estimates that he will sell fifty fewer tickets for every dollar the price is raised or fifty more tickets for every dollar the price is lowered. Write a function $r(x)$ for the estimated revenue if the theater raises the price by x dollars.
    a. $r(x) = -50x^2 - 100x + 6000$
    b. $r(x) = -50x^2 + 100x + 6000$
    c. $r(x) = 50x^2 - 1100x - 6000$
    d. $r(x) = 50x^2 + 1100x + 6000$

13. Compare the graphs of $f(x) = 3^x$ and $g(x) = 3^{x+1}$.
    a. The graph of g is the graph of f shifted one unit down.
    b. The graph of g is the graph of f shifted one unit up.
    c. The graph of g is the graph of f shifted one unit to the left.
    d. The graph of g is the graph of f shifted one unit to the right.

14. Exponential functions grow by equal factors over equal intervals. By what factor does the exponential function $f(x) = 3 \cdot 2^x$ grow by over every interval whose length is 3?
    a. By a factor of 6
    b. By a factor of 8
    c. By a factor of 18
    d. By a factor of 24

15. Of the four functions listed here, which will increase in value the most between $x = 10$ and $x = 20$?

$$f(\ ) = 2^x$$
$$g(x) = x^2$$
$$h(x) = 3x$$
$$j(x) = ln(x)$$

a. $f(x)$
b. $g(x)$
c. $h(x)$
d. $j(x)$

16. Calculate the sixth term $f(6)$ of the sequence defined as:

$$f(n) = \begin{cases} 1 & n = 1,2 \\ f(n-1) + 2f(n-2) & n > 2 \end{cases}$$

a. 8
b. 11
c. 21
d. 41

17. Complex numbers are sometimes drawn as vectors to allow for addition and subtraction on the graph. Identify the equation of complex numbers represented by the following graph of vectors:

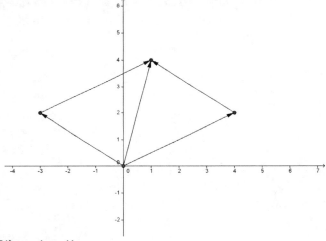

a. $(-3 + 2i) + (4 + 2i) = 1 + 4i$
b. $(4 + 2i) - (-3 + 2i) = 1 + 4i$
c. $(1 + 4i) - (-3 + 2i) = 4 + 2i$
d. $(2 - 3i) + (2 + 4i) = 4 + i$

Answers and Explanations #2

Reading

World Literature

1. B: There is no indication in the passage that the Bennets are interested in becoming friends with Mr. Bingley (choice A), that Mr. Bingley would be a valuable business connection (choice C), or that Mr. Bingley has any prior knowledge of the Bennet daughters (choice D). Mrs. Bennet tells her husband that a new neighbor is moving in: "Mrs. Long says that Netherfield is taken by a young man of large fortune." Mrs. Bennet is sure he will make an excellent husband for one of her daughters: "You must know that I am thinking of his marrying one of them."

2. A: Mrs. Bennet feels that Mr. Bingley is likely to marry one of her daughters. She tells her husband that Mr. Bingley is a "single man of large fortune; four or five thousand a year. What a fine thing for our girls!"

3. C: Mrs. Bennet wants her husband to be acquainted with Mr. Bingley so that he can introduce Mr. Bingley to their daughters: "But it is very likely that he may fall in love with one of them, and therefore you must visit him as soon as he comes."

4. A: Mrs. Bennet remarks to her husband, "But it is very likely that he may fall in love with one of them, and therefore you must visit him as soon as he comes."

5. B: Mrs. Bennet is annoyed and fed up with her husband's seeming indifference to Mr. Bingley: "'My dear Mr. Bennet,' replied his wife, 'how can you be so tiresome!'"

6. B: The evidence in this selection indicates that marrying a man with money was a primary goal for young women. Mrs. Bennet tells Mr. Bennet that Mr. Bingley is "A single man of large fortune; four or five thousand a year." Mrs. Bennet further indicates that she is thrilled with the news because of Mr. Bingley's potential as a husband for one of her daughters: "What a fine thing for our girls... You must know that I am thinking of his marrying one of them."

7. A: "It is a truth universally acknowledged" means that something is understood to be true by the general public.

8. C: "A single man in possession of a good fortune, must be in want of a wife" means that if a man has enough money to support a wife in comfort, he must want to find a wife as soon as possible.

9. A: Mr. Bennet is facetiously asking if the idea of marriage (particularly to one of his own daughters) was Mr. Bingley's intention when he agreed to rent Netherfield Park.

History/Social Studies

Passage 1

10. A: The text indicates that the "rebel fire was hottest, the shells rolling down every street, and the bridge under the heavy cannonade" and "a courier… placed in my hand a crumpled, bloody piece of paper, a request from the lion-hearted old surgeon on the opposite shore, establishing his hospitals in the very jaws of death." Both of these indicate that the soldiers knew that the situation was dangerous, no place for an unarmed lady.

11. A: The text mentions Clara being helpful during several battles. While she may have helped throughout the Civil War, it is not the topic here. Choice C focuses more on other nurses in the war, and Choice D doesn't make sense because Clara was on the battlefield when the fighting was taking place.

12. C: The author mentions that men had been shot while Clara lived, demonstrating an interesting dichotomy of her life: the unarmed nurse who was protected on the battlefield, while the armed men did not seem to be.

13. B: While the other choices may have some truth to them, there is no evidence in the text that the soldier had little money (A). Options C and D give only partial answers.

14. D: From the context of this passage, the surgeon's hospitals were not all destroyed (a), as he continued to treat the wounded. The surgeon is described as old, but nothing indicates he was near dying himself (b). Although a great many soldiers died in the Civil War, not all of them who were treated died (c), and nothing in the passage indicates all of this particular surgeon's patients died. In this context, "the very jaws of death" refers to treating wounded soldiers on (or directly adjacent to) battlefields (d).

15. D: The sentence answering this question is, "It ended the life of the poor lad, but only tore a hole in Clara Barton's sleeve." Clara was not wounded; the bullet missed her. The boy, however, was not merely wounded but killed.

16. C: In this sentence context, "rare" means occurring seldom. Unusually great (a) is another meaning of "rare," e.g. a rare show of bravery. Fine or precious (b) and admirable (d) are other meanings of "rare," but the context describing Barton's courage, dedication, and seriousness informs the correct meaning here.

17. A: *Noble* and *gallant* are evidence of positive feelings toward the North. Excerpt (b) is evidence of Barton's care for both sides' soldiers. Excerpt (c) is evidence of large numbers and unceasing action of Union troops, not positive feelings toward them. Excerpt (d) is evidence of personal experience with war casualties.

18. B: This sentence uses parallelism/parallel structure in a series of phrases beginning with *every*; i.e., "its every church a crowded hospital, every street a battle-line, every hill a rampart..." The repeated structure and words reinforce the description, emphasizing the visual evidence that the *city of death* was a war zone. Alliteration (a) is repeating the same sounds across words. Paradoxes (c) combine contradictory concepts to convey deeper insight. Periphrasis (d) is deliberately using verbiage for grandiose effect, embellishment, and/or distraction from meaning.

Passage 2

19. B: The entire passage makes the argument that Black History Month should be abolished, offering various reasons why this is the best course of action.

20. D: The context of the sentence suggests that post-racial refers to an approach in which race is not a useful or positive organizing principle.

21. D: Clearly both authors think it is important for students to learn about the achievements and experience of African Americans; their debate is whether observing Black History Month is the best way to achieve this goal.

22. C: The author of Passage 2 points out that just because there is a month focused on African American history, this doesn't mean that African American history must be ignored for the rest of the year.

23. C: The author points out in paragraph 3 of Passage 2 that the debate about how to meet the need to teach children about African American history can remind parents that this need is not yet fully met.

24. D: The author of Passage 1 never suggests that people do not learn about African American history during Black History Month.

25. C: Neither author claims that the Emancipation Proclamation was signed in February.

26. A: In paragraph 4, the author of Passage 2 states that the material available is rich and varied.

27. B: Passage 2 states that W.E.B. DuBois was born in 1868; his birth was therefore the first of the identified events.

Science

Passage 1

28. A: Solar radiation is not listed as a component of comet nuclei.

29. B: The second sentence in the passage notes that comets are distinguishable from asteroids by the presence of comas or tails.

30. B: A comet with an orbit of longer than 200 years is a long period comet.

31. C: The third paragraph notes that there are over 3,500 known comets. It also notes that this represents only a small portion of those in existence.

32. C: The second paragraph notes that because they have low mass, they don't become spherical and have irregular shapes.

33. A: The second paragraph notes that some comets may be tens of kilometers across. It also notes that comas may be larger than the sun.

34. D: The sixth paragraph notes that most comets have oval shaped orbits.

35. D: The passage defines single apparition comets as those whose trajectories make them pass the Sun once and then exit our solar system permanently. It also describes most comets as having oval orbits wherein they are nearer to the Sun during part of their orbit, and then move farther away from the Sun *within the solar system* for the rest of the orbit; hence (a) is incorrect. While single apparition comets are only apparent once, they are NOT still in the solar system (b). The passage defines short and long orbital periods, but does not include long orbital periods in that definition (c).

36. A: The last sentence in the second paragraph states, "Because of their low mass, they do not become spherical and have irregular shapes." The first sentence in this second paragraph identifies the content of comet nuclei (b), but these contents are not given as evidence of low mass. The second sentence in this paragraph identifies how large the comas can be (c), but does not use size as evidence of low mass. The first sentence in this paragraph indicates variability in size (d), but this is not given as evidence of low mass.

37. D: The fourth paragraph in the passage states, "If a comet's path crosses the Earth's path, there will likely be meteor showers as Earth passes through the trail of debris." The fifth paragraph states that many comets and asteroids have collided with the Earth (a), but does not say this can cause meteor showers. Nothing in the passage identifies large groups of meteors entering Earth's atmosphere (b) as causing meteor showers. There is no mention of a comet exploding (c) either.

Passage 2
38. D: Following the quoted sentence, the passage author identifies the current periodic table groups by their numbers, which are Arabic numerals 1-18. The names of individual elements (a), e.g., helium, calcium, gold, silver, argon, etc., are NOT the current group naming convention; their *group numbers* are. The groups are not named using lower-case letters (b). Roman numerals (c) are identified as a *previous* group naming convention, but not the current one.

39. B: In the sentence preceding the one quoted, the author writes, "At minimum, a cell includes the symbol for the element and its atomic number." The quoted sentence follows as an example. Since the atomic number is a number, even readers unfamiliar with the subject can assume it is the "1"; thus the "H" must be the symbol. "H" does not represent alphabetical order (a): the following sentence states, "Elements are ordered by atomic number," not alphabetically. "H" is the initial letter of Hydrogen, but (c) is incorrect because not all element symbols are initial letters of their English names; for example, the symbol for sodium is Na, and the symbol for gold is Au (these reflect the first two letters of their Latin names). Even readers not knowing this can distinguish symbol vs. number from context (see above). Since "1" must be the atomic number, (d) is incorrect.

40. A: This sentence first explains that the outer electron shell's configuration has a primary effect on the chemical properties of an element; and then concludes that the periodic table's groups contain chemically similar elements. Sentence (b) identifies the groups as containing elements with similar outer electron shell configurations; but without the explanation from sentence (a) that those similar configurations of their outer electron shells signify similar chemical properties, this sentence alone is not evidence that groups in the periodic table are chemically similar. Sentence (c) describes cells, not groups, in the periodic table. Sentence (d) describes how one chemical property, ionization energy, increases across periods and decreases down groups, not how groups are chemically similar.

41. B: The fourth paragraph, the last in the excerpted passage, describes how atomic radii, electronegativity, ionization energy, and electron affinity increase or decrease from left to right across periods and from top to bottom within groups. These increases and decreases of chemical properties are not mentioned in the first (a), second or third (c) paragraphs; hence (d) is incorrect.

42. B: The first paragraph in the passage defines rows as periods and columns as groups. Since rows are horizontal and columns are vertical, the reader infers the directionality of periods and groups from this information. (a) is the reverse of the correct choice. Cells are not called periods or rows called groups (c); the first paragraph's description states that cells are *arranged* in periods, which are rows; and in groups, which are columns. Therefore (d) is incorrect.

43. A: The periodic trends described are mainly patterns of increasing or decreasing across periods and from top to bottom in groups. Since increases and decreases are progressive linear changes, and since these occur in horizontal or vertical order, the relationship they depict is sequential. Although cause-and-effect underlies these trends; i.e., they occur because of the elements' atomic structures and periodic nature and the periodic table's corresponding arrangement, the trends themselves do not show a cause-effect relationship (b). For example, electronegativity or other properties named increase or decrease in sequence across periods/down groups; a change in the quantity or quality of a property in one cell of a period or group is not an effect caused by the previous cell. The relationship is not parts to whole (c), which might involve something like the similar chemical properties of all elements within one group rather than sequences of change throughout groups and periods. Comparison-contrast (d) would involve distinct similarities and differences between/among parts of the table rather than progressive sequences of increasing or decreasing properties.

44. A: Based on the descriptions in the paragraph, an inverse relationship often occurs between periods and groups in terms of periodic trends; i.e., as one increases, the other decreases and vice versa. The reader might infer this from the information that atomic radii decrease across rows but increase down groups; electronegativity increases across periods but decreases down groups; and ionization energy increases across periods but decreases down groups. The information that electronic affinity increases in negativity across periods but changes little within groups shows that an inverse relationship is not necessarily or always the case. In a converse (b) relationship, such properties would both increase or both decrease both across periods and down groups. The passage does not identify this. A direct (c) relationship and a converse (b) relationship are synonyms. Since (a) is correct, (d) is incorrect.

45. C: The passage's fourth paragraph identifies the number of electrons in the outer shell as determining which group an element belongs to in a block. The passage never identifies an element's atomic number as determining an element's group (a). The number assigned to each period (b) does not *determine* an element's group in a block; rather, as the paragraph states, this period number *corresponds to* and represents the highest-numbered electron shell in use. Group numbers label each group for reference; the fourth paragraph does not identify group numbers (d) as *determining* the group where an element belongs.

46. B: The first paragraph gives a general summary of what the periodic table is and does and how it is organized. The ensuing paragraphs give more specific details about groups, blocks within periods, and trends in properties, respectively; hence (a) is incorrect. Since the first paragraph is more general, (c) is incorrect. (d) is the reverse of the correct answer.

47. D: The purpose of this passage is to explain how the periodic table works, how it is organized, the conventions it uses, and some trends in chemical properties that can be identified in its organization. The other choices are all subordinate topics within this main purpose. For example, (a) is addressed in the first two sentences of the second paragraph. Choice (c) is addressed in one sentence: "It is a common model for organizing and understanding elements." Periods and groups (b) are major organizational features of the periodic table and are discussed throughout, but are still individual components within the larger purpose of explaining the periodic table overall.

Writing and Language

Careers

1. A: The material in the last paragraph of this passage is explicitly introduced by the preceding sentence, "The following are examples of types of dietitians and nutritionists:" with the colon further identifying this sentence as an introduction to what follows. Such an introduction is not used between other or all paragraphs (b). Since (a) is correct, (c) and (d) are necessarily incorrect.

2. D: The first paragraph identifies the functions of dietitians and nutritionists. The second paragraph gives examples of some dietitians and nutritionists' clients. The third paragraph identifies some activities of self-employed dietitians and nutritionists. The fourth paragraph serves as a transition from all preceding paragraphs; establish that specialties exist in these occupations; and introduce the fifth paragraph. The fifth/last paragraph defines some job functions, work settings, and clienteles of three specialties in these fields.

3. B: According to the passage, self-employed dietitians and nutritionists may need to schedule appointments and perform other administrative duties (a); write and/or assemble information (c) to distribute materials to clients to educate them about diet and nutrition; and engage in marketing activities to promote their own services (d).

4. B: The second paragraph includes examples about planning diets to address hypertension, weight loss; and to coordinate patient care, all of which relate to improving health. The last paragraph includes counseling patients about how to live healthier lifestyles; specializing in working with patients having specific diseases; and counseling the public on food- and nutrition-related topics, all of which also contribute to improving health. Therefore (a) is incorrect. However, this information is found in only these two paragraphs, not all of them (c). Since it appears in two paragraphs, (d) is also incorrect.

5. C: The last paragraph of this passage identifies management dietitians as the ones who "...may be responsible for buying food and for carrying out other business-related tasks such as budgeting. Management dietitians may oversee kitchen staff or other dietitians." Clinical dietitians and nutritionists (a) are described as providing medical nutrition therapy, creating nutritional programs, counseling patients, and sometimes specializing by working only with patients having certain diseases. Community dietitians and nutritionists (b) are identified as developing programs, counseling the public, and often working with specific groups like elderly or adolescent age groups. Hence (d) is incorrect.

6. D: A pair of dashes is used to identify a parenthetical statement inserted in a sentence for additional clarification, as used here. (Other uses include adding a further comment; making a dramatic qualification; or indicating a sudden change in thought.) The dashes are not incorrect here; and omitting punctuation (a) would remove the emphasis on the parenthetical statement. The author is emphasizing that nutritional advice involves not only which foods to eat, but *also* those foods to avoid. Although it is a parenthetical statement, parentheses are not preferable (b) here because they imply a less important addition, whereas the intent here is to emphasize that the addition is equally important: *not* eating unhealthy foods is as important to health as eating healthy foods is. Enclosing the added statement in commas instead (c) would not emphasize its importance as enclosing it in dashes does.

7. A: This is a simple sentence despite its length and multiple modifiers because it has only one independent clause and no dependent clause. All modifiers are prepositional phrases, adverbs, and adverbial phrases. A complex sentence (b) contains an independent clause and a dependent/subordinate clause; for instance: "A dietitian might teach a client how to use less salt when preparing meals because the client has high blood pressure." A compound sentence (c) has two independent clauses joined by a coordinating conjunction. For instance: "A dietitian might teach a client to use less salt when preparing meals, and this can lower high blood pressure." A compound-complex sentence (d) includes both two (or more) independent clauses and one (or more) dependent clause(s), e.g.: "A dietitian might teach a client how to use less salt when preparing meals because the client has high blood pressure, and this can help lower it."

8. C: Both have noun agreement, so either one would be correct. Choice (a) preserves the original singular "a diet" and changes plural object noun "patients" to singular "a patient" to agree. Choice (b) changes "a diet" to plural "diets" to agree with the existing "patients". Making no change (d) to the sentence would retain the original disagreement in noun number.

9. B: Following the quoted portion, the sentence context continues, "such as adolescents or the elderly." Hence "people in specific age groups" is the best answer since the author uses two specific age groups as examples. People with specific diseases (a) are identified in this paragraph as examples of people with whom clinical dietitians and nutritionists—not community dietitians and nutritionists—work. While this paragraph says community dietitians and nutritionists counsel the public (c), the general public does not constitute *specific* groups of people; and the paragraph does not equate these. While the paragraph says that community dietitians and nutritionists work in HMOs (d), it also says in the same sentence that they also work in public health clinics, government and nonprofit agencies, and other settings. It does not use HMO members as examples of specific groups of people.

10. D: Because of the word "or", this sentence represents an "either-or" choice; i.e., they *either* meet with patients *or* consult for organizations, not both. Hence the reader must infer (whether true or not*) that when consulting for organizations, self-employed dietitians and nutritionists do not meet with patients. *(This may not always be true: in some cases, physicians, therapists, or other practitioners requesting consults may ask dietitians/nutritionists to meet with a patient as part of the consultation. However, the question does not ask whether this sentence is accurate; it only asks what the reader must infer from it as it is written.) The sentence says that self-employed dietitians/nutritionists may consult for organizations, not that consultants are always self-employed (a). It says that they meet with patients OR consult, not that they only meet with patients WHEN consulting (b). Because of the "or", readers cannot infer dietitians/nutritionists meet with patients whether consulting or not (c).

11. C: Dietitian and nutritionist occupations are not included among business and financial operations occupations or among personal financial advisor occupations; therefore they must be included among "Total, all occupations". The projections shown in the graph indicate that business and financial operations occupations are projected to increase by a greater percentage than the total of all occupations; and personal financial advisor occupations are projected to increase by a greater percentage than business and financial operations occupations. Thus dietitian and nutritionist occupations are expected to increase by a lesser percentage than the other two (c) categories—not than only one of them (b), not by a greater percentage (a) than the others, and not by an equal percentage as the others (d).

History/Social Studies

12. C: A simple past tense verb is necessary in this clause.

13. A: This phrase is most correctly written in the form in which it appears in the passage. All of the verb tenses used in the revision options are inconsistent with the tense used in the rest of the sentence.

14. B: The first paragraph refers to the Spray as a sloop, which is a kind of sailboat, and refers to its being berthed among the docks.

15. B: In the first paragraph the author describes his surprise at the changes in the harbor, and in Lines 8-9 indicates that the changes downtown were much less.

16. C: Lines 11-12 mentions a letter of introduction that had been sent ahead from another of the author's contacts in Montevideo.

17. C: Line 15 mentions the "Standard's" columns, which had contained stories about the Spray's voyage.

18. B: Although "landmarks" are usually monuments or buildings, the author uses the term and goes on to describe a number of merchants who had been present during his earlier visit to the city, and who were significant features of the town in his estimation.

19. C: Line 22 tells us that the lemons went on forever, suggesting that the merchant hardly ever changed them at all.

20. B: The author would have liked to look up the whiskey merchant, but there is nothing in the passage to suggest that he was desperate or anxious to do so.

21. C: The phrase in Line 31, that the waters were not blameless of disease germs, indicates that some germs may have been present in them.

22. B: Throughout the passage, the author is looking for people he had seen on his first visit, and he says of this merchant that he had "survived" (Line 34).

Humanities

23. D: A past tense verb is needed for this sentence.

24. C: The passage speaks of New Zealand being colonized, where previously it was not occupied, so incursion is not an accurate word to describe the coming of the settlers. Influx is a more appropriate description.

25. C: An archipelago is a large group or chain of islands.

26. D: The article deals primarily with the ways the colonists fed themselves: their crops and the foods they hunted. While it also describes New Zealand's prehistory, the main focus is on food sources.

27. B: The article states that the islands were colonized by Polynesians in the fifteenth century but that the first settlers had arrived some 400 years earlier than that.

28. D: The passage states that the first settlers were forced to rely on fishing for their food.

29. A: When an increased population had driven a major food source to extinction, they began to fight for control over the remaining food supply.

30. D: The article tells us that coconuts did not grow in New Zealand, and that some of the other crops would grow only on North Island.

31. C: The sweet potato could be stored, providing a source of food during the winter when other food gathering activities were difficult.

32. A: The sweet potato provided a winter food source through storage, allowing the population to increase.

33. D: All of the reasons given are good ones for locating the camps near the source of food production.

Science

34. A: The only option that both makes a complete sentence and contains a grammatically correct verb form is the one that appears in the passage.

35. C: The sentence needs to be separated into two distinct clauses and this is the only choice that does so in an acceptable way. It would also be acceptable to separate them with a comma-conjunction combination, but the conjunction must indicate a further explanation (e.g., *and* or *so*) rather than a contrast (e.g., *but* or *yet*)

36. B: Cilia and flagella are both organelles, which are defined in the first paragraph as sub-cellular structures that perform a particular function.

37. A: The second paragraph describes the function of cilia as providing fluid flow across the gills or the epithelia lining the digestive tract. The stomach is part of the digestive tract.

38. C: The third paragraph of the text describes 9 peripheral pairs of polymers, and two central ones, or 20 in all.

39. B: Tubulin and dynein are both defined as proteins in the text (Paragraphs 3 and 4). Flagellin is a protein, but it is not mentioned in the text. Sonneborn is not a protein; he was a scientist.

40. B: The mechanism is explained in detail in the fourth paragraph. Dynein causes the outer polymer pairs to slide past each other, not to bend. The inner polymers do not have dynein associated with them, so they are not involved in the bending. And the passage cites no evidence to suggest that the organelles contract. While "flagella beat in a circular, undulating motion that is

continuous" (Paragraph 2), the question is asking for an explanation of this movement, not a description.

41. C: Although the polymers in this passage are made of protein subunits, the definition is more general. Paragraph 3 tells us that in this case the subunits are tubulin proteins.

42. B: The fourth paragraph introduces Sonneborn as "of Indiana University" and describes him doing scientific research.

43. D: The experiment described in Paragraph 5 showed that the cilia always retained their original direction of rotation.

44. D: The first paragraph states that both structures are less than 5 μm in diameter.

Math – Calculator

1. B: Notice that the given system has two equations, and each equation has two variables, x and y. Therefore, the solution of the system of equations must have values for each of the two variables. To find the solution, you can use algebraic methods, graphs, tables, or matrices. For the purposes of this explanation, we will use an algebraic method called substitution.

To begin, notice that the first equation already has y isolated on the left side. Therefore, substitute the left side, $3x + 2$, for y into the second equation, and then solve for x.

$$2x + y = 7$$
$$2x + (3x + 2) = 7$$
$$5x = 5$$
$$x = 1$$

To find the value of y, substitute 1 for x in the first equation.

$$y = 3(1) + 2$$
$$= 3 + 2$$
$$= 5$$

Therefore, the solution of the given system of equations is $x = 1, y = 5$. Check this solution on your own by substituting the values into the second equations to make sure that you get a true equality.

2. D: For each value of $x, f(x) = x^2 + 1$,

$$f(1) = (1)^2 + 1 = (1)(1) + 1 = 1 + 1 = 2$$
$$f(2) = (2)^2 + 1 = (2)(2) + 1 = 4 + 1 = 5$$
$$f(3) = (3)^2 + 1 = (3)(3) + 1 = 9 + 1 = 10$$
$$f(4) = (4)^2 + 1 = (4)(4) + 1 = 16 + 1 = 17$$
$$f(5) = (5)^2 + 1 = (5)(5) + 1 = 25 + 1 = 26$$

3. A: The slope (or ratio of the change in y-values per change in corresponding x-values) may first be calculated. Using the points, $(-3, -21)$ and $(-1, -3)$, the slope can be written as $\frac{-3-(-21)}{-1-(-3)}$ or 9. The slope can be substituted into the slope-intercept form of an equation, or $y = mx + b$, in order to find the y-intercept. Doing so gives $y = 9x + b$. Substituting the x- and y-values of any ordered pair will reveal the y-intercept. The following may be written: $-21 = 9(-3) + b$; solving for b gives $b = 6$. Thus, the equation that represents the relationship between x and y is $y = 9x + 6$.

4. A: The number of possible combinations of gallons of milk and cartons of eggs may be represented by the inequality, $3.50x + 1.75y \leq 21$, where x represents number of gallons of milk and y represents number of cartons of eggs. Solving for y, the inequality may be written as $y \leq -2x + 12$. The inequality may be graphed as $y = -2x + 12$, with shading shown on the side of the line, containing the point, $(0, 0)$. Note. $0 \leq 12$, so the test point, $(0, 0)$, results in a true statement. Only Choices A and C have a y-intercept of 12. The slope of Choice A may be calculated by using any two points on the line. Using the x- and y-intercepts, the slope can be written as $\frac{0-12}{6-0}$ or -2. Thus, Choice A represents the possible combinations of gallons of milk and cartons of eggs she may purchase.

5. B: The easiest pair to test is the third: $y = 4$ and $x = 0$. Substitute these values into each of the given equations and evaluate. Choice G gives $4 = 0 + 4$, which is a true statement. None of the other answer choices are correct using this number set.

6. A: To evaluate $\frac{x^3+2x}{x+3}$ at $= -1$, substitute in -1 for x in the expression: $\frac{(-1)^3+2(-1)}{(-1)+3} = \frac{(-1)+(-2)}{2} = \frac{-3}{2} = -\frac{3}{2}$.

7. B: To solve this problem, all we need to do is substitute -1 for every x in the expression and then simplify: $\frac{2(-1)-2}{(-1)-3} = \frac{-2-2}{-4} = \frac{-4}{-4} = 1$.

8. 0%. (The seller does not profit.): Suppose the seller purchases an item for $100. A mark-up of 25% is $\frac{25}{100} \times \$100 = \$25$, so the store price is set at $125. If that $125 item is marked down 20%, or $\frac{20}{100} \times \$125 = \$25$, the clearance price is $100. Since $100 is the amount of the seller's initial investment, he makes no profit on the sale of clearance merchandise.
A general expression describing the price of the clearance merchandise is $0.80(1.25x)$, where x is the seller's purchase price. The expression simplifies to x, so the clearance price is the same as the seller's investment price.

9. B: The probability of playing a song by any band is proportional to the number of songs by that band, divided by the total number of songs, or $\frac{5}{15} = \frac{1}{3}$ for Band D. The probability of playing any particular song is not affected by what has been played previously, since the choice is random.

10. B: The number of people who voted for the proposition is 9.5% of 51,623. If we only require an approximation, we can round 9.5% to 10%, and 51,623 to 50,000. Then 9.5% of 51,623 is about 10% of 50,000, or $(0.1)(50,000) = 5,000$.

11. B: Since all students who answered her survey said they prefer one of the three flavors, the percentages must add up to 100%. Therefore the percentage of students who prefer strawberry must be $100\% - (35\% + 40\%) = 100\% - 75\% = 25\%$.

12. B: Suppose you put the two hosts in two adjacent seats, as required. (It does not matter which two seats we choose since we are not worried about rotations of the whole arrangement.) Then, the other four guests can be arranged in $4! = 4 \times 3 \times 2 \times 1 = 24$ different orders. However, we have to multiply this answer by 2 because there are two possible ways in which the two hosts can be seated; in other words, if they are sitting side-by-side, the hosts can exchange seats and still be sitting together. The total number of orders is $24 \times 2 = 48$.

13. D: Since 16 chairs are empty, and this represents 2/5 of the total enrollment, then the full class must consist of $\frac{5}{2}(16) = 40$ students.
Alternatively, use proportions:
$\frac{2}{5} = \frac{16}{x}$ Cross multiply.
$2x = 80$ Divide each side by 2 to solve for x.
$x = 40$ students.

14. C: The problem may be solved by writing $P(phil \text{ or } qual) = P(phil) + P(qual) - P(phil \text{ and } qual)$. The probability for philosophy or qualitative and the probability for philosophy may be substituted giving $0.62 = 0.30 + P(qual) - P(phil \text{ and } qual)$. Next find the probability that she chooses both philosophy and qualitative by using the formula, $P(phil \text{ and } qual) = P(phil) \cdot P(qual|phil)$. Substituting the probabilities of 0.30 and 0.40 gives $P(phil \text{ and } qual) = 0.30 \cdot 0.40$, or 0.12. Now, the probability of 0.12 may be substituted into the original equation, giving $0.62 = 0.30 + P(qual) - 0.12$. Solving for $P(qual)$ gives a probability of 0.44. Thus, there is a 0.44 probability that Alisha chooses a qualitative methods class.

15. D: Since the figure represents the number line, the distance from point A to point B will be the difference, B-A, which is 5 – (-6) = 11. The distance from point B to point C will be the difference, C-B, which is 8 – 5 = 3. So, the ratio BC:AB will be 3:11.

16. D: The expected value is equal to the sum of the products of the probabilities and their x-values. The expected value is $(0 \cdot 0.23) + (1 \cdot 0.21) + (2 \cdot 0.17) + (3 \cdot 0.14) + (4 \cdot 0.12) + (5 \cdot 0.09) + (6 \cdot 0.04)$, which equals 2.14.

17. C: The median number of volunteers in Texas is 21, with a mean of approximately 25.9. The median number of volunteers in New Mexico is 33, with a mean of approximately 31.2. Thus, the median and mean numbers of volunteers in Texas are smaller.

18. B: The probability may be written as $P(A \text{ or } B) = \frac{23}{58} + \frac{49}{58} - \frac{37}{58}$, which simplifies to $P(A \text{ or } B) = \frac{35}{58}$.

19. A: The mode is the number that appears most often in a set of data. If no item appears most often, then the data set has no mode. In this case, Kyle achieved one hit a total of three times, two hits twice, three hits once, and four hits once. One hit occurred the most times, and therefore the mode of the data set is 1.

20. B: The mean, or average, is the sum of the numbers in a data set, divided by the total number of items. This data set contains seven items, one for each day of the week. The total number of hits that Kyle had during the week is the sum of the numbers in the right-hand column, or 14. This gives $Mean = \frac{14}{7} = 2$.

21. C: The expected value is equal to the sum of the products of the probabilities and the amount he will win. The probability of rolling a 3 or 4 is $\frac{2}{6}$, the probability of rolling a 2 is $\frac{1}{6}$, and the probability of rolling any other number is $\frac{3}{6}$. Thus, the expected value is $\left(10 \cdot \frac{2}{6}\right) + \left(8 \cdot \frac{1}{6}\right) + \left(12 \cdot \frac{3}{6}\right)$. Thus, he can expect to win approximately $10.67.

22. D: You can solve the quadratic inequality using graphs, tables, or algebraic methods. For this explanation, we will approach the problem algebraically. To begin, solve the equation $2x^2 + 5x - 12 = 0$ by factoring the left side.

$$2x^2 + 5x - 12 = 0$$
$$(2x - 3)(x + 4) = 0$$
$$2x - 3 = 0 \text{ and } x + 4 = 0$$
$$x = \frac{3}{2} \text{ and } x = -4$$

Since the given inequality contains a greater-than-or-equal-to sign (rather than just a greater-than sign), the solution will include $x = -4$ and $x = \frac{3}{2}$.

Furthermore, these two solutions split the number line into three distinct regions: $x < -4$, $-4 < x < \frac{3}{2}$, and $x > \frac{3}{2}$. To determine the solution set, test one value in each region by substituting it in the given inequality. If the test value leads to a true statement, then the whole region it is in is part of the solution set.

Region	Test Value	$2x^2 + 5x - 12 \geq 0$	Conclusion
$x < -4$	-5	$2 \cdot (-5)^2 + 5 \cdot (-5) - 12 \geq 0$ $50 - 25 - 12 \geq 0$ $13 \geq 0$	Part of the solution set
$-4 < x < \frac{3}{2}$	0	$2 \cdot 0^2 + 5 \cdot 0 - 12 \geq 0$ $-12 \geq 0$	Not part of the solution set
$x > \frac{3}{2}$	2	$2 \cdot 2^2 + 5 \cdot 2 - 12 \geq 0$ $8 + 10 - 12 \geq 0$ $6 \geq 0$	Part of the solution set

Therefore, the solution set is $x \leq -4$ or $x \geq \frac{3}{2}$.

23. B: You can solve the equation using graphs, tables, or algebraic methods. For this explanation, we will approach the problem algebraically. To begin, isolate the square-root sign on the left side by subtracting 2 from both sides.

$$\sqrt{4x - 3} + 2 = x$$
$$\sqrt{4x - 3} = x - 2$$

Then square both sides of the equation and simplify the result.
$$\left(\sqrt{4x - 3}\right)^2 = (x - 2)^2$$
$$4x - 3 = x^2 - 4x + 4$$

Now solve the resulting equation by moving everything to one side and factoring the resulting quadratic equation.
$$x^2 - 8x + 7 = 0$$
$$(x - 7)(x - 1) = 0$$
$$x = 7 \text{ and } x = 1$$

Therefore, the possible solutions are $x = 1$ and $x = 7$. Unfortunately, whenever you have to square both sides of an equation to solve it, you run the risk of finding an incorrect solution. Consequently, we cannot automatically say that the solutions are $x = 1$ and $x = 7$. We need to check these solutions in the original equation. To do this, substitute them into the given equations and make sure that the result is a true statement.

$x = 1$:

$\sqrt{4 \cdot 1 - 3} + 2 = 1$

$\sqrt{1} + 2 = 1$

$1 + 2 = 1$ *False*

$x = 7$:

$\sqrt{4 \cdot 7 - 3} + 2 = 7$

$\sqrt{25} + 2 = 7$

$5 + 2 = 7$ *True*

Since only x=7 leads to a true statement, the solution is $x = 7$.

24. C: The roots of a quadratic function $f(x)$ are the values of x for which $f(x) = 0$. Quadratic functions may have two real roots, two imaginary roots, or one real double root. A quadratic function written in the form $f(x) = (x - a)(x - b)$ has roots at $x = a$ and $x = b$. Therefore, to find $f(x)$, substitute the given roots for a and b into $f(x) = (x - a)(x - b)$ and simplify.

$$f(x) = (x - a)(x - b)$$
$$= (x - (-4))(x - 6)$$
$$= (x + 4)(x - 6)$$
$$= x^2 - 2x - 24$$

25. D: The denominator of the second rational expression may be factored as $(x + 8)(x + 2)$. Thus, the least common denominator of the two rational expressions is $(x + 8)(x + 2)$. Multiplying the top and bottom of the first fraction by $(x + 8)$, we see that $\frac{3}{x+2} = \frac{3(x+8)}{(x+2)(x+8)}$. The sum may be written as $\frac{3(x+8)+x}{(x+8)(x+2)}$, which simplifies to $\frac{4x+24}{(x+8)(x+2)}$. Factoring out a 4 in the numerator gives: $\frac{4(x+6)}{(x+8)(x+2)}$.

26. C: Distributing each term in the expression, $x- 8$, across each term in the trinomial, gives $4x^4 - 2x^2 + 4x - 32x^3 + 16x - 32$. Writing the expression in standard form gives $4x^4 - 32x^3 - 2x^2 + 20x - 32$.

27. C: In a parallelogram, consecutive angles are supplementary; that is, the sum of their measures is 180°. Use this to write an equation and then solve for x.

$$m\angle B + m\angle C = 180°$$
$$(4x + 5) + (3x) = 180$$
$$7x + 5 = 180$$
$$7x = 175$$
$$x = 25$$

Now use this value to find m$\angle B$ and m$\angle C$.

$m\angle B = 3x$	$m\angle C = 4x + 5$
$= 3(25)$	$= 4(25) + 5$
$= 75°$	$= 105°$

In a parallelogram, opposite sides are congruent. Thus, m$\angle A$ = m$\angle C$ = 105°.

28. 39.1: The area of a circle is given by the formula $A = \pi r^2$, where r is the length of the radius. A sector is a slice of a circle bounded by two radii. Its area is proportional to the angle between the two radii bounding the sector. Thus, the area of a sector with angle θ (in degrees) is given by the formula

$$A = \pi r^2 \cdot \frac{\theta}{360}$$

Substitute the value of the radius and angle into this formula and simplify. Round the result to the nearest tenth.

$$A = \pi(8)^2 \cdot \frac{70}{360}$$
$$= 64\pi \cdot \frac{70}{360}$$
$$\approx 39.1$$

29. 2825: The pool is a prism, so its volume is calculated by using the formula $V = Bh$, where B is the area of the base (i.e. the area of the given shape) and h is the height (i.e. the depth) of the swimming pool. First calculate B by adding the areas of the rectangle and two semicircles.

The area of the rectangle is given by the formula $A = lw$. Thus,

$$A_{\text{rectangle}} = lw$$
$$= 20 \text{ ft} \times 12 \text{ ft}$$
$$= 240 \text{ ft}^2$$

Now notice that the diameter of each semicircle is 12 ft, so their radius is $r = 12 \div 2 = 6$ ft. Put together, the two semicircles form a complete circle, whose area is given by the formula $A = \pi r^2$. Thus, the total area of the semicircles is

$$A_{\text{semicircles}} = \pi r^2$$
$$= \pi \cdot (6 \text{ ft})^2$$
$$= 36\pi \text{ ft}^2$$
$$\approx 113.10 \text{ ft}^2$$

Then add the two areas to find the total area of the swimming pool.

$$B = A_{\text{rectangle}} + A_{\text{semicircles}}$$
$$\approx 240 \text{ ft}^2 + 113.10 \text{ ft}^2$$
$$= 353.10 \text{ ft}^2$$

Finally, use this value to find the volume of the pool. Recall that its depth is given as 8 ft in the problem.

$$V = Bh$$
$$\approx 353.10 \text{ ft}^2 \times 8 \text{ ft}$$
$$\approx 2825 \text{ ft}^3$$

30. $\frac{5\sqrt{3}}{3}$: The circle intercepts the triangle at the midpoints of its sides. Draw the radius that meets one of these points (marked D below) as well as the line segment, $\overline{AO}$.

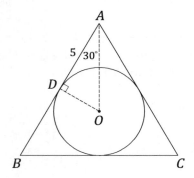

Thus, $AD = \frac{1}{2}(AB) = 5$. Since $\triangle ABC$ is an equilateral triangle with three 60° angles and $\overline{AO}$ bisects $\angle BAC$, we know that m$\angle DAO = \frac{1}{2} \cdot 60° = 30°$. In addition, $\overline{AB}$ is a tangent to circle O, so $\angle ADO$ is a right angle.

Therefore, we see that $\triangle ADO$ is a 30-60-90 triangle. In a 30-60-90 triangle, the ratio of the lengths of the sides is $1: \sqrt{3}: 2$. In this triangle, 5 corresponds to $\sqrt{3}$ and the radius r corresponds to 1. Use a proportion to calculate r.

$$\frac{1}{\sqrt{3}} = \frac{r}{5}$$
$$r\sqrt{3} = 5$$
$$r = \frac{5}{\sqrt{3}}$$
$$r = \frac{5\sqrt{3}}{3}$$

31. C: Start by distributing each coefficient across the parentheses. Next add the complex binomials. Complex numbers have a real part, a, and an imaginary part, b, and are usually written as $a + bi$. When adding imaginary numbers, add the real parts and the imaginary parts separately:
$$4(-3 + 5i) + 6(1 - 3i) = -12 + 20i + 6 - 18i = (-12 + 6) + (20i - 18i) = -6 + 2i$$

Math - No-Calculator

1. C: The linear function $s(h) = 27h + 720$ starts at 720 when $h = 0$ and increases by 27 every time h increases by 1. Therefore, for every hour after 40, the librarian earns $27, so his salary is $27 per hour.

2. D:

$$y = 4x - 2$$
$$y + 2 = 4x$$
$$\frac{y + 2}{4} = x$$
$$\frac{y}{4} + \frac{2}{4} = x$$
$$\frac{1}{4}y + \frac{1}{2} = x$$
$$x = \frac{1}{4}y + \frac{1}{2}$$

3.

First, solve the inequality.

$$2|x + 3| - 9 \geq -1$$
$$2|x + 3| \geq 8$$
$$|x + 3| \geq 4$$

$$x + 3 \geq 4 \qquad -(x + 3) \geq 4$$
$$x \geq 1 \qquad -(x + 3) \geq 4$$
$$x + 3 \leq -4$$
$$x \leq -7$$

Then, graph the solution on the number line. When solving absolute value equations and inequalities, it is good practice to check for extraneous solutions. Choose a number in each shaded region to be sure it satisfies the given inequality.

$$2|-8 + 3| - 9 \geq -1? \qquad\qquad 2|2 + 3| - 9 \geq -1?$$
$$2|-5| - 9 \geq -1? \qquad\qquad 2|5| - 9 \geq -1?$$
$$2(5) - 9 \geq -1? \qquad\qquad 2(5) - 9 \geq -1?$$
$$10 - 9 \geq -1? \qquad\qquad 10 - 9 \geq -1?$$
$$1 \geq -1? \qquad\qquad 1 \geq -1?$$

$1 \geq -1$ is a true statement, so -8 and 2 are indeed included in the solution.

4. A: The positively sloped line has a slope of 2 and a y-intercept of -3; the line is solid, and the region above the line is shaded. Therefore, the graph illustrates the solution to the inequality $y \geq 2x - 3$.

The negatively sloped line has a slope of -3 and a y-intercept of 4; the line is dashed, and the region below the line is shaded. Therefore, the graph illustrates the solution to the inequality $y < -3x + 4$. In choice A, the second inequality when solved for y is equivalent to $y \geq 2x - 3$.

$$4x - 2y \leq 6$$
$$-2y \leq -4x + 6$$
$$y \geq 2x - 3$$

(The direction of the inequality sign changes when multiplying or diving by a negative number.) The solution of the system of inequalities is shown by the region where the two sets of shading overlap.

5. C: The four choices all have the two lines that mark the boundaries of the inequalities plotted identically; the only difference is which sides are shaded. It's therefore not necessary to check that the lines are correct; simply determine which of the areas bounded by the lines pertain to the system of inequalities. One way to do that is to pick a point in each region and check whether it satisfies the inequalities. For instance, in the region on the left, we can pick the origin, $(0, 0)$. Since $0 - 0 \not> 1$ and $2(0) + 0 \not> 2$, this does not satisfy either inequality. From the top region we can choose, for example, the point $(0, 3)$. $0 - 3 \not> 1$, so this fails to satisfy the first inequality. From the bottom region we can choose, for instance, $(0, -2)$. $0 - (-2) > 1$, so the first inequality is satisfied, but $2(0) + (-2) \not> 2$, so the second is not. Finally, from the rightmost region we can choose, for example, the point $(2, 0)$. $2 - 0 > 1$ and $2(2) + 0 > 2$, so both inequalities are satisfied; this is the only region that should be shaded in.

6. D: To simplify the inequality $3 - 2x < 5$, we can first subtract 3 from both sides: $3 - 2x - 3 < 5 - 3 \Rightarrow -2x < 2$. Now, we can divide both sides of the inequality by -2. When an inequality is multiplied or divided by a negative number, its direction changes ($<$ becomes $>$, $\leq$ becomes $\geq$, and vice versa). So $-2x < 2$ becomes $\frac{-2x}{-2} > \frac{2}{-2}$, or $x > -1$.

7. C: If the exam has 30 questions, and the student answered C questions correctly and left B questions blank, then the number of questions the student answered incorrectly must be $30 - B - C$. He gets one point for each correct question, or $1 \times C = C$ points, and loses $\frac{1}{2}$ point for each incorrect question, or $\frac{1}{2}(30 - B - C)$ points. Therefore, one way to express his total score is $-\frac{1}{2}(30 - B - C)$.

8. B: If there are n floors, and each floor has a height of h feet, then to find the total height of the floors, we just multiply the number of floors by the height of each floor: nh. To find the total height of the building, we must also add the height of the spire, 30 feet. So, the building's total height in feet is $nh + 30$.

9. D: First, test each expression to see which satisfies the condition $x > y$. This condition is met for all the answer choices except C and D, so these need not be considered further. Next, test the remaining choices to see which satisfy the inequality $x + y > 0$. It can be seen that this inequality holds for choices A and B, but not for choice E, since:
$x + y = 3 + (-3) = 3 - 3 = 0$. In this case the sum $x + y$ is not greater than 0.

10. B: To simplify the expression, first factor the numerator and the denominator. To factor the numerator, use trial-and-error to find two numbers whose sum is 2 and whose product is -24, and then put those numbers into the form $(x + \_)(x + \_)$. For the denominator, factor out the common factor, which is 5.
$$\frac{x^2 + 2x - 24}{5x - 20} = \frac{(x+6)(x-4)}{5(x-4)}$$

Now there is a common factor, $(x - 4)$, in both the numerator and the denominator. Therefore, you can further simplify the expression by cancelling it out.

$$\frac{(x+6)(x-4)}{5(x-4)} = \frac{x+6}{5}$$

11. C: To simplify the expression, first simplify the expression with parentheses. To raise $3x$ to the third power, raise both 3 and x to the third power separately.

$$x^6 \cdot (3x)^2 = x^6 \cdot 3^2 \cdot x^2$$
$$= x^6 \cdot 9x^2$$

Next, multiply the two terms. Since they have the same base and are being multiplied together, add the exponents of the like base, x.

$$x^6 \cdot 9x^2 = 9x^{6+2}$$
$$= 9x^8$$

12. B: Revenue is the total amount of money the theater makes from ticket sales. In this case, the revenue is the price of each ticket multiplied by the total number of tickets sold. So, to find the estimated revenue, find the price and the number of tickets sold after the price is raised by x dollars. Then multiply the two quantities together.

If the price of a ticket starts at \$10, then the price after it is raised by x dollars will be $10 + x$ dollars. In addition, we are told that the theater sells 50 fewer tickets for every dollar the price is raised. Therefore, the total number of tickets that are sold will be $600 - 50x$. Calculate the revenue function $r(x)$ by multiplying the expressions and simplify the result.

$$r(x) = (10 + x)(600 - 50x)$$
$$= -50x^2 + 100x + 6000$$

13. C: To transform $f(x)$ into $g(x)$, you have to replace x with $x + 1$. This transformation results in a translation, or shift, of the graph. Specifically, for a particular x, $g(x)$ returns the value of the function $f(x)$ one unit further along the x-axis (to the right). This results in shifting the graph one unit to the left.

14. B: The length of an interval is the difference between its endpoints. For example, the length of the interval [2, 4] is 2. To determine how the given function grows over an interval of length 3, determine the value of f at each endpoint of that interval. Since exponential functions grow by equal factors over equal intervals, you can use any interval of length 3, and your answer will apply to all such intervals. For example, you can use the interval [0,3]:

$$f(0) = 3 \cdot 2^{(0)}$$
$$= 3 \cdot 1$$
$$= 3$$

$$f(3) = 3 \cdot 2^{(3)}$$
$$= 3 \cdot 8$$
$$= 24$$

Since $f(0) = 3$ and $f(3) = 24$, the function grows by a factor of $\frac{24}{3} = 8$ over this interval.

15. A: Examine the graph to determine which graph eventually exceeds the other three. In other words, find the function that eventually goes above the other three as the graph goes from left to right. Notice that the function f goes above the other three when $x = 5$.

16. C: Since the function is defined recursively, you need to calculate all of the first six terms. The first and second terms are already given in the problem as $f(1) = 1$ and $f(2) = 1$. To calculate the third term, $f(3)$, take the previous term and add two times the term that is two back:

$$f(3) = f(2) + 2f(1) = 1 + 2 = 3$$

The fourth term is similarly calculated:

$$f(4) = f(3) + 2f(2) = 3 + 2 = 5$$

Continuing in this way, you will find that the first six terms of the sequence are 1, 1, 3, 5, 11, 21. Therefore, the sixth term of the sequence is 21.

17. A: Vectors can be graphically added using the parallelogram method, in which the diagonal of the parallelogram, formed by duplicating each of the two vectors originating at the tip of the other, represents the sum. Complex numbers are of the form $a + bi$; a is an element of the real numbers and is represented on the horizontal axis, bi is an element of the complex numbers and b is represented on the vertical axis. Find the complex numbers representing the legs of the parallelogram by simply counting the horizontal and vertical components; they are $-3 + 2i$ and $4 + 2i$. The diagonal of the parallelogram, the result, is again found by counting: $(-3 + 2i) + (4 + 2i) = 1 + 4i$.

Secret Key #1 – Time is Your Greatest Enemy

To succeed on the PSAT, you must use your time wisely. Most students do not finish at least one section. The time constraints are brutal. To succeed, you must ration your time properly. The reason that time is so critical is that every question counts the same toward your final score. If you run out of time on any passage, the questions that you do not answer will hurt your score far more than earlier questions that you spent extra time on and feel certain are correct.

Success Strategy

Pace Yourself

Wear a watch to the PSAT Test. At the beginning of the test, check the time (or start a chronometer on your watch to count the minutes), and check the time after each passage to make sure you are "on schedule."

If you find that you are falling behind time during the test, begin skipping difficult questions (unless you know it at a quick glance). Once you catch back up, you can continue working each problem. If you have time at the end, go back then and finish the questions that you left behind.

Remember that on most sections you have slightly more than a minute per question, which makes it easy to keep track of your time. If you are spending more than a minute per question, skip it and move on. It is better to end with more time than you need than to run out of time. You can always go back and work the problems that you skipped. Besides, they were difficult or you wouldn't have skipped them. The difficult questions are the ones you are most likely to miss anyway, so it isn't a big loss. If you have time left over, as you review the skipped questions, start at the earliest skipped question, spend at most another minute, and then move on to the next skipped question.

Always mark skipped questions in your workbook, NOT on the Scantron. Last minute guessing will be covered in the next chapter.

Lastly, sometimes it is beneficial to slow down if you are constantly getting ahead of time. You are always more likely to catch a careless mistake by working more slowly than quickly, and among very high-scoring students (those who are likely to have lots of time left over), careless errors affect the score more than mastery of material.

Estimation

For some math questions, estimate. Calculation takes time, and you should avoid it whenever possible. You can usually eliminate three obviously wrong choices quite easily. For example, suppose a graph shows that an object has traveled 48 meters in 11 seconds, and you are asked to find its speed. You are given these choices:

a. 250 m/s
b. 42 m/s
c. 4.4 m/s
d. 1.2 m/s

You know that 48 divided by 11 will be a little over 4, so you can pick out C as the answer without ever doing the calculation.

Scanning

For critical reading sections, don't waste time reading, enjoying, and completely understanding the passage. Simply scan the passage to get a rough idea of what it is about. You will return to the passage for each question, so there is no need to memorize it. Only spend as much time scanning as is necessary to get a vague impression of its overall subject content.

Secret Key #2 – Guessing is Not Guesswork

You have probably heard that guessing on the PSAT is a bad idea, because there is a penalty for giving the wrong answer. On the PSAT that is being administered as of October 2015, this is no longer the case. There is no longer a penalty for wrong answers. So, even if you have no idea about a question, you still have a 25% chance of getting it right and no reason not to fill in an answer for it.

Most students do not understand the impact that proper guessing can have on their score. Unless you score higher than 1300 or so, guessing will probably contribute about 180-240 points to your final score.

Monkeys Take the PSAT

If you have only four answer choices, then you have a 25% chance of getting it correct. What most students don't realize is that to ensure a 25% chance, you have to guess randomly. If you put 20 monkeys in a room to take the PSAT, assuming they answered once per question and behaved themselves, on average they would get 25% of the questions correct. Put 20 high school students in the room, and the average will be lower among guessed questions. Why?

1. The PSAT writers intentionally write deceptive answer choices that "look" right. A student has no idea about a question, so picks the "best looking" answer, which is often wrong. The monkey has no idea what looks good and what doesn't, so will consistently be lucky about 25% of the time.
2. Students will eliminate answer choices from the guessing pool based on a hunch or intuition. Simple but correct answers often get excluded, leaving a 0% chance of being correct. The monkey has no clue and selects randomly.

This is why the process of elimination endorsed by most test courses is flawed and detrimental to your performance: students don't guess, they make an ignorant stab in the dark that is usually worse than random.

Success Strategy

Let me introduce one of the most valuable ideas of this course- the $5 challenge:

You only mark your "best guess" if you are willing to bet $5 on it.
You only eliminate choices from guessing if you are willing to bet $5 on it.

Why $5? Five dollars is an amount of money that is small yet not insignificant, and can really add up fast (20 questions could cost you $100). Likewise, each answer choice on one question of the PSAT will have a small impact on your overall score, but it can really add up to a lot of points in the end.

The process of elimination IS valuable. The following shows your chance of guessing it right:

If you eliminate this many choices:	0	1	2	3
Chance of getting it right	25%	33%	50%	100%

If you accidentally eliminate the right answer or go on a hunch for an incorrect answer, your chances drop dramatically: to 0%. By guessing among all the answer choices, you are GUARANTEED to have a shot at the right answer.

That's why the $5 test is so valuable- if you give up the advantage and safety of a pure guess, it had better be worth the risk.

What we still haven't covered is how to be sure that whatever guess you make is truly random. Here's the easiest way:
Always pick the first answer choice among those remaining.

Such a technique means that you have decided, **before you see a single test question**, exactly how you are going to guess- and since the order of choices tells you nothing about which one is correct, this guessing technique is perfectly random.

Let's try an example:

A student encounters the following problem on a math section:

What is the cosine of an angle in a right triangle that is 3 meters on the adjacent side, 5 meters on the hypotenuse, and 4 meters on the opposite side?
A. 1
B. 0.6
C. 0.8
D. 0.75

The student has a small idea about this question- he is pretty sure that cosine is opposite over hypotenuse, but he wouldn't bet $5 on it. He knows that cosine is "something" over hypotenuse, and since the hypotenuse is the largest number, he is willing to bet $5 on choice A not being correct. So he is down to B, C, and D. At this point, he guesses B, since B is the first choice remaining.

The student is correct by choosing B, since cosine is adjacent over hypotenuse. He only eliminated those choices he was willing to bet money on, AND he did not let his stale memories (often things not known definitely will get mixed up in the exact opposite arrangement in one's head) about the formula for cosine influence his guess. He blindly chose the first remaining choice, and was rewarded with the fruits of a random guess.

This section is not meant to scare you away from making educated guesses or eliminating choices- you just need to define when a choice is worth eliminating. The $5 test, along with a pre-defined random guessing strategy, is the best way to make sure you reap all of the benefits of guessing.

Specific Guessing Techniques

Slang

Scientific sounding answers are better than slang ones. In the answer choices below, choice B is much less scientific and is incorrect, while choice A is a scientific analytical choice and is correct.

Example:
    A. To compare the outcomes of the two different kinds of treatment.
    B. Because some subjects insisted on getting one or the other of the treatments.

Extreme Statements

Avoid wild answers that throw out highly controversial ideas that are proclaimed as established fact. Choice A is a radical idea and is incorrect. Choice B is a calm rational statement. Notice that Choice B does not make a definitive, uncompromising stance, using a hedge word "if" to provide wiggle room.

Example:
a. Bypass surgery should be discontinued completely.
b. Medication should be used instead of surgery for patients who have not had a heart attack if they suffer from mild chest pain and mild coronary artery blockage.

Similar Answer Choices

When you have two answer choices that are direct opposites, one of them is usually the correct answer.
Example:

    A. Passage 1 described the author's reasoning about the influence of his childhood on his adult life.
    B. Passage 2 described the author's reasoning about the influence of his childhood on his adult life.

These two answer choices are very similar and fall into the same family of answer choices. A family of answer choices is when two or three answer choices are very similar. Often two will be opposites and one may show an equality.

Example:
    A. Operation I or Operation II can be conducted at equal cost
    B. Operation I would be less expensive than Operation II
    C. Operation II would be less expensive than Operation I
    D. Neither Operation I nor Operation II would be effective at preventing the spread of cancer.

Note how the first three choices are all related. They all ask about a cost comparison. Beware of immediately recognizing choices B and C as opposites and choosing one of those two. Choice A is in the same family of questions and should be considered as well. However, choice D is not in the same family of questions. It has nothing to do with cost and can be discounted in most cases.

Hedging

When asked for a conclusion that may be drawn, look for critical "hedge" phrases, such as likely, may, can, will often, often, almost, mostly, usually, generally, rarely, sometimes, etc. Question writers insert these hedge phrases to cover every possibility. Often an answer will be wrong simply because it leaves no room for exception. Avoid answer choices that have definitive words like "exactly," and "always".

Secret Key #3 – Practice Smarter, Not Harder

Many students delay the test preparation process because they dread the awful amounts of practice time they think necessary to succeed on the test. We have refined an effective method that will take you only a fraction of the time.

There are a number of "obstacles" in your way on the PSAT. Among these are answering questions, finishing in time, and mastering test-taking strategies. All must be executed on the day of the test at peak performance, or your score will suffer. The PSAT is a mental marathon that has a large impact on your future.

Just like a marathon runner, it is important to work your way up to the full challenge. So first you just worry about questions, and then time, and finally strategy:

Success Strategy

1. Find a good source for practice tests.
2. If you are willing to make a larger time investment, consider using more than one study guide. Often the different approaches of multiple authors will help you "get" difficult concepts.
3. Take a practice test with no time constraints, with all study helps "open book." Take your time with questions and focus on applying strategies.
4. Take a practice test with time constraints, with all guides "open book."
5. Take a final practice test with no open material and time limits

If you have time to take more practice tests, just repeat step 5. By gradually exposing yourself to the full rigors of the test environment, you will condition your mind to the stress of test day and maximize your success.

Secret Key #4 – Test Yourself

Everyone knows that time is money. There is no need to spend too much of your time or too little of your time preparing for the PSAT. You should only spend as much of your precious time preparing as is necessary for you to pass it.

Success Strategy

Once you have taken an official practice test under real conditions of time constraints, then you will know if you are ready for the test or not.

If you have scored extremely high the first time that you take the official practice test, then there is not much point in spending countless hours studying. You are already there.

Benchmark your abilities by retaking practice tests and seeing how much you have improved. Once you score high enough to get accepted into the school of your choice, then you are ready.

If you have scored well below where you need, then knuckle down and begin studying in earnest. Check your improvement regularly through the use of practice tests under real conditions. Above all, don't worry, panic, or give up. The key is perseverance!

Then, when you go to take the PSAT, remain confident and remember how well you did on the practice tests. If you can score a passing score on a practice test, then you can do the same on the real thing.

General Strategies

The most important thing you can do is to ignore your fears and jump into the test immediately- do not be overwhelmed by any strange-sounding terms. You have to jump into the test like jumping into a pool- all at once is the easiest way.

Make Predictions

As you read and understand the question, try to guess what the answer will be. Remember that several of the answer choices are wrong, and once you begin reading them, your mind will immediately become cluttered with answer choices designed to throw you off. Your mind is typically the most focused immediately after you have read the question and digested its contents. If you can, try to predict what the correct answer will be. You may be surprised at what you can predict.

Quickly scan the choices and see if your prediction is in the listed answer choices. If it is, then you can be quite confident that you have the right answer. It still won't hurt to check the other answer choices, but most of the time, you've got it!

Answer the Question

It may seem obvious to only pick answer choices that answer the question, but the test writers can create some excellent answer choices that are wrong. Don't pick an answer just because it sounds right, or you believe it to be true. It MUST answer the question. Once you've made your selection, always go back and check it against the question and make sure that you didn't misread the question, and the answer choice does answer the question posed.

Benchmark

After you read the first answer choice, decide if you think it sounds correct or not. If it doesn't, move on to the next answer choice. If it does, mentally mark that answer choice. This doesn't mean that you've definitely selected it as your answer choice, it just means that it's the best you've seen thus far. Go ahead and read the next choice. If the next choice is worse than the one you've already selected, keep going to the next answer choice. If the next choice is better than the choice you've already selected, mentally mark the new answer choice as your best guess.

The first answer choice that you select becomes your standard. Every other answer choice must be benchmarked against that standard. That choice is correct until proven otherwise by another answer choice beating it out. Once you've decided that no other answer choice seems as good, do one final check to ensure that your answer choice answers the question posed.

Valid Information

Don't discount any of the information provided in the question. Every piece of information may be necessary to determine the correct answer. None of the information in the question is there to throw you off (while the answer choices will certainly have information to throw you off). If two seemingly unrelated topics are discussed, don't ignore either. You can be confident there is a relationship, or it wouldn't be included in the question, and you are probably going to have to determine what is that relationship to find the answer.

Avoid "Fact Traps"

Don't get distracted by a choice that is factually true. Your search is for the answer that answers the question. Stay focused and don't fall for an answer that is true but incorrect. Always go back to the question and make sure you're choosing an answer that actually answers the question and is not just a true statement. An answer can be factually correct, but it MUST answer the question asked. Additionally, two answers can both be seemingly correct, so be sure to read all of the answer choices, and make sure that you get the one that BEST answers the question.

Milk the Question

Some of the questions may throw you completely off. They might deal with a subject you have not been exposed to, or one that you haven't reviewed in years. While your lack of knowledge about the subject will be a hindrance, the question itself can give you many clues that will help you find the correct answer. Read the question carefully and look for clues. Watch particularly for adjectives and nouns describing difficult terms or words that you don't recognize. Regardless of if you completely understand a word or not, replacing it with a synonym either provided or one you more familiar with may help you to understand what the questions are asking. Rather than wracking your mind about specific detailed information concerning a difficult term or word, try to use mental substitutes that are easier to understand.

The Trap of Familiarity

Don't just choose a word because you recognize it. On difficult questions, you may not recognize a number of words in the answer choices. The test writers don't put "make-believe" words on the test; so don't think that just because you only recognize all the words in one answer choice means that answer choice must be correct. If you only recognize words in one answer choice, then focus on that one. Is it correct? Try your best to determine if it is correct. If it is, that is great, but if it doesn't, eliminate it. Each word and answer choice you eliminate increases your chances of getting the question correct, even if you then have to guess among the unfamiliar choices.

Eliminate Answers

Eliminate choices as soon as you realize they are wrong. But be careful! Make sure you consider all of the possible answer choices. Just because one appears right, doesn't mean that the next one won't be even better! The test writers will usually put more than one good answer choice for every question, so read all of them. Don't worry if you are stuck between two that seem right. By getting down to just two remaining possible choices, your odds are now 50/50. Rather than wasting too much time, play the odds. You are guessing, but guessing wisely, because you've been able to knock out some of the answer choices that you know are wrong. If you are eliminating choices and realize that the last answer choice you are left with is also obviously wrong, don't panic. Start over and consider each choice again. There may easily be something that you missed the first time and will realize on the second pass.

Tough Questions

If you are stumped on a problem or it appears too hard or too difficult, don't waste time. Move on! Remember though, if you can quickly check for obviously incorrect answer choices, your chances of guessing correctly are greatly improved. Before you completely give up, at least try to knock out a couple of possible answers. Eliminate what you can and then guess at the remaining answer choices before moving on.

Brainstorm

If you get stuck on a difficult question, spend a few seconds quickly brainstorming. Run through the complete list of possible answer choices. Look at each choice and ask yourself, "Could this answer the question satisfactorily?" Go through each answer choice and consider it independently of the other. By systematically going through all possibilities, you may find something that you would otherwise overlook. Remember that when you get stuck, it's important to try to keep moving.

Read Carefully

Understand the problem. Read the question and answer choices carefully. Don't miss the question because you misread the terms. You have plenty of time to read each question thoroughly and make sure you understand what is being asked. Yet a happy medium must be attained, so don't waste too much time. You must read carefully, but efficiently.

Face Value

When in doubt, use common sense. Always accept the situation in the problem at face value. Don't read too much into it. These problems will not require you to make huge leaps of logic. The test writers aren't trying to throw you off with a cheap trick. If you have to go beyond creativity and make a leap of logic in order to have an answer choice answer the question, then you should look at the other answer choices. Don't overcomplicate the problem by creating theoretical relationships or explanations that will warp time or space. These are normal problems rooted in reality. It's just that the applicable relationship or explanation may not be readily apparent and you have to figure things out. Use your common sense to interpret anything that isn't clear.

Prefixes

If you're having trouble with a word in the question or answer choices, try dissecting it. Take advantage of every clue that the word might include. Prefixes and suffixes can be a huge help. Usually they allow you to determine a basic meaning. Pre- means before, post- means after, pro - is positive, de- is negative. From these prefixes and suffixes, you can get an idea of the general meaning of the word and try to put it into context. Beware though of any traps. Just because con is the opposite of pro, doesn't necessarily mean congress is the opposite of progress!

Hedge Phrases

Watch out for critical "hedge" phrases, such as likely, may, can, will often, sometimes, often, almost, mostly, usually, generally, rarely, sometimes. Question writers insert these hedge phrases to cover every possibility. Often an answer choice will be wrong simply because it leaves no room for exception. Avoid answer choices that have definitive words like "exactly," and "always".

Switchback Words

Stay alert for "switchbacks". These are the words and phrases frequently used to alert you to shifts in thought. The most common switchback word is "but". Others include although, however, nevertheless, on the other hand, even though, while, in spite of, despite, regardless of.

New Information

Correct answer choices will rarely have completely new information included. Answer choices typically are straightforward reflections of the material asked about and will directly relate to the question. If a new piece of information is included in an answer choice that doesn't even seem to relate to the topic being asked about, then that answer choice is likely incorrect. All of the information needed to answer the question is usually provided for you, and so you should not have to make guesses that are unsupported or choose answer choices that require unknown information that cannot be reasoned on its own.

Time Management

On technical questions, don't get lost on the technical terms. Don't spend too much time on any one question. If you don't know what a term means, then since you don't have a dictionary, odds are you aren't going to get much further. You should immediately recognize terms as whether or not you know them. If you don't, work with the other clues that you have, the other answer choices and terms provided, but don't waste too much time trying to figure out a difficult term.

Contextual Clues

Look for contextual clues. An answer can be right but not correct. The contextual clues will help you find the answer that is most right and is correct. Understand the context in which a phrase or statement is made. This will help you make important distinctions.

Don't Panic

Panicking will not answer any questions for you. Therefore, it isn't helpful. When you first see the question, if your mind goes blank, take a deep breath. Force yourself to mechanically go through the steps of solving the problem and using the strategies you've learned.

Pace Yourself

Don't get clock fever. It's easy to be overwhelmed when you're looking at a page full of questions, your mind is full of random thoughts and feeling confused, and the clock is ticking down faster than you would like. Calm down and maintain the pace that you have set for yourself. As long as you are on track by monitoring your pace, you are guaranteed to have enough time for yourself. When you get to the last few minutes of the test, it may seem like you won't have enough time left, but if you only have as many questions as you should have left at that point, then you're right on track!

Answer Selection

The best way to pick an answer choice is to eliminate all of those that are wrong, until only one is left and confirm that is the correct answer. Sometimes though, an answer choice may immediately look right. Be careful! Take a second to make sure that the other choices are not equally obvious. Don't make a hasty mistake. There are only two times that you should stop before checking other answers. First is when you are positive that the answer choice you have selected is correct. Second is when time is almost out and you have to make a quick guess!

Check Your Work

Since you will probably not know every term listed and the answer to every question, it is important that you get credit for the ones that you do know. Don't miss any questions through careless mistakes. If at all possible, try to take a second to look back over your answer selection and make sure you've selected the correct answer choice and haven't made a costly careless mistake (such as marking an answer choice that you didn't mean to mark). This quick double check should more than pay for itself in caught mistakes for the time it costs.

Beware of Directly Quoted Answers

Sometimes an answer choice will repeat word for word a portion of the question or reference section. However, beware of such exact duplication – it may be a trap! More than likely, the correct choice will paraphrase or summarize a point, rather than being exactly the same wording.

Slang

Scientific sounding answers are better than slang ones. An answer choice that begins "To compare the outcomes..." is much more likely to be correct than one that begins "Because some people insisted..."

Extreme Statements

Avoid wild answers that throw out highly controversial ideas that are proclaimed as established fact. An answer choice that states the "process should be used in certain situations, if..." is much more likely to be correct than one that states the "process should be discontinued completely." The first is a calm rational statement and doesn't even make a definitive, uncompromising stance, using a hedge word "if" to provide wiggle room, whereas the second choice is a radical idea and far more extreme.

Answer Choice Families

When you have two or more answer choices that are direct opposites or parallels, one of them is usually the correct answer. For instance, if one answer choice states "x increases" and another answer choice states "x decreases" or "y increases," then those two or three answer choices are very similar in construction and fall into the same family of answer choices. A family of answer choices is when two or three answer choices are very similar in construction, and yet often have a directly opposite meaning. Usually the correct answer choice will be in that family of answer choices. The "odd man out" or answer choice that doesn't seem to fit the parallel construction of the other answer choices is more likely to be incorrect.

Additional Bonus Material

Due to our efforts to try to keep this book to a manageable length, we've created a link that will give you access to all of your additional bonus material.

Please visit http://www.mometrix.com/bonus948/psat to access the information.